D0691333

Innovative Sewing

Other books in the Creative Machine Arts Series, available from Chilton:

Claire Shaeffer's Fabric Sewing Guide

The Complete Book of Machine Embroidery, by Robbie and Tony Fanning

Creative Nurseries Illustrated, by Debra Terry and Juli Plooster

Creative Serging Illustrated, by Pati Palmer, Gail Brown, and Sue Green

Distinctive Serger Gifts and Crafts: An Idea Book for All Occasions, by Naomi Baker and Tammy Young

The Expectant Mother's Wardrobe Planner, by Rebecca Dumlao

The Fabric Lover's Scrapbook, by Margaret Dittman

Friendship Quilts by Hand and Machine, by Carolyn Vosburg Hall

Innovative Serging: The Newest, Best, and Fastest Techniques for Overlock Sewing, by Naomi Baker and Tammy Young

Know Your Bernina, by Jackie Dodson

Know Your Brother, by Jackie Dodson with Jane Warnick

Know Your Elna, by Jackie Dodson with Carol Ahles

Know Your New Home, by Jackie Dodson with Judi Cull and Vicki Lynn Hastings

Know Your Pfaff, by Jackie Dodson with Audrey Griese

Know Your Sewing Machine, by Jackie Dodson

Know Your Simplicity, by Jackie Dodson with Jane Warnick

Know Your Singer, by Jackie Dodson

Know Your Viking, by Jackie Dodson with Jan Saunders

Know Your White, by Jackie Dodson with Jan Saunders

Owner's Guide to Sewing Machines, Sergers, and Knitting Machines, by Gale Grigg Hazen

Petite Pizzazz, by Barb Griffin

Sew, Serge, Press, by Jan Saunders

Sewing and Collecting Vintage Fashions, by Eileen MacIntosh

Simply Serge Any Fabric: A How-to Handbook for Today's Textiles, by Gail Brown and Tammy Young

Other Books by Gail Brown:

Creative Serging: The Complete Guide to Decorative Overlock Sewing

Sensational Silk

Sew a Beautiful Wedding

Sewing with Sergers: The Complete Guide for Overlock Sewing

Super Sweater Idea Book

Ordering Information:

For ordering information, see pages 174 – 177.

Special Offer:

For a free sampler of articles and ideas from past issues of *Sewing Update*, send a business-sized, self-addressed. stamped envelope to: *Sewing Update* Sampler Offer, 2269 Chestnut, Suite 269BK, San Francisco, CA 94123.

Innovative Sewing

The Newest, Best, and Fastest Sewing Techniques

Gail Brown and Tammy Young

Chilton Book Company
Radnor, Pennsylvania

Copyright ©1990 by Gail Brown and
Tammy Young

All Rights Reserved

Published in Radnor, Pennsylvania
19089 by Chilton Book Company

No part of this book may be repro-
duced, transmitted, or stored in any
form or by any means, electronic or
mechanical, without prior written per-
mission from the publisher.

Color photographs by Lee Phillips
Designed by Martha Vercoutere
Cover design by Kevin Culver
Illustrations by Chris Hansen
Dressmaking by Naomi Baker, Gail
Brown, and Virginia Fulcher
Traffic Control: Tom Vercoutere

Manufactured in the United States of
America

II. Title. III. Series.
LC #89-42853
ISBN 0-8019-7999-4

1 2 3 4 5 6 7 8 9 0   9 8 7 6 5 4 3 2 1 0

Contents

Foreword

By Clotilde

Years ago, sewing techniques were handed down, dressmaker to dressmaker. Laborious sample books were made of how to make a buttonhole, to sew on a snap, to make each kind of seam. Sewing was tedious—and **boring**.

Gradually, though, women who worked in garment factories "leaked" secrets of how to do techniques faster and easier, while still maintaining top quality.

I was fortunate. I had a mother who loved to sew and who didn't need a spy from the garment factory to teach her new ways to sew. She came by many shortcuts naturally. And lucky for me, she didn't graduate from the Rip-Rip-Rip Sewing School. Instead, she passed on to me her love of creating clothes. Now my goal is to show the whole world what fun, enjoyable, and rewarding results can come from making your own clothes—made the way **you** want them.

In this excellent book, Gail and Tammy are continuing that love of sewing, of how to make it "easier, faster, and simpler." Our grandmothers would probably faint to see their speedy, simple sewing techniques. What? Finish a dress without facings? Finish a hem with just a lettuce-leaf edge or a 1/4" machine-stitched hem, let alone a fused hem? Never! Yet Gail and Tammy know that many of today's designer clothes **are** sewn with these bare-bones construction methods. And their fresh, clear-cut descriptions of how to make sewing simpler and easier will continue to help thousands of sewers.

For example, their altering "second-time-around" jackets and slacks chapter is a tremendous help for women who have no time to sew from scratch. The extensive supply and source directory is a book in itself. Because they give brand names, it makes it so much easier to buy the correct product.

Gail and Tammy take away the drudgery and put the fun back into sewing and home decorating. So blow the dust off of your machine, get out your scissors and pins, and start sewing today's fashions—today!

Preface

The Story Behind
Innovative Sewing

This book began as a series of news-letters: While managing the *Palmer/Pletsch* workshops, Tammy was en-couraged by teachers, students, and associates to fill a void in the sewing world: concise, updated information in a streamlined but fully illustrated newsletter format. Tammy took their suggestions seriously: she introduced the *Sewing Update* with the October 1986 issue. The editorial emphasis was sewing innovation—the newest, fast-est, and best techniques—presented by top professionals in the field. Gail, a well-known author and coauthor of such books as *Sew a Beautiful Wedding*, *Sensational Silk*, *Sewing with Sergers*, and *Creative Serging Illustrated*, agreed to collaborate as a featured columnist. (Later, in April 1987, Tammy also began the *Serger Update* in response to demand from serger enthusiasts for specialized information.)

Robbie Fanning, our editor-to-be, suggested that the *Update* newsletter research deserved book-format expo-sure. We welcomed the opportunity to integrate our information in a "best of" book. *Innovative Sewing* was born. (We composed the companion text, *Innovative Serging*, in similar fashion; for more information about that title, see "Refer-ences," page 175).

Our intent for *Innovative Sewing* was to assemble and organize the very best of *Sewing Update*—all the ingenious and timesaving methods not found in other books or periodicals. We then edited it again, updating and augment-ing the compilation with our other current work. And because we know that many of our *Sewing Update* readers don't own a serger, you'll notice that in this book serging is mentioned only as an alternative, not as the exclusive element on which the method is de-pendent.

Busy production schedules keep us from sewing as much as we'd like (a frustration many of you share, no doubt). We, and our writers, do, how-ever, test every technique and project. The time we spend experimenting and making mistakes will save you time. Several approaches are always tried before arriving at the most practical method that produces the best results.

To accommodate your busy life and necessarily short reading sessions, we've also organized the book modu-larly. Chapter subheadings are not dependent on one another, so you can read only a page or two and still glean tips that can significantly speed or improve your sewing. Continue to delight in your discovery of innovative sewing.

Gail Brown and Tammy Young

We'd love to hear from you. (Yes, even the critics.) Write us c/o the *Up-date Newsletters*, 2269 Chestnut #269BK, San Francisco, CA 94123.

Acknowledgments

Our special thanks to the knowledgeable sewing professionals who have written for the *Sewing Update* newsletters, helping us develop the materials included in this book: Ann Price, Naomi Baker, Lori Bottom, Jackie Dodson, Karen Dillon, Sue Green, Barbara Griffin, Gale Grigg Hazen, Janet Klaer, Nancy Kores, Judy Lindahl, Jan Saunders, Claire Shaeffer, Ann Marie Soto, Marilyn Thelen, Barbara Weiland, Leslie Wood, and Nancy Zieman.

Also, this book could not have been written without the ongoing support of and essential information from the major sewing machine companies and their local dealers. Our thanks to the following firms (listed in alphabetical order and paired with their respective brand names): Allyn International (Necchi); Bernina of America (*Bernina*); Brother International Corp. (*Brother*); Elna, Inc. (*Elna* and *Elnita*); Fabri-Centers of America (*Sonata Compu-Sew*); Juki Industries of America (*Juki*); New Home Sewing Machine Co. (*New Home*); Pfaff American Sales Corp. (*Pfaff*); Riccar America (*Riccar*); Sears Roebuck Co. (Kenmore); Simplicity Sewing Machines (*Simplicity*); Singer Sewing Machine Co. (*Singer*); Tacony Corp. (*Baby Lock*), Viking Sewing Machine Co. (*Viking*); and White Sewing Machine Co. (*White*). Addresses are listed on page 159.

It's also been our considerable advantage to work with sewing specialists Naomi Baker (coauthor of *Distinctive Serger Gifts and Crafts* and *Simply Serge Any Fabric*) and Virginia Fulcher. Because we haven't figured out how to type and sew simultaneously we rely on their expertise and critiques. And when there's test sewing to be done, or garments to complete for photography, they always, somehow, produce samples that are the envy of the industry.

In addition, we must recognize Chris Hansen, who single-handedly produced the illustrations for this book (and the *Sewing Update* newsletters). (He is, by the way, one of the few illustrators we know who is also an avid sewing enthusiast.) Chris continues to provide us with his ingenuity, encouragement, and professional evaluation of our techniques.

We are also blessed with families and friends who kindly persevere when we go underground to finish books. Thank you for your patience and tolerance for TV dinners.

Finally, we once again (but no less heartily) thank our editor, Robbie Fanning. Her love of sewing, writing, and books is contagious and inspiring.

Introduction

How to Make This Book Work for You

We know you never have enough reading or sewing time, so we have tried to organize our information to make the most of the moments you have to spare. In brief:

• **Read as little or as much as you like**. This book is organized modularly, so one project or chapter is not dependent on another. If there are cross-references, page numbers are cited.

• **Find specific techniques within the chapters** by referring to the Index.

• **Look up unfamiliar terms** in the Index. Page numbers are cited, so you can look up and read about the term in context.

• **Skim the book quickly** by focusing on the fashion or project illustrations that immediately follow chapter subhead introductions.

• **Don't miss the ☞ Update tips and ✎ Notes.**

☞ **Update tips** are special insights about or angles on the specific technique or product.

✎ **Notes** are items of particular importance that you may have overlooked, or answers to common questions related to the subject.

• **Notice the sources for products** listed at the end of related techniques and projects. We always encourage our readers to shop locally first, but when items are unavailable in your area stores, these source lists are indispensable. Addresses are given on pages 160 – 173, in the "Sew-by-Mail Directory."

• **Notice the references** listed at the end of related techniques or projects. These are books or videos that have inspired us, and that cover the subject in greater detail. Also, see "Sewing Books," on pages 174 – 177 of "References."

✎ **Note:** *You don't have to own a serger to utilize this book.* We have intentionally excluded those techniques and projects that call for serging exclusively. (Where serging is an option, it is listed, but not featured.) Although we are avid serging enthusiasts, we also realize that many sewing enthusiasts haven't, and perhaps never will, purchase a serger. If you have questions about serging, please consult *Innovative Sewing's* companion book, *Innovative Serging,* and *Creative Serging Illustrated,* another book that Gail coauthored (see "References," page 174, for information and addresses).

1. Finally—Fashion Disaster-Proof Sewing

- **Practical Wardrobe Planning: Sew to Look Your Best** *Every Day*
- **Go Ahead—Break Some Fashion Rules**
- **Sew Fashion That Flatters: A Pictorial Guide**

What you are going to make is a more important decision than how you are going to make it. Perfect construction can still spell fashion disaster: that is, a garment that—because of the color, fabric, styling, or fit—just isn't your best look. This chapter includes professional guidelines that have helped us avoid fashion disasters. (We still make mistakes, but not as many.) If we could sum it up, it would be: Be honest about your lifestyle, figure, and image. Then assess what you have, need, and like, wardrobe-wise. Oh yes, and have fun breaking a few fashion rules along the way.

Practical Wardrobe Planning: Sew to Look Your Best *Every Day*

Do you find yourself sewing only for special occasions? Or wearing your new outfits only when you need to "dress up"? Many of us do, but perhaps we should adopt a new approach.

Psychologists tell us that the way we feel is directly related to the way we look. *Why not give yourself the advantage of looking and feeling good every day?* With everything we hear about improving the quality of our life, the place to start might well be our own closet. And think how much easier it will be to dress from a well-planned wardrobe. Your sewing time investment will prove more profitable too.

Analyze Your Lifestyle

Do you go to an office every day? Do you attend numerous meetings, events, and social activities? Do you spend

most of your time at home? Do you have other activities which require special clothing—sports, gardening, or work? Think through a typical week and decide what percentage of your time is spent in each different dressing category.

Inventory Your Closet

Set aside a block of time to go through your closet. If you have a friend who will be honest with you, invite her to assist you. Move all of your out-of-season clothes to one section of the closet, to another closet, or to some other storage method. Consider only the garments suitable for the current season. (Obviously segmenting by season is unnecessary if you don't experience season changes.)

Try on anything you haven't worn lately. Be merciless. If something is too small, give it away, or store it. If it's worth altering, put it in a separate place and alter it, or have it altered as soon as possible. If it's worn or you just don't feel good in it, get rid of it. (You might want to save one or two old outfits for the occasional dirty job, such as painting, but you won't need a closetful.)

List All Pieces By Category

Draw columns on a blank piece of paper for each different category you have analyzed in your lifestyle. Label them and add the approximate percentage of time spent at each.

Now, list everything by type, like jackets, tops, bottoms, and other. If you wish, divide tops into sweaters and blouses, or bottoms into pants and skirts. Put dresses and jumpsuits under the "other" category. If an item fits into more than one category, put it under each category it is worn (e.g., a favorite sweater for work and social).

Study Your Chart

Are your lifestyle percentages in scale with your percentages of categorized items? You may discover that some of your clothes have to cover for a lot of your time. That's one of the first categories to consider adding to.

Another place to add is where you have "holes." Find these by going down each column to make certain all the tops and bottoms go together. Do you have some garments that don't match anything? Either add a coordinate soon or discard them. When filling in the holes, try to make sure that each addition is mixable with several items on your list.

When making additions to your wardrobe, ask these questions:

1. **How comfortable will the style be?** Pull-on waistbands are very fashionable now—hurray!

2. **Will special care be required?** If you tend to wear your machine-wash, tumble-dry clothes a large percentage of the time, that's an important feature. Lots of us have perfectly good clothes we seldom wear because they must be ironed, hand-washed, or dry-cleaned. Make what you'll be most apt to wear regularly.

3. **Will the outfit be flattering?** If it's a style you haven't worn before, try on a comparable look in ready-to-wear before sewing. Don't use a color or fabric you dislike because it's on hand

Lifestyle/Wardrobe Chart*
* Change, customize, and add categories as necessary.

Work/Office	Home/Casual	Social (dressier casual)	Sportswear	Semiformal/ Formal
___% time	___% time	___% time	___% time	___% time
Jackets:				
Tops: Blouses				
Sweaters				
Bottoms: Skirts				
Slacks				
Accessories:				
Other:				

Photocopy this chart to use for your wardrobe inventory and analysis. (Enlarge the chart, if necessary.)

or on sale. *Keep reminding yourself: What colors and looks do I feel great in?*

4. Do you have a jacket you love? A neutral color in a fingertip length will go over both skirts and pants (even jeans) and any length of top.

5. Have you tried the new knits? Nothing beats them for comfort and ease of care. There's a wider variety available now than ever before. And you'll find lots of fashionable, super-fast-to-sew knit patterns.

References: For a more detailed explanation of wardrobe planning, refer to *Clothes Sense...Straight Talk About Wardrobe Planning,* by Barbara Weiland and Leslie Wood, ©1984, $8.20 ppd., from Palmer/Pletsch Associates, P.O. Box 12046, Portland, OR 97212-0046, and *Fashion That Flatters,* by Marilyn Thelen, ©1989 (see "References,") page 177.

Go Ahead—Break Some Fashion Rules

Develop your own style and fashion sense through open-minded experimentation and critiquing. Get ready to break self-imposed fashion rules. Then create some fresh, flattering looks.

• **Rule:** *"I'm short, so I stick with single-color outfits."*

• **Reality:** You're limiting yourself unnecessarily. Successful color mixing is a function of degree and proportion. To lend the illusion of one-color dressing, mix colors of equal intensities, such as taupe with heather gray or vivid turquoise with an equally bold fuchsia. See Fig. 1-1.

Fig. 1-1

Proportion is a factor, too. One rule is still universally applicable: the two-thirds/one-third ratio. For example, a pink blouse worn with full-length black slacks, black-tone hose, and black shoes is a winner on just about any figure.

• **Rule:** *"Horizontal stripes and seams make me look shorter and heavier."*

• **Reality:** Not in every case...subtle color and shade differences can minimize the widening effect of horizontal lines (for example, a beige/ivory stripe). Where the stripe or seam line falls is crucial. If the line falls through the upper bodice, the line brings the eye up as shown; when it's positioned at the fullest part of the hip, it only accentuates a problem area.

If broken vertically by a placket, zipper, or intersecting seam, the horizontal dominance is reduced. Also, notice that a stripe, seam, or embellishment that runs horizontally across a dolman-sleeved top doesn't remain horizontal when worn; the line curves down at the shoulders, softening the illusion of horizontal width. See Fig. 1-2.

Fig. 1-2

• **Rule:** *"With my legs, I could never wear those narrow-cut knit pants."*

• **Reality:** Topped with a long shirt or sweater extending beyond the hip or high thigh, narrow knit pants (also called leggings) are surprisingly slenderizing for any figure type. (This is proven by the proliferation of the long top/skinny pant outfits in large-size and maternity catalogs.) This look

creates the flattering two-thirds/one-third proportion, too. See Fig. 1-3.

Fig. 1-3

If your legs are heavy through the calves, the pants should not be skin-tight, but not sweatpant baggy either. Those with well-shaped calves can wear leggings tighter. Whatever your shape or size, begin by using stretchy interlocks, *Lycra*®-blend, or ribbed knit fabrics. Cut out the pants with at least

1" ease through the legs and hips, then try them on and take in equal, incremental amounts along the inner and outer seams.

☞ **Update tip:** Lengthen and slenderize your legs visually with twin-needle topstitching sewn along the center front of the pant legs. The stitching stabilizes the knit (discouraging knee bagging) while simulating pressed crease-lines. See Fig. 2-30 on page 23.

• **Rule:** *"I'm overweight, so bright colors are out."*

• **Reality:** Brights are beautiful on 16-plus sizes. The secret seems to be the fabric, rather than the color or its intensity: Pick one that is not textured, such as jersey or gabardine, that drapes to skim (not cling to) body contours.

The two-thirds/one-third proportion ratio plays an important role when breaking this rule. Don't cut yourself in half when dividing colors; wear a long top over a skirt or a short jacket with trousers or a long skirt.

Other secrets to wearing brights successfully are focus and fit. Direct the eye to one focus only, with accessories or embellishments. For example, tie a dark-print challis scarf over a bright red dress; you'll accentuate your face and diminish silhouette size (Fig. 1-4).

Fit? Unfortunately, brights showcase pull-lines, strained seams, and

Fig. 1-4

too-revealing contours considerably more than dark shades. Fit carefully in front of a mirror and, if possible, an honest friend.

• **Resolution:** *Break at least one of your long-standing fashion rules this season.*

Then delight in the compliments, the wardrobe renovation, and a newfound inspiration to sew.

Reference: *Fashion That Flatters*, by Marilyn Thelen, ©1989 (for more information, see "References," page 177).

Sew Fashion That Flatters: A Pictorial Guide

SHINY FABRICS ADVANCE VISUALLY— USE TO CREATE EMPHASIS!

FLATTER A FLAT DERRIERE: TWO-PIECE DRESSES WITH TOP WORN OUT

A SCARF TIED AT THE NECK CREATES A FOCAL POINT

BEFORE: AFTER: ADD SHOULDER PADS TO BALANCE HIPS

A LARGE, SQUARE SHAWL DRAPED AT THE SHOULDER LENGTHENS THE TORSO.

2. *Newest Knit Know-How*

- **Multiple Choices: Knits and Knit-likes**
- **Before You Sew...**
- **Sewing How to's**
- **The Best Knit Hems**
- **Update: Pro Tips for Today's Most Popular Knits**
- **Twin-needle Sewing**

When Gail first worked in New York's garment district, "knits" meant stable polyester doubleknits. (*Remember leisure suits?*) But during the last twenty-five years, knit options have multiplied dramatically. The current selection couldn't be more enticing—forgiving interlocks, drapable jerseys, stretch-to-fit *Lycra*®-blends, and a whole new generation of fluid, flattering doubleknits. The fibers are as varied as the knit constructions—acrylics, cottons, wools, rayons, silks, polyesters, spandex, and a variety of blends.

Multiple Choices: Knits and Knit-likes

Once we faced the problem of limited knit selection; today, we are confronted with such myriad stretch-fabric options that narrowing down to the right one can be a dilemma. Selection is easier, however, if you understand the inherent qualities and stretchability of knits and knit-likes, outlined below.

Sewing Staples: The Knit Basics

✎ **Note:** Also see "Update: Pro Tips for Today's Most Popular Knits," on pages 26 – 34.

• **Interlocks** are now enjoying unprecedented popularity, and for good reason. This stretchy, drapable knit is actually a fine double rib (Fig. 2-1). The rib pattern is nearly indiscernible, but

you'll recognize interlocks by their beefy hand and crosswise stretchability. *Suitable as its own edge finish. Can be reversed for use on either side; many fibers available. Up to 50% stretch, good recovery.*

• **Singleknit jerseys** come in an incredible range of weights, textures, and fibers (Fig. 2-1). Most common are the fine T-shirt weights, but this category includes much heavier sweatshirting, brushed on the wrong side for comfort and body. *Up to 50% stretch, fair recovery.* (Also, refer to "Update: Pro Tips for Today's Most Popular Knits," pages 26-34).

•THE KNIT BASICS•

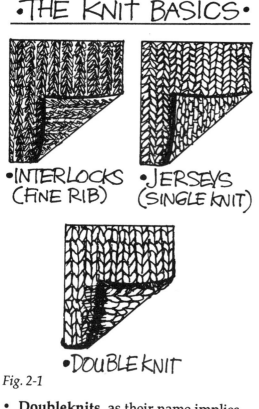

•INTERLOCKS (FINE RIB) •JERSEYS (SINGLE KNIT)

•DOUBLE KNIT

Fig. 2-1

• **Doubleknits,** as their name implies, are double—the yarn loops interlock from front to back (Fig. 2-1). This double construction enhances stability, although it may inhibit stretchability. Today's doubleknit cottons, rayons, wools, and blends are a welcome world apart from the stiffer synthetics of the leisure suit/pantsuit era. *From 12% to 25% stretch, excellent recovery.*

• **Sweaterknits** are generally (but not always) heavier-gauge singleknits (Fig. 2-2). Most are very stretchy but lack resiliency because of the jersey stitch and yarn weight. Compensate by controlling edge stretch with top-quality ribbings or more stable bindings. *From 50% to 75% stretch, poor to fair recovery.* Or consider using **sweaterknit ribbing-by-the-yard** for the entire sweater (Fig. 2-2). *Up to 100% stretch, poor to fair recovery.*

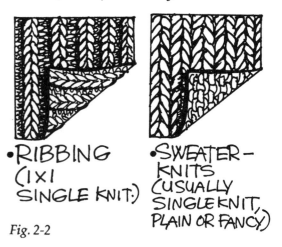

•RIBBING (1×1 SINGLE KNIT) •SWEATER-KNITS (USUALLY SINGLE KNIT, PLAIN OR FANCY)

Fig. 2-2

• **Ribbing** is another singleknit, readily distinguishable because of its unparalleled stretchability and alternating knit-purl stitch. Sold by the yard or as finished-edge bands and collars. The key to selection is resiliency; after being stretched crosswise, the ribbing should spring back. The best sewing techniques can't redeem ribbing that lacks resiliency. Bands, when available, are probably your best bet. *Generally 100% stretch, good to excellent recovery.*

☞ **Update tip:** Occasionally we've been lucky enough to locate *Lycra®*-blend ribbing. This ribbing absolutely will not stretch out of shape. When Gail finds it in any other color than chartreuse, she buys the bolt.

The Knit Newcomers

Although you'll rely on the knit basics, don't miss out on the sewing and fashion excitement of the newest knits, including:

• **Two-way stretch knits**, once relegated to swim and aerobic wear only, now are being sewn into trendy dresses and separates. Most are singleknits that inherit their stretch from the *Lycra®* (spandex) fiber, generally from 8% to 20% of the total blend. Performance bonuses: minimal bagging and wrinkling. *Usually 100%-plus stretch in both the lengthwise and crosswise directions, full (100%) recovery.*

• **Pucker knits** offer all-new surface texture, created by knitting two layers of singleknits together; then the smaller, interlocking lining layer draws in the outer layer, forming puckers. Press carefully, if at all. *Up to 50% stretch, good recovery.*

• **Reversible jerseys** are also two interlocking layers of contrasting-color singleknits, but the right and wrong side are the smooth jersey stitch. *Most have about 25% stretch, excellent recovery.*

The Knit-Likes: Stretch Wovens

When is a stretchy fabric not a knit? When it's a stretch-woven, like these:

• **Crinkled stretch crepes** are elegantly lightweight and conveniently stretchable, thanks to a percentage of *Lycra®* in the blend. *Stretchability can range from about 12% to 25%, excellent recovery.*

• **Stretch gabardines** are great for slenderizing pull-on slacks or skirts; because of the weave and/or *Lycra®*-blending, this flat-surfaced, tightly woven fabric has give. *Limited crosswise stretch, from 12% to 18% (well-suited for most woven, not knits-only, patterns) and recovers completely.*

• **Bubbled or smocked wovens** are made knit-like with an elastic thread used in the bobbin of the decorative surfacing stitching. Check stretchability. *The stretch variance is wide (from 12% to 50%) within this category, and the recovery is excellent.*

The How's and Why's of Stretch Ratios

To determine the stretch ratio of your fabric, simply stretch 4" in the true crosswise direction. If it stretches 1/2", the ratio is about 12.5%, 1" is 25%, 2" is 50%, and so on (Fig. 2-3). Some patterns specify two different ratios for the same style; 50% or more stretch may be needed for the ribbed bands, but only 25% may be required for the main portion of the garment.

Recovery is the degree of resilience or the amount the knit springs back into shape. Give any prospective knit a test stretch, not only for pattern compatibility but to forecast its performance under wearing conditions. *Does it spring back or remain stretched out?* Forget ribbings that don't recover.

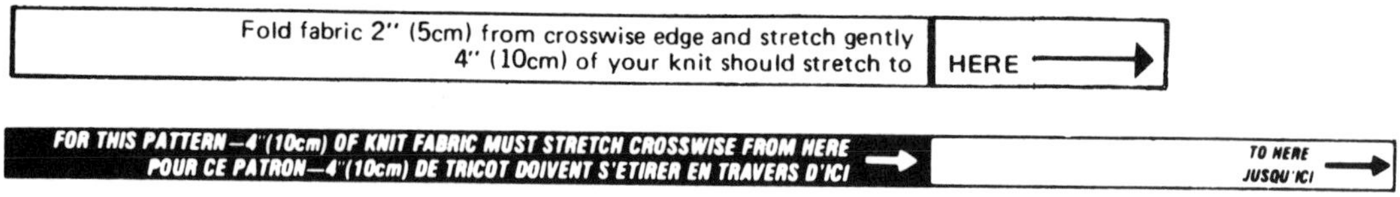

Fold fabric 2'' (5cm) from crosswise edge and stretch gently
4'' (10cm) of your knit should stretch to HERE ⟶

FOR THIS PATTERN—4''(10cm) OF KNIT FABRIC MUST STRETCH CROSSWISE FROM HERE ⟶
POUR CE PATRON—4''(10cm) DE TRICOT DOIVENT S'ETIRER EN TRAVERS D'ICI ⟶   TO HERE ⟶
JUSQU'ICI

Fig. 2-3

Why is it crucial to follow stretch guidelines? Because the stretch allows the pattern designer to exclude fitting features like darts and wearing ease; the knit shapes to and moves with the body without darted-in contours or extra ease. Also, stretch and recovery minimizes inner construction and fasteners; facingless edges can be turned and topstitched (even on curves); garments can be pulled on without zippered openings.

If you use a knit that doesn't stretch to pattern specifications, your finished garment may be too tight, distorted, or, worse yet, impossible to pull on over your head or hips.

Savvy Shopping

• **Open the yardage flat** to search for permanent foldlines, recurring flaws, or needle holes.

• **Don't assume the knit is 60" wide**—ribbed, puckered, or tubular knits are often narrower.

Before You Sew...

Knit Fit

Fitting knits is not an exact science; rather it's an easily acquired aptitude because the fabric is so forgiving.

• *The stretchier the knit, the tighter the fit can be.*

• Compensate for knits with 50% or more stretch and marginal recovery (like 100% cotton interlocks and sweaterings) by sizing down a pattern size. Cut out your standard size and, after a fitting check, sew wider (1") seam allowances.

• If using a knit that stretches less than the pattern suggests, offset the difference by cutting the pattern larger—try an extra 1/2" along all major seamlines. Pin-fit before final seaming.

• Unless otherwise specified, *the greatest stretch goes around the body, arms, and legs.*

• Cut seam allowances wider and hems deeper if you're uncertain about the fit and fabric. After fitting, excess allowances can be trimmed. Or test a pattern by using a similar but less expensive knit.

• Allow skirts and dresses to hang at least 24 hours prior to hemming. (You'll compensate for any extra or uneven stretching of the hemline, caused by the weight of the garment.)

Preparation and Precautions

• **Absolutely, positively prelaunder your washable knits.** Lately, we've calculated 100% cotton interlock shrinkage to be as much as 8" in length per yard (nearly 25%!). Machine wash and dry twice. Dry-clean-only knits should be thoroughly steamed by the dry cleaner, if possible; with hefty steam treatment, shrinkage can be as much as 4" in length per yard.

☞ **Update tip:** To offset yardage lost to shrinkage, buy an extra 1/4-yard of a 100% cotton knit for each yard required and an extra 1/8-yard of other knits (cotton-blends, wools, and wool-blends) for each yard required.

• **Investigate for permanent foldlines.** Refold, if necessary, so that the line will be cut away. Or, if layout is tight, position the line in an inconspicuous area like the center of the sleeves.

• **Consider adding a modesty layer.** When making jersey or interlock tops and dresses, Gail cuts out two fronts. She then sews them as one layer. The extra layer serves as a buffer between undergarments and the outer layer, while adding opacity and body.

• **Follow "with nap" layouts,** if possible, because of the one-way directional knit construction.

• **To secure pattern pieces, use weights** (either specially made weights or unopened pet food cans work well) or fine, sharp long pins with large heads.

• **Reserve rotary cutters for other less bulky projects.** Clean cutting could be a strong-arm task: the rotary action can also stretch the fabric, distorting seam widths.

• For accuracy, **cut out puckered and heavier novelty knits single layer.**

• When extra stability is required, **interface with fusibles;** they move and drape with the knit. It's generally safer to fuse to the facing rather than to the garment; to decrease bulk, trim off about 1/2" from the interfacing seam allowances before fusing. See Fig. 2-4. Some fusible favorites of ours include all the knit fusibles and Pellon's *Stretch-Ease*. (See the "Interfacing Selection Guide" on pages 112 – 113.)

Test swatches on fabric scraps to assess suitability.

Fig. 2-4

Sewing How-to's

Seaming—Not for Sergers Only

Unfortunately, some seamsters have been told that knits can't be sewn without a serger. Fortunately, that isn't true—even the stretchiest *Lycra®*-blends can be straight stitched successfully. (Of course, the inherent stretch of the serged stitch makes it perfect for, but not essential to, seaming stretch knits.) First test any of the following tips on fabric scraps.

• **Change to a new ball or universal point needle,** size 11 (European 75); if available, use needles specially engineered for preventing skipped stitches, like the Singer *Yellow Band Needle* (fits other brands too). Blunt needles can make permanent holes in the fabric along the stitching lines. Adjust the needle size up or down for very light or heavy knits.

• To prevent stretching while sewing, **lighten the presser foot pressure** (see your owner's manual).

• To ensure smooth, jam-free starts when beginning to sew or serge, **gently pull the threads under the foot to the back of the machine.**

• **Use name-brand quality polyester or cotton-wrapped polyester thread.** Cotton has a tendency to break. Or experiment sewing or serging with one of the new woolly stretch nylon threads; thread the eye of the needle with a common wire needle threader.

• **Lengthen stitches** to 8 – 10/inch.

• When straight stitching seams that must stretch, **stretch as you sew** to provide give and to prevent puckering and popping (Fig. 2-5). The seam allowance width will narrow as it is stretched and stitched; readjust the seam width (usually to about 3/8" – 1/2") so that it will measure 5/8" when relaxed.

☞ **Update tip:** Remember, *not all knit seams must stretch,* so stretching while you sew isn't always mandatory. In fact, some knits, like sweaterknits, which tend to stay stretched out after being stitched, require stable seaming and possibly some easing.

• **Don't stretch while serging;** over-locked stitches are inherently stretchy.

• If you have problems with wavy, stretched-out seams or edges, **ease plus**

STRETCH AS YOU SEW, PREVENTING SEAMS FROM PUCKERING & POPPING.

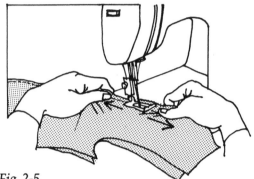

Fig. 2-5

as you stitch. With one index finger, hold the fabric behind the presser foot. With your other hand, force-feed the fabric under the foot faster than the feed dogs are taking it in. See Fig. 2-6. The resulting seam will be slightly eased. A roller or even-feed foot can help too. Adjust sergers with the differential feed feature to the 2.0 ratio setting to automatically ease plus without manipulating the fabric.

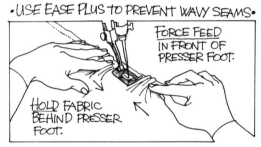

• USE EASE PLUS TO PREVENT WAVY SEAMS •

FORCE FEED IN FRONT OF PRESSER FOOT.

HOLD FABRIC BEHIND PRESSER FOOT.

Fig. 2-6

• **Use single-shank triple and double needles** to enhance the stretchability of straight stitching while reflecting topstitching trends on ready-to-wear sportswear. All you need is a zigzag machine that threads from the front to the back. For easiest threading, wind your thread onto empty bobbins and stack them on the top thread rod (alternating unwinding directions to minimize tangling). The double (or twin) needle can be used for seaming and topstitching; save the triple needle for topstitching (Fig. 2-7). Also, see "Twin-needle Sewing," page 32.

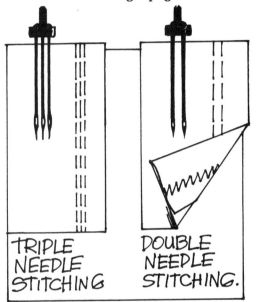

Fig. 2-7

• **Take a few moments to practice** sewing or serging seams on your project scraps. On most knits, traditional pressed-open seams seldom stay that way. Therefore, you can straight stitch, press open, and topstitch the seam layers to both or one side of the seamline; for accuracy, topstitch from the right side. See Fig. 2-8. This more decorative topstitched seam treatment is frequently utilized in tandem with similarly turned and topstitched facingless edge finishes (see pages 17 – 19).

Or sew narrower stitched and trimmed seams; this will minimize

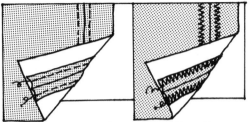

CONVENTIONAL KNIT SEAMING OPTIONS:

STRAIGHT STITCH, PRESS OPEN & TOPSTITCH WITH STRAIGHT OR ZIGZAG STITCHING.

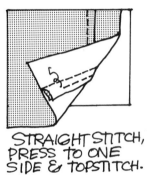

STRAIGHT STITCH, PRESS TO ONE SIDE & TOPSTITCH.

Fig. 2-8

bulk, curling, and raveling. Of those conventional knit seaming options shown in Fig. 2-9, the double-needle and stretch-stitch seams are the stretchiest and most suitable for *Lycra*®-blend knits and other projects that demand seam stretch. But for most knits, the other double-stitched seams work well.

☞ **Update tip:** Investing in a stitch-and-trim attachment (also called a "mini-serger") can cut down on your time spent trimming after seaming; it screws on in place of the standard presser foot and trims as you stitch. (For more information, see pages 139 – 140.)

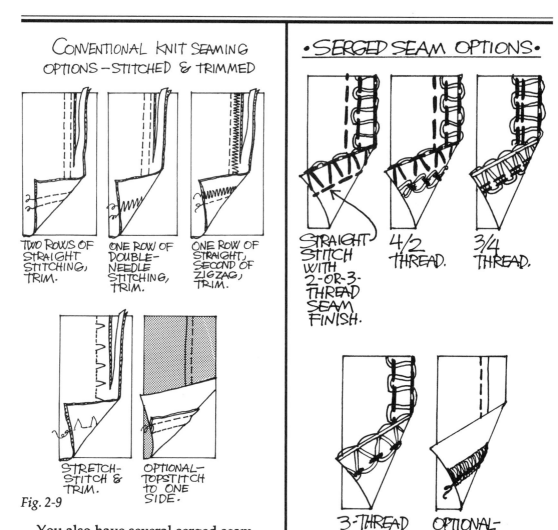

CONVENTIONAL KNIT SEAMING
OPTIONS — STITCHED & TRIMMED

TWO ROWS OF STRAIGHT STITCHING, TRIM.

ONE ROW OF DOUBLE-NEEDLE STITCHING, TRIM.

ONE ROW OF STRAIGHT, SECOND OF ZIGZAG, TRIM.

STRETCH-STITCH & TRIM.

OPTIONAL-TOPSTITCH TO ONE SIDE.

Fig. 2-9

•SERGED SEAM OPTIONS•

STRAIGHT STITCH WITH 2-OR-3-THREAD SEAM FINISH.

4/2 THREAD.

3/4 THREAD.

3-THREAD

OPTIONAL-TOPSTITCH TO ONE SIDE.

Fig. 2-10

You also have several serged seam options, as shown in Fig. 2-10. Choose a more stable stitch, such as a straight/serged stitch combination or 4/2-thread overlocking, when stretched-out, wavy seams are a problem; stretchy 3-thread overlocking will withstand the rigorous stretching that Lycra®-blend activewear is subjected to.

• Whether you sew or serge, you have the option to **topstitch narrow seams to one side** (this will limit seam stretch). See Figs. 2-9 and 2-10.

• **Stabilize shoulder seams** by simply pressing open and topstitching 1/4" on both sides of the seamline. We like this fast, flat technique because it also prepares a smooth surface for mounting shoulder pads. For invisible stabilizing, serge or straight stitch over preshrunk lining selvage strips, twill, or seam tape. See Fig. 2-11.

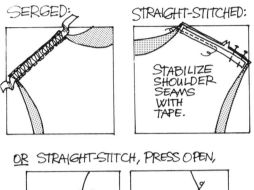

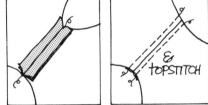

Fig. 2-11

• **Grade, but don't clip seams** (Fig. 2-12). Clipping leaves telltale impressions on the right side of the garment and can weaken the seam. Instead, just trim in layers close to the seamline, as shown; knits are ravel resistant, so narrow seam allowances won't fray out.

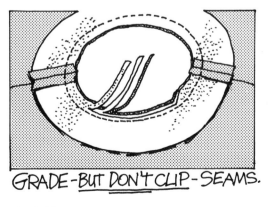

GRADE-BUT DON'T CLIP-SEAMS.

Fig. 2-12

Fast, Facingless Edges

☞ **Update tip:** Before edge-finishing, binding, or trimming a neckline or sleeve, try the edge over your head, arm, or hand (it should be large enough to pull on and off easily). If not, trim the edge in 1/4" increments until the fit is correct.

• On knits with 25%+ stretch, you can **finish edges by simply turning and topstitching** the allowance (Fig. 2-13). You'll love the sewing ease and look of this lightweight knit finish. Test on garment scraps first to see if this method provides enough stability and allows the edge to turn smoothly.

1. Turn the allowance to the wrong side and pin intermittently. Finishing the edge first is unnecessary.

2. Topstitch about 3/8" from the fold, using a single or twin needle and straight or zigzag stitching. The twin-needle topstitching and zigzagging are stretchier and best for edges that will be stretched, like a neckline or a slim sleeve.

3. Trim the allowance to the topstitching on the wrong side. *Optional:* Serge the edge, trimming off 1/8" – 1/4", turn to the right side (see Fig. 2-13) and edgestitch inconspicuously along the serged needle line.

• **Bind with ribbing-by-the-yard or self fabric** (Fig. 2-14). An advantage of this binding is that the neckline or edge will never stretch out. The finished binding should be no wider than 1".

1. Cut crosswise strips three times the finished binding width plus 1". The length will be the edge measurement plus 1".

FACINGLESS FINISHES:
TURN to WRONG SIDE & TOPSTITCH.

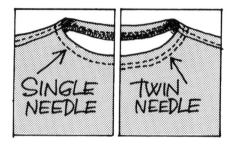

OR SERGE, TURN TO RIGHT SIDE,
& EDGESTITCH.

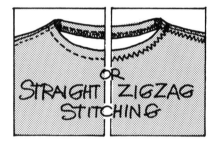

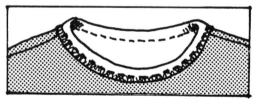

Fig. 2-13

2. Sew one shoulder seam.

3. Right sides together, straight stitch the binding to the edge. The seam allowance should be the width of the finished trim. Stretch slightly around curves so that the finished binding will lie flat.

4. Straight stitch the other shoulder seam, through the binding, and press open. Trim the seam bulk.

BINDING WITH RIBBING

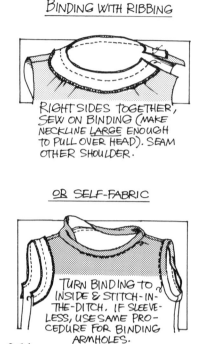

RIGHT SIDES TOGETHER, SEW ON BINDING (MAKE NECKLINE <u>LARGE</u> ENOUGH TO PULL OVER HEAD). SEAM OTHER SHOULDER.

<u>OR</u> SELF-FABRIC

TURN BINDING TO INSIDE & STITCH-IN-THE-DITCH. IF SLEEVE-LESS, USE SAME PROCEDURE FOR BINDING ARMHOLES.

Fig. 2-14

5. Fold the binding over the seam. Stitch-in-the-ditch to secure the binding in place. Trim to narrow and neaten the unfinished binding edge. Follow the same procedure for binding the armhole edges.

• **Finish with self-fabric bands** (Fig. 2-15). Opt for this method when light to medium-weight knits call for a

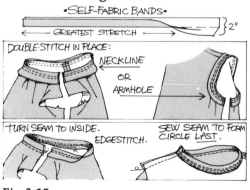

Fig. 2-15

stable but soft edge finish. The flat construction method allows for taking in or letting out the last band seam, helpful when making fit adjustments.

1. Cut the self-fabric band length along the crosswise or the greatest stretch direction. Cut the band 2" wide by the edge measurement plus 1". Fold the band in half lengthwise and finger press.

2. Straight stitch one shoulder seam and press open.

3. Right sides together, double-stitch (one row of twin-needle stitching or two rows—1/4" apart—of straight stitching) the band to the edge with a 1/2" seam allowance.

4. Turn the seam allowance to the wrong side. *From the right side*, edgestitch through all layers 1/8" on the garment side of the seamline.

5. Straight stitch the other shoulder seam (forming a circle). Hide any seam allowances that show along the finished edge by hand-tacking to the wrong side.

Follow the same procedure for finishing armhole edges.

The Best Knit Hems

Conventionally Machine-stitched Hems

• Turn up the hem 1/4" to the wrong side. Zigzag along the edge with a medium-width, medium-long stitch. Trim to the zigzagging. See Fig. 2-16. Try this method on a range of knits, from T-shirt singleknits to interlocks.

• Turn up the hem 1/4" twice to the wrong side and edgestitch 1/8" or so from the hemline. See Fig. 2-17. Suggested for lightweight singleknits—great for flared hems.

• Turn up 3/4" – 2-1/4" to the wrong side and triple or twin-needle topstitch 1/2" – 2" from the hemline fold. Trim to the topstitching. See Fig. 2-18. Suitable for most knits, even heavier sweaterings.

TURN UP ¼", ZIGZAG & TRIM.

Fig. 2-16

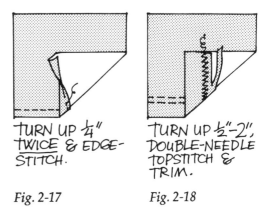

TURN UP ¼" TWICE & EDGE-STITCH.

Fig. 2-17

TURN UP ½"-2", DOUBLE-NEEDLE TOPSTITCH & TRIM.

Fig. 2-18

• **Blindstitch by machine.** Turn up and fold. For a discreetly stitched hem, the zigzag portion of the stitch should barely catch the fold. See Fig. 2-19. Adjust the stitch length and width to achieve the most inconspicuous hem. Always test on scraps. Durable and a real timesaver for T-shirt and sweat-shirt hems.

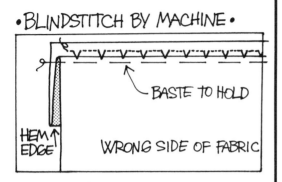

• BLINDSTITCH BY MACHINE •

BASTE TO HOLD

HEM EDGE

WRONG SIDE OF FABRIC

Fig. 2-19

• Make machine-stitched pant hems completely invisible. Allow no less than a 3" hem depth. Just turn up, aligning the out-seams and the in-seams. Then, stitch-in-the-ditch from the right side. See Fig. 2-20. This method is super-quick and truly invisible, but care must be taken when stepping into the pant leg. Perfect for straight and tapered leg pants made of any weight knit.

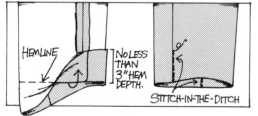

• INVISIBLE MACHINE-STITCHED PANT OR SLEEVE HEMS •

HEMLINE

NO LESS THAN 3" HEM DEPTH.

STITCH-IN-THE-DITCH

Fig. 2-20

Serged hems:

• Simply serge-finish with narrow rolled or balanced hemming (Fig. 2-21). Lengthen the stitch for a lighter, less decorative hem (our preference). A fast, swingy finish for flared jersey skirts and dresses. Also, finish in this

manner before pleating knits—there's no bulk to interfere with pressing.

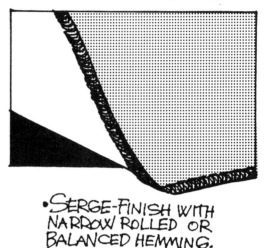

• SERGE-FINISH WITH NARROW ROLLED OR BALANCED HEMMING.

Fig. 2-21

• Serge, turn up 1/2" to the wrong side, and topstitch 1/4" from the hemline (Fig. 2-22). *Optional:* Topstitch with a double or triple needle. Recommended for most knits.

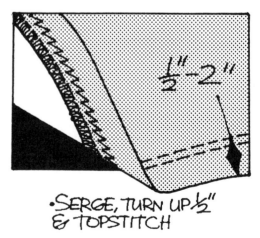

$\frac{1}{2}$"-2"

• SERGE, TURN UP $\frac{1}{2}$" & TOPSTITCH

Fig. 2-22

• Serge, turn up to the wrong side and double- or triple-needle topstitch 1/2" – 2" from the hemline (Fig. 2-23). Suitable for most knits, but we use it mainly on two-way stretch knits, interlocks, and doubleknits.

•SERGE, TURN UP & DOUBLE-NEEDLE TOPSTITCH.

Fig. 2-23

☞ **Update tip:** Flounce (lettuce leaf) edges or hems easily. Stretch as you zigzag with a short to medium length stitch. When serging, there are two possible methods: stretch after satin-serging (see Fig. 2-24) or stretch as you serge. The more stretch, the more flounce. If possible, flounce before seaming in a circle, so the hem edge is flat for easier, more even stretching.

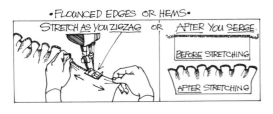

Fig. 2-24

Fast-fused hems:

• Use 3/8"-wide strips of fusible transfer web (with paper or film backing, such as *Aleene's Hot Stitch Fusible Film™*, *Trans Web™ Fusible Web*, *Magic Fuse™*, *Heat N Bond*, or *Wonder-Under™*, positioned 1/4" down from the hem edge. See Fig. 2-25. Fuse following the package or interleaf instructions. Be careful not to press over the raw hem edge, which can leave an undesirable impression on the garment right side. For extra durability, combine fusing with stitching-in-the-ditch of seamlines (as in Fig. 2-20).

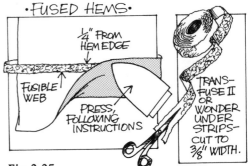

Fig. 2-25

Invisible catchstitched hems:

• Turn up the hem and machine baste in place 3/8" from the raw edge. Fold back as shown and catchstitch from left to right, barely catching the garment. See Fig. 2-26. The stitches should be

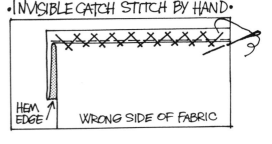

Fig. 2-26

loose enough to be invisible and allow flexibility. After catchstitching, remove the basting. Utilized primarily for medium to heavy knits.

Machine Buttonholes in Knits

• **Work with, not against, the knit.** On ribbed fabrics, place buttonholes parallel with the ribbing. On other knits, buttonholes should run parallel to the lengthwise knitting grain. Also, choose smooth buttons that will glide easily through buttonholes.

• **Make a buttonhole pattern.** (Using this innovative approach, you won't need to remark the buttonhole placements that have disappeared during garment construction!) Place water-soluble or tear-away nonwoven stabilizer over the pattern. Then trace the stitching, fold, and buttonhole placement lines. See Fig. 2-27.

Carefully pin the buttonhole pattern to the garment and work machine buttonholes as marked. Tear away most of the stabilizer. When using water-soluble stabilizer, spritz with water to remove any remaining traces.

• **Lengthen your normal buttonhole stitch** to about 10/inch. Shorter stitches may stretch the buttonhole.

☞ **Update tip:** Protect lightweight knits with a layer of tear-away stabilizer placed over the throat plate, so the knit won't be pulled into the feed dogs during stitching.

• **Cord buttonholes to help stabilize** stretchy knits. For cording, use matching buttonhole twist, crochet thread, or embroidery floss. To stitch a corded buttonhole, place cording over the

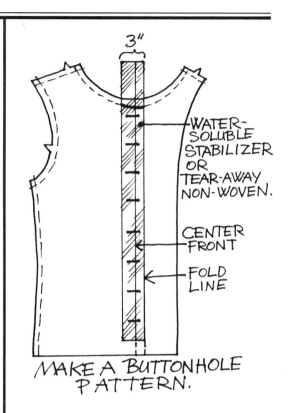

MAKE A BUTTONHOLE PATTERN.

Fig. 2-27

buttonhole, marking with a loop at one end. (Some buttonhole feet have a prong on the back to anchor the cord while sewing. Otherwise loop cording around the head of a pin.) See Fig. 2-28.

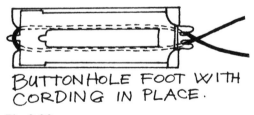

BUTTONHOLE FOOT WITH CORDING IN PLACE.

Fig. 2-28

Lower the presser foot and complete the buttonhole over the cording. Pull the cording taut so no loop remains, then pull a little more to slightly pucker the buttonhole. Clip the cord next to the bartack, or use a large-eyed needle to pull both cording ends to the wrong side and tie them off.

• **Clip buttonholes with a sharp seam ripper**. Starting at one bartack, poke the seam ripper through the fabric and cut toward the middle of the buttonhole. Repeat, slicing from the other bartack. See Fig. 2-29. After cutting buttonholes open, dot the cut edges with seam sealant to enhance stability.

Fig. 2-29

Pressing Pointers

• **Don't overpress knits,** especially synthetics. A low steam setting is suitable for most knits.

• **Control stretching and distortion** while pressing by working on a larger surface; excess fabric is not pulled over the edge of the board.

• **Simulate pant front creaselines** with twin-needle topstitching. (Knits resist permanent creases.) Press-mark the center front. Then, from the right side, double-needle topstitch along the creaseline. See Fig. 2-30. The vertical stitching streamlines stretch-prone soft knit pants.

• Permanently **crease knit pleats**: hem first, press in place, and edgestitch the pleat folds with a single needle.

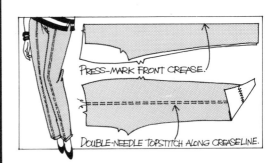

Fig. 2-30

Elastic Waistband Wonders

• Create the latest waistband look in just five minutes. Buy the wide decorative **waistband elastic** (Fig. 2-31)—about your waistline measurement (*watch out—the elastic will buckle unattractively if it is too tight*). Apply flat, before seaming in a circle. Lap the ruffled edge 1" over the right side of the pregathered skirt or pant waistline, distributing the ease evenly. Sewing with the elastic on top, topstitch to the fabric with a twin needle. Straight stitch the last seam, through the elastic, to form the waistline circle. Finger press the elastic seam open and secure with topstitching 1/4" on both sides of the seamline.

Fig. 2-31

• **Make an all-in-one elastic waistband**. It's less bulky and faster than a separate waistband application. Allow 2-1/2 times the elastic width for the casing. Fold the casing over the elastic and twin-needle topstitch, being careful not to catch the elastic. After sewing the casing, fit the elastic; finish by stitching the opening closed. Stitching-in-the-ditch along seamlines prevents the elastic from turning and twisting. See Fig. 2-32.

☞ **Update tip:** Stretch & Sew founder, Ann Person, *doesn't cut the elastic, but marks the waistline measurement and leaves it on the roll* so that the casing doesn't have to be gathered as she stitches. After stitching the casing, the elastic is pulled up, cut, overlapped, and topstitched.

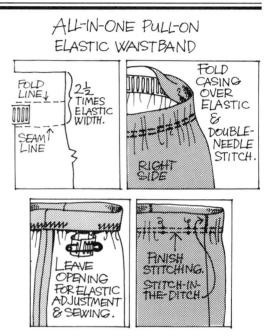

ALL-IN-ONE PULL-ON ELASTIC WAISTBAND

FOLD LINE↓

2½ TIMES ELASTIC WIDTH.

SEAM LINE↑

FOLD CASING OVER ELASTIC & DOUBLE-NEEDLE STITCH.

RIGHT SIDE

LEAVE OPENING FOR ELASTIC ADJUSTMENT & SEWING.

FINISH STITCHING. STITCH-IN-THE-DITCH.

Fig. 2-32

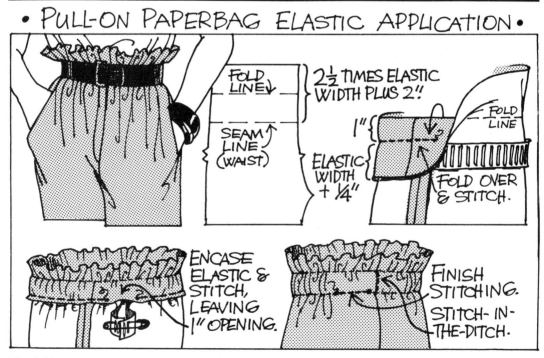

• PULL-ON PAPERBAG ELASTIC APPLICATION •

FOLD LINE↓

SEAM LINE (WAIST)↑

2½ TIMES ELASTIC WIDTH PLUS 2".

1"

ELASTIC WIDTH + ¼"

FOLD LINE

FOLD OVER & STITCH.

ENCASE ELASTIC & STITCH, LEAVING 1" OPENING.

FINISH STITCHING. STITCH-IN-THE-DITCH.

Fig. 2-33

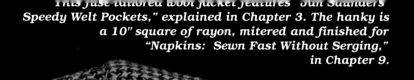

This fine-tailored wool jacket features "Jan Saunders' Speedy Welt Pockets," explained in Chapter 3. The hanky is a 10" square of rayon, mitered and finished for "Napkins: Sewn Fast Without Serging," in Chapter 9.

Gail's daughter's bicycle outfit was sewn without a serger; all seaming and topstitching was done with a twin needle. The same twin-needle technology was applied when making Gail's velour jumpsuit. See Chapter 2.

Sewing coats doesn't have to be time-consuming. This short coat was sewn in three hours—notice the wide top-stitching, extended facings, and edges bound in contrasting wool jersey. See Chapter 3. To make the belt, simply cut a strip of Ultraleather®—no sewing required. See Chapter 6.

Real leather is surprisingly sewable. The fringe and roll-up buttons on the teal-blue coat were easily fashioned from the coat leather. Made from durable smooth-finished pigskin, the burgundy coat was quickly machine-sewn and glued together. See Chapter 6.

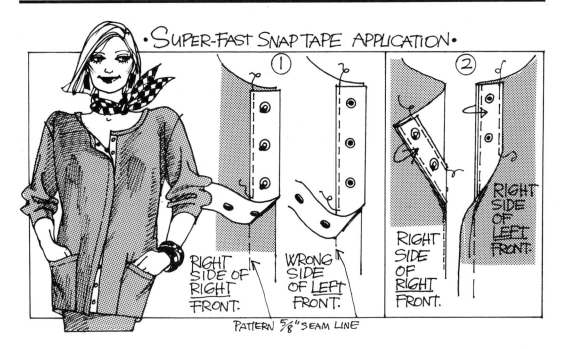

·SUPER-FAST SNAP TAPE APPLICATION·

(1) RIGHT SIDE OF RIGHT FRONT. WRONG SIDE OF LEFT FRONT.

(2) RIGHT SIDE OF RIGHT FRONT. RIGHT SIDE OF LEFT FRONT.

PATTERN 5/8" SEAM LINE

Fig. 2-34

☞ **Update tip:** Paperbag elastic applications are all the rage. Copy the ruffled-top by easily altering the all-in-one waistband. Add an additional 2" to the top of the waistline. Form the ruffle by turning over the casing and straight stitching 1" from the fold. Then proceed as shown in Fig. 2-33, just like the "all-in-one" technique described above.

• **Sew-through elastic waistbands** are another variation of the all-in-one style. For step-by-step instructions, see page 64 – 65 of Chapter 4, "Simply Flattering Slacks."

Super-fast Fasteners

• **Substitute snap tape for buttons.** Add 1-3/4" to both center front pieces (if not already allowed for by the pattern). Straight stitch the tape in place as shown in Fig. 2-34, being careful to align corresponding snap parts. Turn the tape, covering the raw edge and edgestitch; a zipper foot will assist in keeping stitching straight next to snaps. See Fig. 2-34. Bind the top edge as shown on page 18 (Fig. 2-14).

Update: Pro Tips for Today's Most Popular Knits

✎ **Note:** Although most of the knit tips we've already given apply to these popular knits, special exceptions and notable techniques have been highlighted.

A WOOL JERSEY WONDER!

NO ZIPPERS! NO DARTS! THE FABRIC DRAPES THE FIT.

Wool Jersey

• **Always preshrink wool and wool-blend jersey.** Before cutting, have the fabric steamed at the dry-cleaners; it will also remove sizing, which can cause skipped stitches.

• **Cut with care,** using a with-nap layout. Check for the knit's right side

by pulling across the grain; the horizontal cut edge will curl to the right side (Fig. 2-35).

CROSSWISE GRAIN

← STRETCH →
JERSEY WILL ROLL TO THE RIGHT SIDE.

Fig. 2-35

• **Don't over-press.** From the wrong side, steam press in the direction of the lengthwise ribs, using a slightly dampened press cloth (Fig. 2-36). Stop pressing while the fabric is still steaming and slightly damp. Because wool absorbs moisture, allow extra time for cooling.

✎ **Note:** Wool jersey is easily molded and eased by steam pressing, a definite advantage for necklines, sleeve caps, and hems.

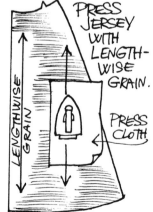

PRESS JERSEY WITH LENGTH-WISE GRAIN.

LENGTHWISE GRAIN

PRESS CLOTH

Fig. 2-36

- For the flattest, least-conspicuous seam, **straight stitch a standard 5/8" seam** and press open.

- **Stabilize shoulder seams** (see Fig. 2-11, on page 17). For soft stabilization of a waistline seam, place *Seams Great®* on the seamline, then sew or serge over it.

Interlocks

- **Try sewing with 100% cotton interlock,** even if it is the most expensive. Why? It's less clingy, less prone to pilling, and has more body than the synthetic blends. (However, many knit lovers swear by less expensive cotton/polyester, if only for its availability, shrinkage resistance, and affordability.)

- **Prewash and dry any washable interlock knit twice.** The extra time

spent will yield long-term benefit—eliminating any residual shrinkage and compacting the fabric yarns, adding body.

- **Follow a "with-nap" layout,** if yardage allows.

- **If using a run-prone synthetic interlock,** effectively prevent running by cutting out garment pieces so that the fabric runs up from the hems (which are subject to less stress).

- **Press conventional seams open;** they won't curl like singleknit jerseys. However, they will tend to lap to one side or the other through washing and wearing. So, either topstitch the allowances to one side or use narrow seaming.

- **Make buttonholes vertical,** not horizontal. Refer to "Machine Buttonholes in Knits," pages 22 – 23.

- **Keep flared hems narrow**—no wider than 3/4".

- **Allow skirts and dresses to hang** at least 24 hours before hemming. Hems will "grow" as much as 2".

Ribbing

- **Sew a deep-lapped "V."**

1. Measure *the V depth and ribbing width carefully*. Remember, the finished ribbing width will "fill" the V; cut down the V proportionately. The V-point seamline on most ready-made tops is positioned about 3" – 5" below the bust point line (see the illustration, on page 28). The finished ribbing width is generally 3" – 4"; cut, allowing 1/4" seams and doubling the width if using ribbing by the yard rather than a

DEEP CROSS-OVER "V" NECKLINE.
LAPPED

ribbed band. Ribbing length should be 1" longer than the cut edge of the neckline.

☞ **Update tip:** To better estimate how much to trim away for the V-neckline, cut out the top with a shallow V, seam the shoulders, pin baste the ribbing in place, and try on. *Caution:* If you'll be wearing the top without a shirt underneath, be careful not to cut the V too low, making it inappropriate for daytime or office dressing.

2. Staystitch 2" on either side of the V point. Start stitching at the center front and stitch up the left side; repeat for the right side.

3. Pin the ribbing to the right side of the neckline, stretching slightly and allowing 1" for lapping at the center front. With the garment on top, straight stitch from the center front to the right shoulder seam. See Fig. 2-37. Stretch the ribbing more (about a 2:3 ratio) between the shoulder seams, pin and stitch, distributing the ease evenly. Stop stitching where shown on Fig. 2-37.

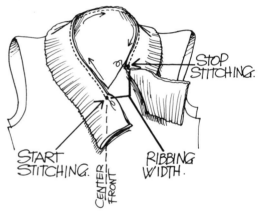

Fig. 2-37

4. Pin the ribbing to the left side of the neckline, stretching slightly. Stop stitching before reaching the V point, *leaving an opening that equals the finished ribbing width measurement.* See Fig. 2-37.

5. Lay the top out on a flat surface, right side up. Tuck the ribbing inside, lapping the left side under the right. See Fig. 2-38. Adjust and pin until smooth and flat. Try on to check fit.

6. *From the wrong side,* straight stitch the opening closed. Pivot at the V point and secure the underlap to the right seam allowance. Trim seam allowances.

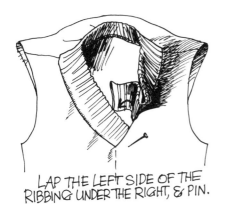

LAP THE LEFT SIDE OF THE RIBBING UNDER THE RIGHT, & PIN.

Fig. 2-38

☞ **Update tip:** After checking the neckline fit, restitch the seam next to the raw edges or serge to neaten and add durability.

• **Sew a wide, mitered "V."**

WIDE MITERED "V" RIBBING.

1. Follow Steps 1 and 2 of the deep-lapped V, pages 27 – 28.

2. Stitch one shoulder seam. *With the ribbing on top,* stitch to the neckline. Stretch the ribbing slightly on the left and right front edges and more (about a 2:3 ratio) along the back neckline.

3. Stitch the other shoulder seam through the ribbing.

4. Miter the V by folding it in half, as shown in Fig. 2-39. Pin baste from the top center front fold line to the ribbing edge; try on the garment. Adjust the seam so that the garment fits smoothly at the neckline and across the bustline.

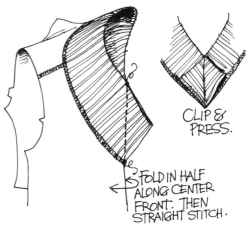

CLIP & PRESS.

FOLD IN HALF ALONG CENTER FRONT. THEN STRAIGHT STITCH.

Fig. 2-39

5. Stitch from the ribbing seam to the ribbing edges, taking care to align the seams and edges accurately. Clip the miter fold and press back. Hand-tack or straight stitch the ribbing raw edges to the seams.

Sweaterknits

Discourage stretching and "waves over the ocean" by following these tips:

• **Cut out the sweater using 1" seam**

EVERITT SWEATER KITS
(NO PATTERNS REQUIRED)
SIZED: S - L .

allowances (seams stretch less when stitching is further away from the raw edges).

• **Lighten the pressure on the presser foot** (refer to your owner's manual).

• **Change to a roller, dual-feed, or even-feed foot**, for smoother feeding.

• **Lengthen stitches to 8 – 10/inch.**

• **Ease plus as you stitch** (see Fig. 2-6 on page 14).

• After stitching the seams, **try on the garment to check the fit**. After making any necessary alterations, straight stitch the allowances together 1/4" from the seamline. Trim to the second stitching.

☞ **Update tip**: Can't find sweater-knits? Look under "S-T-R-E-T-C-H & Knit Fabrics," in the "Sew-by-Mail Directory," pages 166 – 167.

Lycra®-blend Stretch Fabrics

• The degree of stretchability varies, so **test stretch in both directions before**

buying (the more resiliency, the better). A warning about color: without lining, light colors and prints are see-through when wet. (Seen any of these at the pool lately?) If you're modest, stick with intense or darker shades. Another option is to line with self-fabric or swimsuit lining.

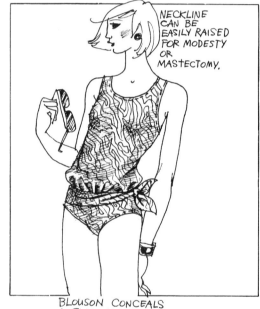

NECKLINE CAN BE EASILY RAISED FOR MODESTY OR MASTECTOMY.

BLOUSON CONCEALS A FULL WAISTLINE.

☞ **Update tip:** Many of our students line just the front of the suit, and some actually use three layers through the front bust area.

• Buy your swimsuit, bodysuit, or leotard pattern by the bust measurement. Then **compare your measurements to the pattern tissue measurements.** Body length seems to give home-sewers the most trouble; after measuring, follow the pattern instructions for shortening or lengthening. Remember, make half of the total length change on the back and the front. Also check the leg opening cut (alter for high or normal) and crotch width (can be narrower or wider).

• **Lay out carefully;** the greatest stretch of the knit should go around the body. Arrange motifs strategically so they enhance your best figure features (*watch out for the bull's-eye effect at the bust or derrière*). Use the main pattern pieces to cut out the lining.

• **Rely on a rotary cutter and mat** for the fastest cutting out. Because of the fabric density, we prefer weights to pins.

• **Sew stretchable seams.** If using a late-model or basic machine, double-stitch with two rows of narrow zigzag or straight stitching. Or use twin-needle stitching for seaming and edge finishing (see "Twin-needle Sewing" on page 32). If using a newer or fully featured machine, try some of the automatic stretch stitches. Whichever you use, *test first on scraps of the actual fabric.* Fine-tune the stitch, *stretching the seam as you sew.*

• **Use a new, fine ballpoint needle,** size 70/10 or 80/12 .

• If using a serger, **insert new needle(s) and test knife sharpness.** Also check length, width, and tension settings. Either a 3- or 3/4-thread overlock will provide a strong, flexible seam; *do not stretch as you serge.* However, with the more stable 2/4-thread seam, stretching as you serge is required. For soft, strong serged seams, use woolly stretch nylon in both loopers.

• **Buy chlorine-resistant swimwear elastic,** generally the 3/8" width for finishing edges. No matter what pattern you use, the ratio of elastic to the leg opening is normally 1:1 in the front and 1" – 2" smaller than the leg opening in back (to keep the suit snug under the fanny). Armholes and necklines, unless specially indicated, are generally a 1:1 ratio, elastic to opening measurements.

• **Apply elastic using the casingless method.**

1. After cutting the elastic to length, sew it to the wrong side of the openings along the raw edge. Use a wide, medium-length zigzag and stretch as you apply, or a long, medium-width overlock or overedge and do not stretch as you serge. Stitch or serge with the elastic on top.

2. Turn the stitched or serged edge to the inside of the suit, encasing the elastic (Fig. 2-40). Twin-needle top-stitch the elastic in place, about 1/4" from the edge. Stretch the fabric and elastic as you topstitch. (The zigzag stitch that forms on the back adds stretch to the stitch.) If you don't have a twin needle, a single row of stitching will suffice.

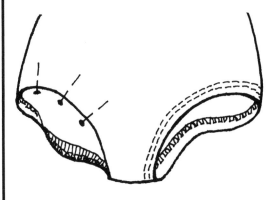

Fig. 2-40

Twin-needle Sewing

Cotton/*Lycra*®-blend knits have made fastenerless sewing possible, and on the simplest zigzag machine. All seaming and finishing is done with a twin needle, maximizing sewing efficiency (Fig. 2-41).

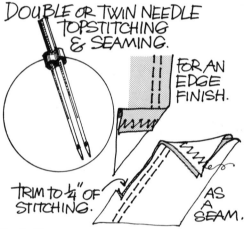

DOUBLE OR TWIN NEEDLE TOPSTITCHING & SEAMING.

FOR AN EDGE FINISH.

TRIM TO ¼" OF STITCHING.

AS A SEAM.

Fig. 2-41

• **Shop.** First, look for patterns—a "for knits only" style requiring 50% stretch (4" of crosswise grain needs to stretch 2" or more), no zippers or buttons, ribbings or facings. Then, buy the fabric—a cotton/*Lycra*®-blend or interlock with at least 50% stretch. (To better understand stretch percentages, see "The How's and Why's of Stretch Ratios" on pages 11 – 12.)

• **Round up new twin needles.** (Have two extras as backups in case of breakage or tip damage; blunt tips make holes in knits.) Because the twin needle will be used for both seaming and topstitching, opt for the widest needle configuration your machine will accommodate. For *Lycra*®-blend and interlock knits, we prefer the 3- to 4mm-width stretch or universal point,

in a size 11/75 or 12/80. Until recently, the wider-width twin needles were only available in sizes 14/90 and 16/100. Mail-order merchant Clotilde introduced us to the Schmetz Stretch Twin Needle size 11/75, sold in the 3mm and 4mm widths. These new, finer sizes are designed for skip-free twin-needle seaming and topstitching. (Unfortunately, the 3- to 4mm-wide 11/75 twin needles are also more susceptible to breaking than the same widths in sizes 14/90 and 16/100.)

To use these single-shank, twin needles, your machine must have the zigzag capability and thread from the front to the back. Ask your dealer about needle availability and adaptability to your make and model.

Quality polyester or cotton-wrapped polyester is recommended for the needles and bobbin. *Optional:* Use woolly stretch nylon thread for soft, very durable seams and topstitching (use common wire needle threaders for threading this limp, crimped nylon).

• **Refer to "Double Needles: Double Your Options"** for more machine set-up information, on pages 95 – 97.

• **Plan sewing strategies.** To streamline the process, you will be using the twin needle for both seaming and topstitching. No needle changing is necessary and the stitch will stretch. Minimize bulk and curling by trimming the allowances close to the stitching.

• **Follow the fastest flat-construction sewing order.** For accuracy, topstitch from the right side of the garment. Unless otherwise specified, all topstitching is 3/8" from the edge. To hide

Fig. 2-42

seams that show at neckline or hem edges, hand-tack allowances to the wrong side.

For the dress (Fig. 2-42):

1. Turn up the sleeve hems and topstitch.

2. Sew one shoulder seam. Hold the allowances to the back bodice side of the seam and topstitch.

3. Turn under the neckline 5/8" and topstitch.

4. Sew the other shoulder seam and topstitch as in the second step.

5. Set-in the sleeves.

6. Sew the center back and center front seams of the skirt. Press to one side.

7. Sew the skirts to the bodices. Hold the allowances to the bodice side of the seam and topstitch.

8. Sew one side and underarm seam. Press to one side.

9. Turn up the bottom hem and topstitch.

10. Sew the other side seam.

For the top (Fig. 2-43):

1. Turn up the sleeve hems and top-stitch.

2. Sew three of the sleeve seams, leaving one open, as shown. Hold the allowances to the sleeve side of the seam and topstitch.

3. Turn under the neckline 5/8" and topstitch. Sew the other sleeve seam.

4. Sew one side and underarm seam.

5. Turn up the bottom hem and top-stitch.

6. Sew the other side and underarm seam.

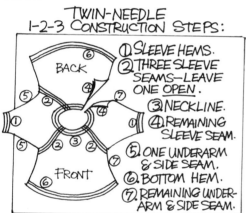

TWIN-NEEDLE
1-2-3 CONSTRUCTION STEPS:

① SLEEVE HEMS.
② THREE SLEEVE SEAMS—LEAVE ONE OPEN.
③ NECKLINE.
④ REMAINING SLEEVE SEAM.
⑤ ONE UNDERARM & SIDE SEAM.
⑥ BOTTOM HEM.
⑦ REMAINING UNDERARM & SIDE SEAM.

Fig. 2-43

Sources: *For all types of knits*—check with your local fabric retailer (if the type you're looking for isn't available, refer to "S-T-R-E-T-C-H & Knit Fabrics," in the "Sew-by-Mail Directory," pages 166 – 167). *For even-feed or roller feet, fusible transfer web, stabilizers (water-soluble or tear-away nonwoven), chlorine-resistant elastic, twin needles, and woolly stretch nylon*— Clotilde, Inc., Nancy's Notions, Ltd., Serge & Sew Notions, Sewing Emporium, Stretch & Sew Fabrics, The Perfect Notion, and Treadleart. *For interlocks and two-way stretch cotton/Lycra®*—Cottons, Etc., Jehlor's, Green Pepper, Kieffer's, LG Fashions and Fabrics, Marianne's Textile Products, Nancy's Notions, Ltd., Serge & Sew Notions, Sew Natural® Fabrics by Mail, and Stretch & Sew Fabrics.

3. Timesaving Tailoring: Better, Faster Jackets and Coats

- Sew Better Jackets: Semi-lined Rather Than Unlined
- Wrap-up Collars and Lapels
- Simple-to-Sew Soft Coat
- Secrets to Tailoring Light-colored Fabrics
- Coats: Pro Pointers, in Brief
- Jan Saunders's Speedy Welt Pockets
- Interfacings for Tailoring
- Restyling Menswear: Fast and Affordable Man-tailoring for Women

Neither of us has the time we once did to tailor. (When she was fifteen, Gail kept track of the hours she spent on making her 4-H Dress Revue entry, a coat—total construction time: 150 hours!) Well, those more leisurely sewing days are over. Like most of you, we now must contend with schedules jammed with family, work, and community-service obligations.

Still, there's nothing we need more, or like better to wear, than a beautiful jacket or coat. With the help of *Sewing Update's* talented writers, we've devised tailoring that's timesaving, without sacrificing quality construction. Steal the few hours you'll need to sew a smashing jacket or coat—your time investment will pay off in long-term fashion and sewing satisfaction.

Sew Better Jackets: Semi-lined Rather Than Unlined

Peruse the pattern catalogs for jackets. Unlined styles are the prevailing trend, except for a very few fully lined classic blazers and coats. The unlined method suits more fluid, oversized silhouettes and our time limitations. Nonetheless, most jackets fit and look better if they are semi-lined rather than unlined. This modification requires only 30 extra minutes of cutting and sewing; the professional results speak for themselves.

• **Purchase lining.** We know this sounds like a contradiction, *but you will be lining the sleeves.* The reason? For the ease in putting the jacket on and taking it off. Plus, lining automatically hems the jacket sleeve without handstitching and adds body, preventing stretching at the elbow. Buy enough durable lining for two sleeve lengths, about 3/4 – 1

yard. We prefer tightly woven polyester linings because they wear so well.

• **Alter the facing(s) shape and size.** *This is the most important step.* On most unlined jacket patterns, the facings aren't wide enough to add body, and they tend to turn to the right side unless tacked down (then the stitches show on the garment). Also, shoulder

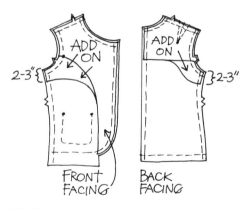

Fig. 3-1

pads must be covered because they show.

By simply extending the front and back facing, all these problems will be prevented. The facings then also double as front and back stays; your jacket will keep its shape and wrinkle less. Pin the facings to the front and back pattern pieces. Using a piece of tissue paper, waxed paper, or nonwoven interfacing (nonfusible), make new facing pieces (Fig. 3-1). The shape of the new facings should look familiar—you've seen the same in many partially lined men's jackets.

• **Cut out the jacket,** using the new, extended facings. Uncertain about fit? Allow about at least 1" side, shoulder, and center back seams (they can always be trimmed, if necessary). Also, you'll want the seams to lie flat after being finished, which is difficult if they are too narrow.

✎ **Note:** Because most fall jackets will be sewn from wider-width fabric, the usual yardage requirements will suffice. However, extra fabric may be needed if you are a size 14+ Misses, if the jacket is oversized, or if the fabric used is narrower than 54" wide. Use your cutting mat or board to plot the layout after you've altered the facings and widened the jacket seam allowances.

☞ **Update tip:** If your pattern doesn't have a separate, larger piece for the upper collar, or the lapel facing is not larger than the jacket lapel, add to the outer edges. To allow for "turn of the cloth," add 1/8" for light- to medium-weight fabric, 1/4" for medium- to heavy-weight fabric, and 3/8" for heavy coatings.

• **Fuse interfacing to the facing and jacket pieces** (Fig. 3-2). As a guide for interfacing selection, review Chapter 8, "Interfacing Update," pages 101 – 114 and pages 50 – 53 of this chapter. It's crucial to preshrink the interfacing and the fashion fabric. You'll avoid unsightly bubbling of the fabric surface later.

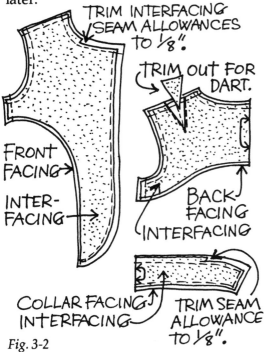

TRIM INTERFACING SEAM ALLOWANCES TO ⅛".

TRIM OUT FOR DART.

FRONT FACING→

INTER-FACING→

BACK FACING INTERFACING

COLLAR FACING INTERFACING

TRIM SEAM ALLOWANCE TO ⅛".

Fig. 3-2

• **Seam the facing and upper collar pieces.** Press open, clipping for smoothness. Because fusible interfacing is used on the facings and hems, edge finishing is a snap. Straight stitch and pink, or serge (routinely or decoratively). Avoid bulky finishes that could make an impression on the right side.

• **Seam the jacket shoulder, under collar, and side seams.** Clip the collar seam. Press. Finish the side seams.

☞ **Update tip:** For a professional finish, bind the seam and facing edges with bias strips of the lining fabric. Cut the strips about 1 – 1-1/4" wide. Bind as shown in "Bind with ribbing or self fabric" on page 18 of Chapter 2 (Fig. 2-14, Step 3). The seam and finished binding width should be about 1/4". Even though the underside of the binding is unfinished, the bias-grain raw edge will not ravel. (Also see photographs of jackets with bound seams on the color pages.)

• **Try on the jacket** with the upper collar and facing piece wrong sides together over the jacket and under collar pieces. Adjust the fit. Stitch the collar/lapel/facing seam. The "Wrap-up Collars and Lapels" how-to's on pages 38 – 41 of this chapter will give you a perfect notched collar every time.

• **Line the sleeves.** Be sure the pattern length is correct (measure with your elbow bent). To cut the sleeve lining, simply use the jacket pattern minus the hem allowance. With a 5/8" seam allowance, seam the lining to the sleeve, right sides together. Grade the seam. Press the seam toward the lining. Right sides together, sew the jacket and lining seam (Fig. 3-3). Press the seam open. Turn the sleeve right side out, aligning the fabric and lining seam.

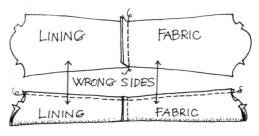

LINING   FABRIC

WRONG SIDES

LINING   FABRIC

Fig. 3-3

• **Set in the sleeve.** Sew to the jacket only, folding away the extended facing piece and the sleeve lining. After setting in both sleeves, insert and position the shoulder pads, then tack in place. Machine stitch the facing pieces in place just inside the sleeve/armhole seam, sandwiching the shoulder pads between.

• **Hand-blindstitch the sleeve lining in place,** hiding the sleeve/armhole seam. Fold under the seam allowance, pin intermittently, and handstitch.

• **Delight in your finished jacket.** The extra time spent will be well worth it when you effortlessly slip it on or lay it over a chair, exposing the lovely extended facings and lined sleeves.

References: *Easy, Easier, Easiest Tailoring,* by Pati Palmer and Susan Pletsch, ©1983 (revised edition), $8.20 postpaid from Palmer/Pletsch Associates, P.O. Box 12046, Portland, OR 97212-12046, *Sew Smart* supplement, by Clotilde, ©1984, by Clotilde (see "Sew-by-Mail Directory"), $7.50 postpaid, and *The Busy Woman's Sewing Book,* by Nancy Zieman, ©1988, Open Chain Publishing (see "References," page 176.)

Wrap-up Collars and Lapels

Telltale signs of tailored-at-home jackets are uneven collars and lapels. But professional-quality detailing is only a technique away. Nancy Zieman, of cable and public television's *Sewing with Nancy,* calls it the "wrapped corner." This simple process folds and stitches seam allowances to the underside, forming smooth corners on both the collar and lapels.

1. **Mark accurately.**

• Mark collars at center back, shoulder seams, and the lapel dots.

• Mark the lapel dots on the jacket front and facing.

• Mark the roll line of the collar (as outlined on the pattern).

2. **Construct the collar.**

• Pin the under collar to the jacket neckline. The shoulder seams, center back, and particularly the lapel dots should match as precisely as possible.

• Stitch the seam *with the collar on top and the jacket layer next to the feed dogs;*

the two layers automatically ease together. Start and stop stitching at the lapel dots. To lock the stitches, the length should be "0" at the beginning and end of the seam. Then change to a standard length (10 – 12/inch) for the rest of the seam.

• Press the neckline seam flat. Clip the neckline seam allowances to the stitching. The first and last clips should be at the lapel dots.

• Stitch the seam again for reinforcement. Press the neckline seam open over a pressing ham.

• Repeat these steps for the upper collar and facing/lining.

3. **Sew the lapel and collar together** (Fig. 3-4).

• Place the two jacket collar units right sides together, aligning the neckline seams. Pin along the neckline seam to prevent shifting while sewing. The lapel dots of the under and upper collars should match exactly. Other critical areas to match are the two shoulder seams and the collar center back seam.

• Pin the upper and lower collar units together, as shown. Baste stitch, sewing toward the lapel dot from the outer edge of the collar. Then baste stitch, sewing toward the lapel dot from the outer edge of the lapel. Leave long thread tails in case you have to remove the stitches. See Fig. 3-4. *Do not stitch through the neckline seam allowances* (doing so can create pulling and bulk in the finished lapel notch). The allowances fold away easily because they haven't been trimmed.

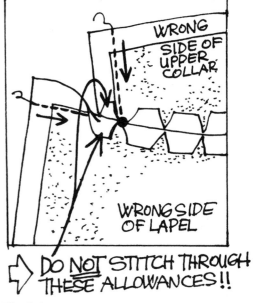

Fig. 3-4

• Finger-press the seams just stitched. Check the stitching accuracy by turning the collar/lapel right side out. Do the two stitching lines meet exactly at the lapel dot? If not, remove the basting and try again. Restitch the lapel seams using a 12 – 15/inch length. To lock the stitches at the lapel dot, set the stitch length on "0." Press the seams flat, then open.

• Grade (layer) the seam allowances and trim the under-collar neckline seam allowances to 1/4". Trim the upper-collar/facing seam allowances to 3/8".

4. **Wrap the corners.**

• Wrap the graded collar seam allowance to the under-collar side. Place the stitching line on the fold. Pin together between the two wrapped collar ends. Next, sew the seam, using a short

(18/inch) length. The collar corners are now wrapped and secured underneath. See Fig. 3-5. Press the outer seam edge of the collar flat, then open as far as possible. Grade the under-collar seam to 1/4", the upper-collar seam to 3/8". Trim away any excess bulk from the collar corners.

Fig. 3-5

☞ **Update tip**: If your fabric ravels readily, seal the corner edges with seam sealant like *Fray Check*™ or *No Fray*.

• Trim the neckline seam allowances that are pressed to the inside of the collar to 3/8". The side of the seam pressed downward from the seamline should remain 5/8". Turn the collar right sides out.

• From the right side, align the two neckline seams, *wrong sides together*. Pin into the seamlines of the two seams. Working from the wrong side of the jacket, zigzag the two neckline seam allowances together (Fig. 3-6).

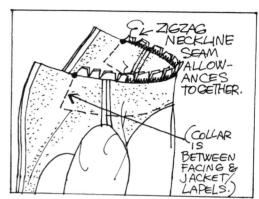

Fig. 3-6

5. Finish the jacket front.

• Pin the front facing to the jacket front, right sides together. Match the roll-line notches. Wrap the neckline seam allowances *to the interfaced jacket side of the seam* (which will be the underside of the lapel). Holding the wrapped seam in place, stitch the front seam. Sew with the jacket on top, automatically easing the longer facing side of the seam. See Fig. 3-7. Press the front seams flat, then open as far as possible.

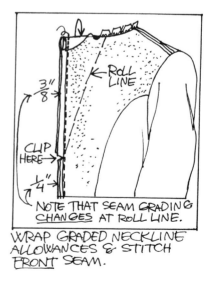

Fig. 3-7

☞ **Update tip:** Press the front seams over a narrow board to eliminate seam-edge imprints from showing on the right side.

• Clip to the seamline at the lower end of the roll line, as shown in Fig. 3-7. Above the clip, grade the facing seam allowance to 3/8" and the jacket to 1/4". Below the clip, grade the facing seam allowance to 1/4" and the jacket to 3/8".

• Turn the jacket right side out. Press along the edge of the facing, aligning the seamline at the folded edge.

Simple-to-Sew Soft Coat

A soft-tailored coat is one of the newest fashion looks. And it's a savvy sewing choice if you shy away from making any jacket or coat requiring traditional tailoring methods. The soft coat's subtle shaping is constructed with quick and easy techniques.

Fabric Choices

Ready-to-wear is featuring coat fabrics with lots of surface texture. Wool fleece, bouclé, mohair, and camel hair all lend themselves well to soft tailoring. These fabrics give the appearance of a thicker, heavier coating but are surprisingly lightweight to wear, particularly when unlined.

Design Choice

A loose-fitting design with a softly rolled collar or no collar is best. Patch or side-seam pockets are easier to construct in softer fabrics than are welt pockets. All of the pattern companies have suitable designs for softly tailored coats; the coat shown on this page is a good example. The modified raglan sleeve requires little fitting and, because there is no sleeve insertion, is easy to sew. Collarless detailing, easy lined pockets, and a speedy sleeve-cuff application add up to a coat that can be made in just hours.

Soft Construction

A traditionally tailored garment usually combines firm fabric with crisp details and built-in shaping. In a softly tailored or unstructured coat, dressmaking techniques are combined with traditional tailoring methods.

✎ **Note:** Be reassured that these faster and easier techniques are also used in the finest ready-to-wear.

Cutting Out and Pressing

• Because most soft coat fabrics are napped, **use the "with-nap" layout,** cutting all pieces in the same direction. Cut *with the nap running down* for longer wearability.

• **Avoid flattening the surface texture** by placing the right side of the fabric against thick terry toweling and pressing from the wrong side.

• **Keep straight seams straight when pressing;** press curved seams on shaped pressing equipment.

• **Lightly steam lining hems.** For a softer look, do not press flat.

Interfacing

As in any tailored garment, interfacing is needed to stabilize and support softer coat fabrics. Today's fusible interfacings can do so without imparting too much crispness.

• **Choose a light- to medium-weight fusible** interfacing the same or lighter weight than the fashion fabric. See the "Interfacing Selection Guide," on pages 112 – 113.

• **Stabilize without stiffness** with tricot knit and weft-insertion interfacings. Both can be used on either knits or wovens. (The knit stretches in the crosswise direction; the weft-insertion is stable on both the lengthwise and crosswise grain.)

• **Use different weights of interfacings** in different parts of the garment to achieve desired results. A medium-weight interfacing is best for support in the facing and neckline and a lighter-weight interfacing is best for shaping in the hem.

• **Test fuse** on a 6" square of fabric, making certain that the interfacing doesn't make the fabric too crisp. On the other hand, avoid an interfacing that's too soft; if it is, the fabric will look too limp.

• **Fuse interfacing stays** to prevent the upper part of the coat from stretching.

1. Cut fusible interfacing to fit the upper area of the fronts, backs, sleeve fronts, and sleeve backs as shown in Fig. 3-8, from the shoulder seams down 10".

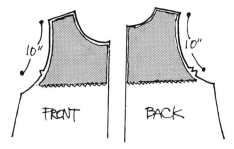

FUSE INTERFACING STAYS to UPPER AREA OF COAT SLEEVES AND BODY- PINK LOWER EDGES

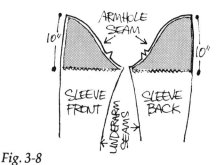

Fig. 3-8

🖝 **Update tip**: Trim the bottom edge of each interfacing piece with pinking shears. A pinked edge will not create a ridge on the right side when fused.

2. Trim 1/2" from the outer edges of heavier-weight interfacing stays. Fuse stays in place.

Collarless Neckline Tips

• **Stabilize the neckline.**

1. After cutting the garment pieces, stay-stitch the neckline 1/2" from the cut edge using a short stitch length (12 – 15/inch). See Fig. 3-9.

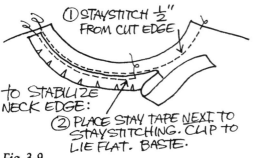

Fig. 3-9

2. Use a narrow (1/4" – 3/8"), light-weight, and pliable cotton or linen stay tape or nylon *Stay Tape*™. (Twill tape can make the seam too rigid.)

✎ **Note**: Pretreat cotton stay tape in hot water and allow to dry completely before using. Do not iron dry.

3. Place the tape next to the stay-stitching line. Clip the tape to allow it to lie flat and baste it into position. See Fig. 3-9. The tape will be caught in the seam stitching.

4. Topstitch the neckline to further stabilize and prevent stretching from wear.

Interfacing the Hem

Interfacing gives body and shape to the hem while also serving as a buffer between the cut hem edge and the right side of the coat.

1. Lightly steam and finger-press the hem up at the lower edge.

2. Cut a bias strip of interfacing 1" wider than the hem depth by the measurement of the lower edge plus 1". **(Note:** A weft-insertion (*Whisper Weft, Suitmaker*™, or *Tailor Fuse*™) or woven (*Stacy Shape-Flex® All Purpose, Form-Flex*™ *All Purpose,* or *Classic Woven*™) fusible interfacing is preferable.) Add seam allowances and piece if necessary.

3. Place the interfacing along the hemline so it extends 1/2" into the depth of the hem and 1/2" into the front facings. Fuse. *The interfacing will extend approximately 1/2" above the cut edge of the pressed hem.* See Fig. 3-10.

4. Hand-catchstitch the hem to the interfacing only.

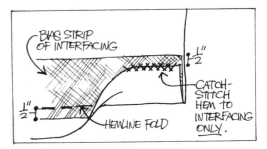

Fig. 3-10

Seam Finishing

• **Bind seam and facing edges with bias strips of the lining fabric or crosswise strips of wool jersey.** Cut the strips about 1 – 1-1/4" wide. Bind as in "Bind with ribbing or self fabric" on page 18 of Chapter 2 (Fig. 2-14, Step 3). The seam and finished binding width should be about 1/4". Even though the underside of the binding is unfinished, the bias-grain raw edge will not ravel. (Also see the soft, teal-blue coat with seams bound in hot-pink wool jersey on the color pages.)

Topstitching

• **Allow wider—7/8"—seams** for seams that will be topstitched. After seaming, press the seam allowances to one side and topstitch at 5/8". See Fig. 3-11. Topstitch around the neckline edge, at sleeve seams, and down the center front 5/8" from the seam or edge.

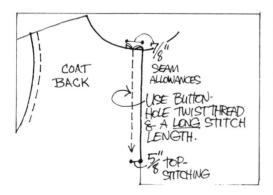

Fig. 3-11

• **Use topstitching or buttonhole twist thread.** To avoid skipped stitches, use a large (size 14/90 – 16/100) needle and loosen the upper needle tension slightly.

• **Adjust for a long stitch length** (8/inch) and stitch slowly for better control of the fabric.

Buttonholes

• **Make corded buttonholes** by stitching over a strand of buttonhole twist. Cording reinforces the buttonhole to prevent stretching.

• **Lengthen the stitch.** A satin stitch will stretch the buttonhole and give it a home-sewn look.

• Using permanent marking pen in a matching color, **camouflage any interfacing** that's showing through along the cut edges of the buttonhole.

Secrets to Tailoring Light-Colored Fabrics

Lighter-colored fabrics present intriguing tailoring advantages and challenges. With greater reflective capacity than darker hues, both perfect detailing (like topstitching) and flaws (like prominent outlines of inner construction) are magnified. Unfortunately, just one or two glaring problems can overpower otherwise skillful sewing. Beat the home-made-look blues with these proven strategies for working smarter and faster:

• **Practice fabric and pattern savvy.** Wrinkles are more conspicuous in lights and whites. If these horizontal creases add unwanted pounds or conflict with your image of neatness, avoid crushable and creasable materials. Consider more carefree blends, knits, or linens and cottons tightly constructed enough to be more

resilient. Remember, wrinkling is a matter of degree—nearly every warm-weather-weight woven does to some extent. Also, most will wrinkle more after cleaning removes surface finishes.

• **Steer clear of tightly constructed, super-resilient synthetics** for notched-collared, tailored jackets. The "iron-free" label can be taken quite literally—you'll tear your hair out trying to do the steam-shaping essential for lapel roll-lines and easing sleeve caps.

• **Play it smart when choosing patterns** too. Fewer sewing precautions will be required of a loosely fitted jacket. An oversized jacket, even if unlined, can generally be sewn following the pattern, whereas a fitted style demands special facing, interfacing, lining, and finishing techniques.

Similarly, coordinate the weight and drape to the silhouette; use light-colored, lighter-weight fabric for draped, easy-fitting styles that subdue facing and seam allowance outlines or "shadows."

• **Fuse an underlining layer to white or light tailored jackets**; it will make the formerly see-through fabric opaque, so inner construction elements like shoulder pads won't shadow through to the garment.

Simply underline the jacket bodice, front facing, upper collar, and pocket pieces (not the sleeves) with light-weight fusible interfacing like *Stacy Easy-Knit*® (or comparable knit types) or *Sof-Shape*® (or other nonwoven types with crosswise or all bias give). Then interface and line as usual. The underlining layer also serves to buffer the bulk of seam layers, minimizing ridge formations on the right side of crucial areas like the notched collar.

✎ **Note:** For other interfacing ideas, refer to the "Interfacing Selection Guide" on pages 112 – 113.

• **Banish unsightly bubbling.** Bubbling on the right side of fused sections will be impossible to hide on light colors. Luckily, this frustrating condition is preventable. Caused by "differential shrinkage," the fusible interfacing can be shrunk more than the fashion fabric. Preshrink any fusible according to the instructions given in the "Interfacing Update," Chapter 8, pages 105 – 106.

Coats: Pro Pointers, in Brief

When making any coat, bulk lurks in every seam, corner, and hem. Help trim the excess bulk in these ways:

FACING

LINING

BINDING

LINER

• **Don't be afraid to closely trim and grade collar and facing seams.** Enclosed seams in coating fabrics can be very bulky, especially with the addition of interfacing. Beveling is especially effective for coat fabrics. Simply hold the scissors at a slant while trimming so one layer of the seam ends up slightly narrower (Fig. 3-12).

BEVEL TO MINIMIZE BULK.

Fig. 3-12

• **Avoid lumpy coat hems** by trimming seam allowances within the hem allowance to 1/4" (Fig. 3-13).

TRIM HEM SEAMS to $\frac{1}{4}$"

Fig. 3-13

Jan Saunders's Speedy Welt Pockets

Nothing screams "loving-hands-at-home" more than poorly executed pocket welts—those that are too long, or have raveling corners, or have lips that are unequal in width. Fortunately, author and *Sewing Update* writer Jan Saunders has developed a nearly goof-proof approach: she uses her innovative bound buttonhole technique for the pocket welts. It's fast and easy because the machine does all the work. (Nonetheless, make a practice run before you sew the real one on the garment.)

✎ **Note:** Zigzag stitches add enough body to the welt so that interfacing is optional.

1. Carefully mark the pocket location on the welt facing piece and the garment, using tailor tacks for accuracy. Trace the welt rectangle on the welt facing with a dressmaker's marking pencil. If your pattern calls for a separate pocket lining, stitch it to the welt facing piece following pattern instructions.

2. Place the right side of the welt facing to the right side of the garment, matching markings (Fig. 3-14).

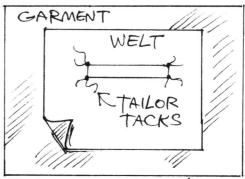

PLACE WELT FACING/LINING TO GARMENT, RIGHT SIDES TOGETHER, MATCHING MARKS.

Fig. 3-14

3. Set your machine for a short (1mm), narrow (3 – 6mm) zigzag stitch; select a width slightly narrower than the finished width of each lip. *With the outer swing of the needle at the tailor tack,* stitch from end to end on one long side of the welt rectangle. Stop with the

needle in the right side of the stitch. Lift the foot and pivot 180 degrees. See Fig. 3-15.

Fig. 3-15

4. Zigzag down the other side, stopping at the tailor tack at the end of the welt. (You have just made a big buttonhole without the bartacks.) See Fig. 3-15.

5. Straight stitch around and as close to the zigzag stitches as possible, creating a box (Fig. 3-16).

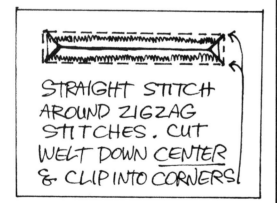

Fig. 3-16

☞ **Update tip:** Be sure to straight stitch *outside* the zigzag stitches or they will be visible after the lips have been made.

6. Cut the welt open through the center, clipping diagonally to the corners (Fig. 3-16). (Clipping through a few zigzag stitches at each end is

okay.) Turn the welt facing/lining through the opening to the inside (Fig. 3-17).

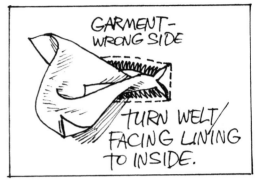

Fig. 3-17

☞ **Update tip:** For perfectly square corners, clip as close to the corner as possible without cutting the straight stitches. Using your thumbs and index fingers, twist the welt back and forth at each corner.

7. *From the wrong side*, press the zigzagged sides toward the center of the welt (Fig. 3-18). To form the welt lips, fold the welt facing back over the zigzagged edges (Fig. 3-19). Press the lips in place from the top, using a see-through press cloth and steam.

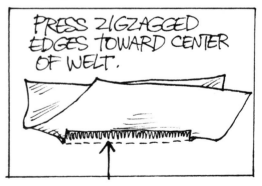

Fig. 3-18

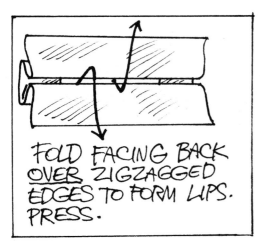

FOLD FACING BACK OVER ZIGZAGGED EDGES TO FORM LIPS. PRESS.

Fig. 3-19

8. From the right side, fold back the ends of the welt to reveal the clipped triangular ends. Sew a few locking stitches over each triangle, catching the welt facing fabric. See Fig. 3-20.

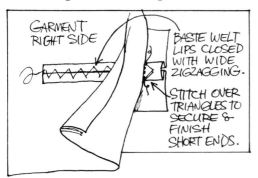

GARMENT RIGHT SIDE

BASTE WELT LIPS CLOSED WITH WIDE ZIGZAGGING.

STITCH OVER TRIANGLES TO SECURE & FINISH SHORT ENDS.

Fig. 3-20

9. Using a long, wide zigzag stitch and a loosened upper thread tension, baste the welt lips closed (Fig. 3-20). This prevents the pocket from stretching or becoming distorted during the rest of its construction. Return the upper tension to normal.

☞ **Update tip:** Use a contrasting bobbin thread when basting. To remove the basting, pull the bobbin

thread. Loosened upper tension allows both threads to pull out easily without distorting the fabric.

10. *From the right side*, stitch-in-the-ditch on the long sides of the welt (Fig. 3-21). To create the pocket, fold the facing/lining down over the back of the welt and stitch according to pattern instructions (Fig. 3-22).

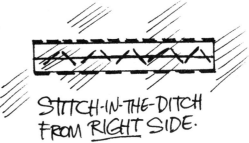

STITCH-IN-THE-DITCH FROM RIGHT SIDE.

Fig. 3-21

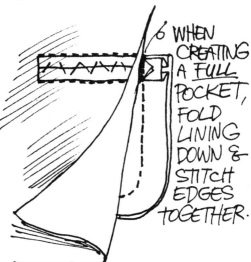

WHEN CREATING A FULL POCKET, FOLD LINING DOWN & STITCH EDGES TOGETHER.

Fig. 3-22

Variation: Make a welt with a pocket flap.

1. Stitch, grade, turn, and press the flap according to pattern instructions.

2. Construct the welt through Step 8. *Do not baste the lips closed.* Insert the flap under the top lip. Stitch-in-the-ditch from the right side on the long sides of the welt, catching the seam allowance of the pocket flap in the stitching. See Fig. 3-23.

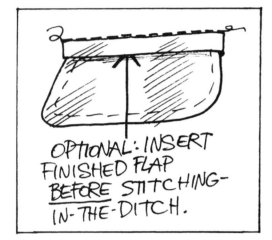

OPTIONAL: INSERT FINISHED FLAP BEFORE STITCHING-IN-THE-DITCH.

Fig. 3-23

3. Trim the flap seam allowance to 1/4", then fold the pocket lining over to create the pocket. Stitch the pocket according to the pattern instructions.

Interfacings for Tailoring

Interfacing gives shape to tailored garments through the shoulders, chest, and armholes. It supports the back and hem edges and defines design details. And it helps produce smooth rolls in collars and lapels.

In **custom tailoring**, hair-canvas interfacing (*Acro, Fino II , P-26 Red Edge, Sewers' Choice™*) is hand-basted and pad-stitched to the undercollar and garment front, producing a soft

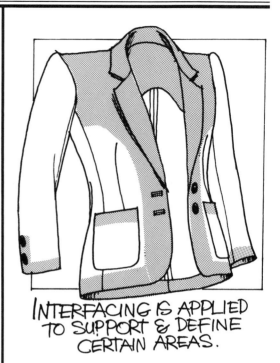

INTERFACING IS APPLIED TO SUPPORT & DEFINE CERTAIN AREAS.

roll at the turn of the collar and lapel (Fig. 3-24). Custom tailoring is time-consuming and requires skill. Consult one of the many tailoring books for how-to's (see "References" on pages 174 – 178).

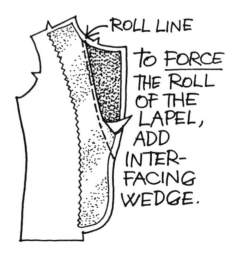

ROLL LINE
To FORCE THE ROLL OF THE LAPEL, ADD INTER-FACING WEDGE.

Fig. 3-24

Select a hair canvas that is pliable, firmly woven, and resilient. Crush and release a small piece in your hand. If noticeable wrinkles remain, choose another hair canvas. Check the fiber content blend: Wool makes the canvas supple and easier to shape with steam pressing. Goat hair makes it resilient and wrinkle-resistant and helps the canvas grab the fashion fabric so the two fabrics act as one. A high percentage of rayon or cotton (instead of wool) reduces the price, but the canvas may not be as resilient or as responsive to shaping. As a rule, the higher the wool and hair content, the higher the quality and price.

✎ **Note:** Use fusible hair canvas (*Fusible Acro*) only when a very firm hand is desired.

In today's **fused tailoring,** fusible interfacing replaces hair canvas and the pad-stitching. The interfacing is fused in place on a flat surface. When fused properly, the fusible resin becomes embedded in the structure of the fabric, taking the place of hand-worked pad-stitches to attach the interfacing. The heat-sensitive fusible resin can now be reshaped while warm and damp, and it will maintain any steamed-in shape when allowed to cool in place. Collar and lapels are quickly "fuse-tailored"— shaped and steam pressed over a tailor's ham and allowed to cool in the new shape (Fig. 3-25).

• **Make a stay to support the back of a tailored jacket** or coat using a light-weight woven interfacing (*Armo Press® Soft, Shape Maker™, Shapewell®*), muslin, batiste, or a lightweight broadcloth that matches or blends with the fashion fabric. Cut a stay from the jacket back

USING A STEAM IRON HELD 1" AWAY, SHAPE FUSED COLLAR & LAPELS OVER A TAILOR'S HAM; LET COOL IN PLACE.

Fig. 3-25

pattern (Fig. 3-26). Fusible interfacings are not as safe to use for the back stay because the bottom edge of the fused interfacing may create a noticeable ridge on the outside of the completed garment. (Although Gail has used fusibles successfully, she reserves their use for darker, textured fabrics that camouflage the fused interfacing ridge line.)

• In fuse-tailored coats and jackets, **interface the upper collar and the front facing** as well as the front and undercollar. Choose a fusible knit or a lightweight, nonwoven fusible. This extra layer of interfacing stabilizes the fabric, making it more compatible with other interfaced areas and easier to handle during construction. The interfacing also cushions trimmed seam allowances so they're less conspicuous from the right side. Topstitching the collar and lapel edges is also easier.

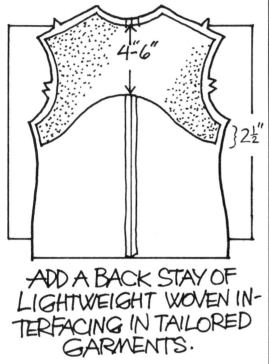

ADD A BACK STAY OF LIGHTWEIGHT WOVEN INTERFACING IN TAILORED GARMENTS.

Fig. 3-26

• **Pink the inner edge of front fusible interfacings.** Pinking creates a "buffer" so the interfacing is less likely to leave a ridge on the right side of the finished garment. See Fig. 3-27. If the pinked edge shows on your test sample but the interfacing is not too heavy for the fabric, apply the interfacing to the entire front, or fuse to the facing rather than to the garment.

• **Double up on interfacing in the undercollar and lapel** of fuse-tailored garments. Interface the entire undercollar, then cut a wedge of a lighter-weight interfacing for the stand of the

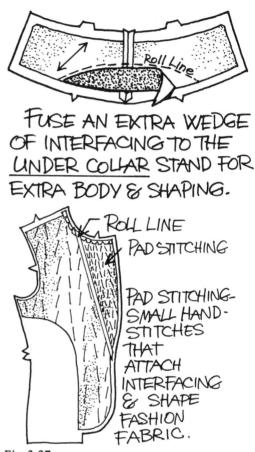

FUSE AN EXTRA WEDGE OF INTERFACING TO THE UNDER COLLAR STAND FOR EXTRA BODY & SHAPING.

ROLL LINE
PAD STITCHING

PAD STITCHING-SMALL HAND-STITCHES THAT ATTACH INTERFACING & SHAPE FASHION FABRIC.

Fig. 3-27

collar between roll line and neckline seam. Fuse in place for added body. Doing the same thing in the lapel from roll line to seamlines will force the lapel to roll. See Fig. 3-27.

Darts in Interfacing

When using heavy sew-in interfacings, stitch the darts in the interfacing separately from the garment:

1. Transfer all dart markings and cut dart wedges from the interfacing.

2. Bring the raw edges of the dart opening together and stitch to a strip of

muslin or seam tape, or fuse to a 3/4"-wide strip of fusible knit interfacing. Reinforce the points with zigzag stitching. See Fig. 3-28.

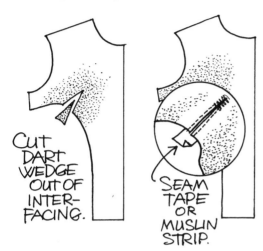

Fig. 3-28

When using fusible interfacings, eliminate the dart wedge entirely: Cut out the dart in the interfacing and fuse the interfacing to the fabric before stitching the dart. Follow the cut edge of the interfacing to stitch the dart. See Fig. 3-29.

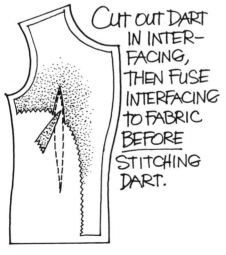

Fig. 3-29

References: *For custom tailoring—Classic Tailoring Techniques, A Construction Guide for Women's Wear*, by Roberto Cabrera, ©1984 Fairchild Publications, 7 East 12th Street, New York, NY 10003 ($26.50 postpaid). *For custom and fused tailoring—Easy, Easier, Easiest Tailoring* (see information on page 38), and *Tailoring*, by Barbara Weiland O'Connell, ©1988, Cy DeCosse Inc., available from the Singer Sewing Reference Library, 5900 Green Oak Drive, Minnetonka, MN 55343 ($16.45 postpaid).

Restyling Menswear: Fast and Affordable Man-tailoring for Women

Tammy has a friend who justified a $2500 trip to Hong Kong with the purchase there of several exquisitely man-tailored suits. "Where else," her friend rationalized, "can a woman buy this quality of tailoring, fabric, and detailing? Just look at the beautifully molded shoulder line, flawless welt pockets, handworked keyhole buttonholes, and bound seams. These suits will last forever."

You don't have to fly to the Orient to be classically man-tailored. Instead, make an excursion to your local thrift, antique clothing, or rummage retailer. Selective shopping can yield a man's jacket or suit that has withstood the test of time and that may even rival those of the garments custom-made overseas. Fit is the obstacle, but hardly insurmountable for the cunning seamster—simply follow these alteration shortcuts.

☞ **Update tip:** If you're very curvy (a 12" or more difference between your bust/waist or waist/hip), alterations would be too expensive. Instead, alter menswear for a straighter-figured friend or daughter.

• **Buy the finest quality, best-fitting jacket you can find.** It may cost you as little as $5 or as much as $40 (still a bargain, relatively speaking). Gail is a tall size 12, so jackets around a size 40 are just roomy enough—gauge your size up or down from that. Avoid any moth-eaten or perspiration-stained garment. Choose wool (the easiest fiber to alter) in a color and texture that flatters. If you're shorter and heavier than Katharine Hepburn, forget matching tweed or plaid trousers (if the jacket is sold only as a suit, salvage buttons and other findings).

*Initial fit shouldn't be too far off—*shoulders not more than 3/4" wider than desired on each side, bottom hem no more than 1" too long, hips no tighter than snug. The roll line can be raised for better bustline contouring. Inspect your prospective purchase closely, both off and then on, in front of a mirror.

☞ **Update tip:** Dry clean your jacket or suit immediately to freshen the fabric, kill moth larva, and ready it for safe alteration pressing.

• **Narrow the shoulders,** if necessary, by blindstitching a small tuck in the top layer of fabric along the neckline seam edge of the under collar, as

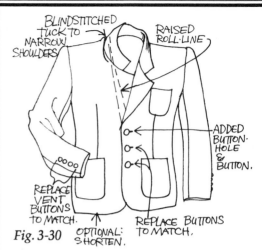

Fig. 3-30

shown. Taper gradually on both ends. For additional narrowing across the upper back, take in the center back seam; take in no more than 1/4" (1/2" total), tapering the alteration into the seam to prevent puckering. See Figs. 3-30 and 3-31.

• **Raise the roll line,** if necessary. After trying on to check the pinned alteration, press hard using a press cloth and wool steam setting. When the roll line is raised, a button and buttonhole will need to be added, spaced to match the existing buttonholes. The new buttonhole should match the others in thread color, shape (generally keyhole), and length; carefully sewn by machine, the newcomer won't look new. Or hire a tailor to handwork the buttonhole (costs about $6 – 10 each). See Fig 3-30.

• **Buy new buttons** that epitomize the menswear look—marbled suit buttons are perfect and easy to find. A slightly smaller size in the same button style can decorate the sleeve vent (to replicate authentic haberdashery, sew at least three on each sleeve, close together—see Fig. 3-30).

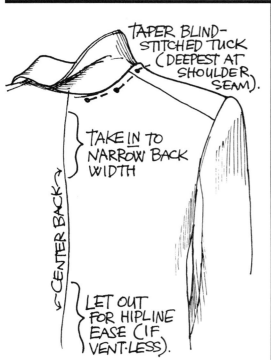

TAPER BLIND-
STITCHED TUCK
(DEEPEST AT
SHOULDER
SEAM).

TAKE IN TO
NARROW BACK
WIDTH

CENTER BACK

LET OUT
FOR HIPLINE
EASE (IF
VENT·LESS).

Fig. 3-31

• **Add waistline and hipline width**
first by moving the button positions. If
you need more width, let out through
the center back seam, tapering for a
smooth seamline. Because Gail frequently alters this center back seam
and likes a neat hem, she covets
harder-to-find ventless jacket styles.

• **Shorten jacket sleeves** as required,
repositioning or adding vent buttons.
Press up the sleeve hem (trim it down
to *no deeper than 2"*) and secure by
restitching the lining in place with
hand blindstitching. Be sure to allow
for lengthwise lining ease (1" minimum), which allows unrestricted
movement and prevents pull lines on
the right side of the sleeve.

✎ **Note:** The bottom hem of the jacket
can be shortened, although this can be
a time-consuming process because it
involves ripping and restitching the
front facing. Avoid this alteration if
possible.

4. Simply Flattering Slacks

- **Sure-fire Pant-fit Strategies**
- **European Pant-fit Secrets**
- **Tummy Flattening Without Dieting**
- **Sew Slenderizing Slacks**
- **Sew-through Waistband Elastic**
- **Double-duty Drawstring Elastic**

- **Neat Waistbands**
- **Flattering Shorts From Favorite Slacks**
- **Modifying Man-tailored Slacks (for Women)**

There's a common goal among the women we know who sew: to make flattering pants. As you know too well, finding ready-mades that fit is impossible for 98% of the female public shaped differently and weighing more than the *Sports Illustrated* bathing-suit-issue models. (Take solace: Cheryl Tiegs probably can't find pants long enough for her mile-long, thin-thighed legs.) Fortunately, for seamsters, there's hope. Put some of the methods featured in this chapter to work; you'll make flattering pants faster and more professionally than ever.

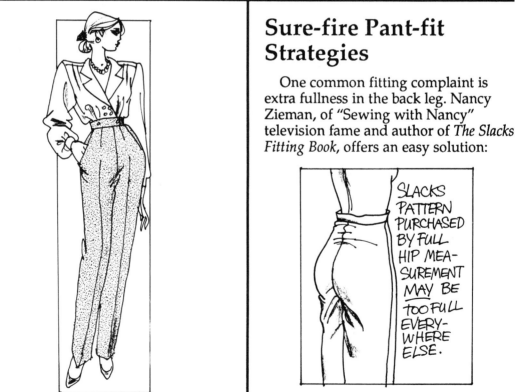

Sure-fire Pant-fit Strategies

One common fitting complaint is extra fullness in the back leg. Nancy Zieman, of "Sewing with Nancy" television fame and author of *The Slacks Fitting Book*, offers an easy solution:

SLACKS PATTERN PURCHASED BY FULL HIP MEASUREMENT MAY BE TOO FULL EVERYWHERE ELSE.

Fig. 4-1

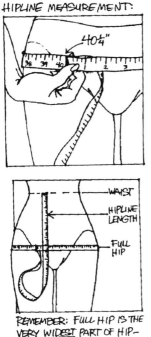

HIPLINE MEASUREMENT:

40¼"

WAIST
HIPLINE LENGTH
FULL HIP

REMEMBER: FULL HIP IS THE VERY _WIDEST_ PART OF HIP— SO IT MAY NOT BE RIGHT AT HIP_BONE_ IF YOU HAVE HIGH, ROUND BUTTOCKS, FOR INSTANCE.

Fig. 4-2

• **Increase the hipline on a smaller size that fits the thigh and back leg.** Why? For slacks, traditional sizing recommends buying a pattern according to the hipline measurement. But if your hips are large in proportion to your waist, a pattern purchased for the hips will fit there but not through the waist, thighs, or legs (Fig. 4-1). It's almost impossible to take away this upper-leg fullness once pants are cut out.

To determine the pattern size to fit your thighs:

1. Dress in a leotard or undergarments.

2. Using a firm measure, have a partner measure the fullest part of your hip. Remember, the full hip is the very widest part of the hip, so it may not be right at the hipbone (if you have a high, round bottom, for instance). Be sure to keept the tape measure parallel to the floor. See Fig. 4-2.

✎ **Note:** Hold the tape over one finger to prevent the measurement from being taken too tightly. Round off the measurement to the nearest 1/2" and record for future reference.

3. Locate your hip measurement on a pattern sizing chart (Fig. 4-3). Purchase your slacks pattern *two sizes smaller than recommended.* It will fit in the thigh and can be easily altered for the hip. For altering how-to's, refer to your

• HIP MEASUREMENT (OR NEAREST FULL SIZE)

STANDARD BODY MEASUREMENTS	WAIST:	24	25	26½	28	30	32	34	INCHES
	HIP-9" BELOW WAIST:	33½	34½	36	38	40	42	44	"
	SIZES:	8	10	12	14	16	18	20	

• PURCHASE 2 SIZES SMALLER

Fig. 4-3

pattern guide sheet directions (instructions are included in styles specified as basic pant-fitting patterns) or any of the many pant-fitting books on the market (see "References," below).

✎ **Note:** If your measurement falls between sizes, choose the one that would more likely fit your thigh size—the larger one for heavy thighs; the smaller one for slender thighs.

References: *Pants for Any Body*, by Pati Palmer and Susan Pletsch, ©1983, Palmer/Pletsch Associates, P.O. Box 12046, Portland, OR 97212-0046 ($8.20 postpaid) and *The Slacks Fitting Book*, by Nancy Zieman, ©1989, Nancy's Notions, P.O. Box 683, Beaver Dam, WI 53916 ($11.95 postpaid).

European Pant-fit Secrets

Sewing expert Sandra Betzina has been teaching pant-fitting for 20 years. From experience, she has come to the conclusion that a contoured seat fit, aspired to by most women, can be achieved effortlessly by starting with a European pattern such as Burda.

The reason lies in the cut of the European pant pattern, which has a longer, slightly deeper back crotch than its American counterpart. This cut enables the curve to fit around and under the derrière without wrinkling under the seat. The European pant pattern also has a shorter front crotch, which eliminates extra fabric above the crotch during sitting or walking. See Fig. 4-4.

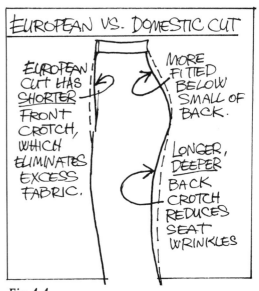

Fig. 4-4

Reference: *Pants That Fit*, a Burda pant-fitting video hosted by Sandra Betzina, ©1988, available for $20 postpaid from Power Sewing, 185 5th Avenue, San Francisco, CA 94118.

Tummy Flattening Without Dieting

"Because of my tummy, I'm a size 14 in front and a size 12 in back." This is a common dilemma facing those with a mature figure. When asked about this in her pant-fitting classes, Karen Dillon tells her students, *"Your figure is not the problem. It's just a different shape than the pattern."*

A round tummy causes horizontal wrinkles near the waistband and a too-snug crotch fit. It requires more length and width than the standard pattern fit allows.

REPLACE DARTS WITH EASING.

Fig. 4-5

🖙 **Update tip:** Sew a gingham (1/4" checks) fitting pant, then transfer the adjustments to the pattern tissue.

1. Begin by shortening, narrowing, curving, or eliminating the front darts to compensate for the tummy roundness—allow a smooth fit over the tummy and enough room through the waist (Fig. 4-5). Most fuller figures look more attractive in pants with soft easing at the waistline rather than darts. (Darts can lead the eye to the problem area.)

2. Let out the front side seams at the waistline. From the side seam notch, draw a straighter line to the waist, as shown. This added width eliminates waistline wrinkles. Those with "love

handle hips" should also use this widening method. See Fig. 4-6.

3. Add more length to the center-front seam at the waistline. You may need to add at least an inch. Then taper this raised waistline seam to the side seam. (Karen has noticed that many mature waistlines are higher in the front, sloping to the back.)

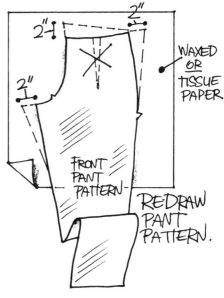

Fig. 4-6

4. If the crotch fit is too tight, lengthen the center-front seam, increasing the depth up to 2" (Fig. 4-6). For most pants, the crotch seam should hang about 3/4" from the body (1" ease for fuller figures).

5. Lengthen the waistband, corresponding to the dart and side seam alterations.

☞ **Update tip:** To simplify making alterations, trim the pattern pieces to the cutting lines. Glue-stick a larger sheet of tissue paper under the pattern. Make the alterations on the tissue, complete with cutting and seamlines.

Sew Slenderizing Slacks

Looking ten pounds thinner seems a universal goal, particularly in body-revealing slacks and shorts. Here's how to create a sleeker illusion now.

• **Select flattering fabrics.** Flat surface fabrics are best. The favorite among sewing professionals is gabardine. Fine wool "gab," when unlined, can actually be worn all year in most climates. In hotter, humid temperatures, try cotton/polyester blends. Linen can be lovely—on the bolt. But it wrinkles, and those horizontal lines add pounds. Stick with less wrinkle-prone linen-look blends.

• **Take advantage of color illusions.** De-emphasize hip and thigh width by choosing darker or neutral colors for your slacks or shorts and light or bright colors for your top or jacket. Selecting

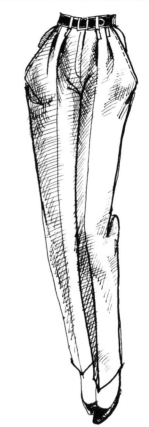

basic colors like taupe, beige, black, brown, gray, or navy will not only slenderize but will multiply wardrobe coordination possibilities as well. If you'd like to look taller, match your top or jacket with slacks or shorts of the same color.

• **Experiment with jacket and top lengths.** For most, a length just below the fullest part of the hips is flattering. Make your pants first, then pin-baste jacket or top pattern pieces and try on both in front of a full-length mirror.

• **Search for the most slenderizing style.** Let's face it. Straight young bodies and some thin older ones can wear skinny pants. For the rest of us, who live with cellulite and stretch-marked tummies, a modified pleated front style slenderizes if fitted and sewn correctly (Fig. 4-7). There's enough ease to smooth the figure without being so full that the effect is widening.

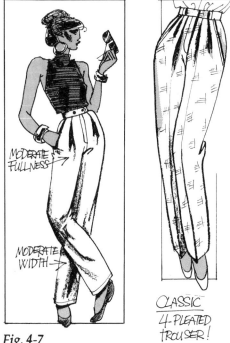

MODERATE FULLNESS →

MODERATE WIDTH →

CLASSIC 4-PLEATED TROUSER!

Fig. 4-7

☞ **Update tip:** Full, wide-legged pants are making a major comeback. All figures can wear the full pant, but only if the fabric is very drapey, allowing it to hang close to the body. Soft rayon suiting or heavy cotton interlock are ideal options.

• **Buy the right size pattern.** See "Sure-Fire Pant-fit Strategies," pages 56 – 58.

• **Follow fitting guides before cutting out.** Pay attention to both length and width measurements. Straight legs, which most are this season, can touch the top of your shoes in the front (narrower legs must be shorter). For shorts, length and width are crucial. They should be long enough to cover the fullest part of your thigh, yet not so long that they "cut your leg in half" (a 1/3:2/3 shorts-to-leg ratio is more slenderizing). And wider-cut shorts make your legs appear thinner.

☞ **Update tip:** Allow 1" seam allowances throughout, 1" – 2" at the inseams if you're full-figured. We call it fitting insurance. Remember, pants that are too tight also make you look bigger, not smaller.

• **Add a stay for tummy control.** Ready-made tummy-control pants with girdle-like power net stays are best-sellers. This nifty tummy-flattening feature can be copied on any trouser. Because the stay is joined in the side seams and fly front stitching, it prevents the pockets and pleats from pooching out.

Place the pocket pattern over the front pant pattern. Pin the pleats in the front. Place the tissue over all and trace the waistline, center front, slanted edge, and bottom curve of the pocket. Extend the pocket pattern to the center front; this is the new stay pattern. See Fig. 4-8. Use it to cut the pocket out of a durable cotton-blend lining (this fabric controls the tummy, is less bulky, more comfortable, and easier to find than power net). After sewing and topstitching the tucks in the pants, sew the stay to the pocket edge, turn to the wrong side, and baste to the pants at the center front.

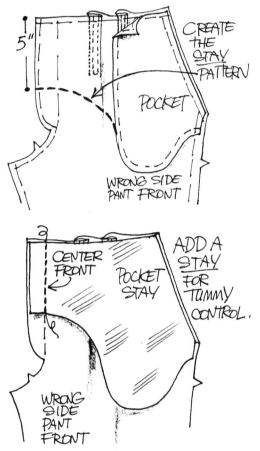

Fig. 4-8

• **Accentuate vertical lines.** Let out the seam allowances as necessary to eliminate horizontal drag lines and to camouflage the tummy and thighs. Topstitch the tucks and pockets in place after trying on to check the fit (Fig. 4-9). When the slacks or shorts are finished, crease the legs.

Highlight the strongest vertical line—the front creaselines—by perma-

Fig. 4-9

nently setting the creases. Place the pants on a pressing surface with outseams and inseams aligned (the crease should be in the center of the leg). Use a press cloth, good steam iron, and pounding block to form sharp creases (Fig. 4-10). The front crease should extend from the tuck closest to the center front (or just below the dart) to the hem. In the back, the crease should extend from the crotch line to the hem.

☞ **Update Tip:** Our irrepressible test seamstress and associate Naomi Baker recommends another permanent creasing technique. With matching thread on top and *ThreadFuse*™ melt adhesive thread (see page 73) in the bobbin, baste along the creaseline. Press the creaselines again; the creases will be permanent. Removing the basting is optional.

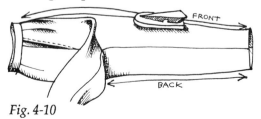

Fig. 4-10

• **Tame trouble areas.** Large-hipped figures can rely on the classic four-pleated trouser, too. *The key is to select a style with a shallow slanted pocket* that ends above the widest part of the hip. See Fig. 4-11.

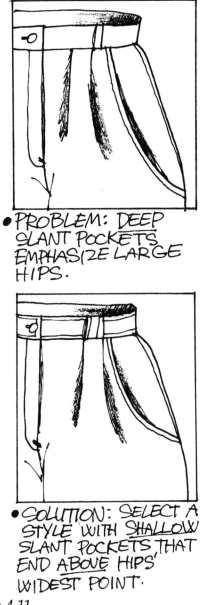

• *PROBLEM: DEEP SLANT POCKETS EMPHASIZE LARGE HIPS.*

• *SOLUTION: SELECT A STYLE WITH SHALLOW SLANT POCKETS THAT END ABOVE HIPS' WIDEST POINT.*

Fig. 4-11

☞ **Update tip:** When sewing with lighter weights and colors, consider fake pockets. Sew the slanted pockets as a seam, pressing the allowances down and topstitching. The pocket seam slant gives the illusion of a smaller waist without the bulk or shadowing of a pocket.

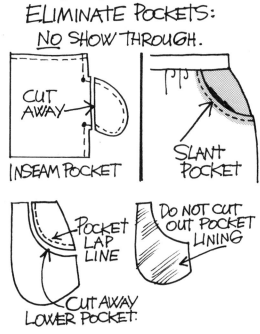

ELIMINATE POCKETS: NO SHOW THROUGH.

CUT AWAY — INSEAM POCKET

SLANT POCKET

POCKET LAP LINE — CUT AWAY LOWER POCKET.

DO NOT CUT OUT POCKET LINING

Fig. 4-12

As shown in Fig. 4-12, it's as elementary as trimming away pocket extensions on in-seam styles; seam to close the pocket. On trouser-style slacks and skirts, trim away the lower portion of the pocket; fold down the slant-line 5/8", lap over the top pocket section, then topstitch.

• **Wear all-in-one control-top pantyhose** to smooth curves and hide blouse hemlines. Bone or other light hose shades are suggested for wearing under light-colored pants.

Sew-through Waistband Elastic

For flattery and comfort, replace rigid waistbands with more comfortable one-piece elastic applications. This shirred waistband is fashion-right, seen on expensive silks as well as sporty knits. And you don't have to worry about shadowing of seams or lingerie; instead of dart-shaping, the fabric is eased softly over the waist and hips.

First, you must use elastic specifically designed for stitching through—Stretch & Sew has carried its brand, called *Sport Elastic*, for years, and now most fabric retailers and mail-order suppliers stock a facsimile (usually about 1-1/2" wide).

✎ **Note:** There are two different types of *Sport Elastic*—one has stitching grooves, one does not. If using the one with grooves, follow them as stitching guides for the casingless application.

This elastic does "grow" when stitched through; compensate by cutting it 3-5" shorter than the waistline measurement (or about 15" smaller than your hips). The heavier the fabric, the more the elastic will grow, so shorten accordingly. This casingless elastic is not suggested for full, gathered styles; the amount of stretch is limited.

This elastic application is the least bulky too—there's no waistband seam, and the fabric is single layer.

1. To adapt any pattern, straighten the side seams up from the hipline and add 1-3/4" above the waistline.

Fig. 4-13

2. Turn down 1/2" to the wrong side at the waist edge (Fig. 4-13).

3. Lap the ends of the elastic 1/2" to form a circle and zigzag. Quarter-mark both the elastic and the garment waist edge.

4. With the elastic on top, stretch the elastic to fit the edge (about 1/4" below the fold), matching quarter-marks. *Starting from the top-edge fold,* topstitch in place with rows about 1/4" – 3/8" apart. Keep stitch length long—about 8/inch. See Figs. 4-14 and 4-15.

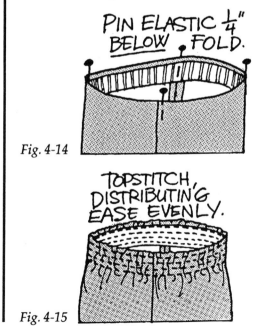

Fig. 4-14

Fig. 4-15

☞ **Update tip:** Activate more elastic recovery by generously steaming the elastic with an iron.

SEW-THROUGH ELASTIC COVERED WITH FULL CASING.

Fig. 4-16

Variation: Cut the casing twice the elastic width plus 1/2". Follow Step 1. Then fold the casing over the elastic, with a 1/2" allowance extending beyond the lower edge of the elastic. Proceed with Steps 2 and 3. See Fig. 4-16 and the photograph on the color pages.

Sources: If unable to locate sew-through elastic in your area, contact these mail-order firms: Clotilde, Inc., Nancy's Notions, Ltd., Serge & Sew Notions, and Stretch & Sew Fabrics. (For addresses, see the "Sew-by-Mail Directory," pages 160 – 173.)

Double-Duty Drawstring Elastic

Drawstring elastic is often seen in ready-made activewear and now it's available to home-sewers. In a single operation, you can achieve the comfort of elastic and the flattering adjustability of a drawstring waistband.

Composed of a soft knit elastic, the drawstring is threaded through the center (Fig. 4-17). When pulled, the drawstring extends to twice the elastic

DRAWSTRING ELASTIC— DUPLICATE READY-TO-WEAR!

DRAWSTRING ELASTIC

DRAWSTRING ENCASED IN ELASTIC.

Fig. 4-17

length, allowing excess for tying and knotting.

The most common width of drawstring elastic is 1-1/2", but 3/4" and 2" widths are also available. If the elastic width is different from the pattern requirement, *the self-casing width will require adjustment*. Measure the difference between the elastic width and the elastic width specified by the pattern, then multiply it by 2. Adjust the pattern by this amount. For example, if the pattern calls for 1-1/4" elastic and you're using 2"-wide elastic, adjust the pattern by adding 1-1/2" to the top of the pattern; if you're using 3/4"-wide elastic, trim 1" off the pattern.

To add a drawstring waistband to a self-casing-style garment:

1. For 2"-wide elastic, cut the elastic the same as your waist measurement; for 1-1/2"- and 3/4"-wide elastic, cut the elastic 2" – 4" less than your waist measurement, depending on the weight of the fabric used (4" for lightweight fabric and 2" for heavier fabric).

2. Lap the elastic ends 1/2", zigzag over each end to secure, then stitch again through the center of the lap (Fig. 4-18). Backstitch, but be careful not to cut the drawstring by excessive stitching.

3. Quarter-mark the elastic with pins, using the seam as one of the marks (Fig. 4-19).

4. Construct the garment following the pattern guidesheet. For a clean-finished casing, press under 1/4" to the wrong side at the waist edge.

5. For a drawstring that ties *on the inside of the garment*, stitch and cut a

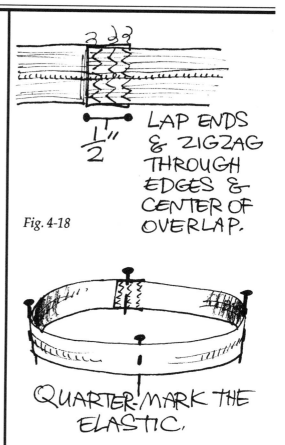

Fig. 4-18

LAP ENDS & ZIGZAG THROUGH EDGES & CENTER OF OVERLAP.

QUARTER-MARK THE ELASTIC.

Fig. 4-19

3/8"-long buttonhole 1/2" from each side of the center front and half the elastic's width down from the garment edge (Fig. 4-20).

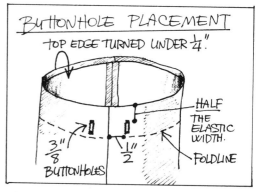

BUTTONHOLE PLACEMENT
TOP EDGE TURNED UNDER 1/4"

HALF THE ELASTIC WIDTH.

FOLDLINE

3/8" BUTTONHOLES   1/2"

Fig. 4-20

6. Quarter-mark the garment edge with pins. Pin the *right side of the elastic* to the *wrong side of the waist*, with the edges even, matching the center back seamlines and the quartermark pins (Fig. 4-21).

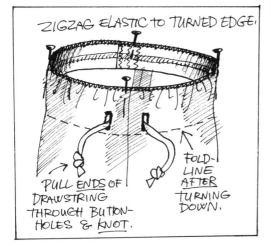

Fig. 4-21

7. *At the exact center front* of the elastic, use a needle or loop turner to pull approximately 12" of the drawstring toward the garment; cut the drawstring extension at the center to form two tails.

8. Zigzag or serge the elastic to the waist edge as pinned, using a long, wide stitch while stretching the elastic to fit between the pins (Fig. 4-21).

9. Using a needle or loop turner, pull the drawstring tails through the buttonholes and knot the ends (Fig. 4-21).

10. Fold the elastic to the wrong side of the garment, enclosing the elastic and keeping the elastic snug against the folded edge. Straight stitch the lower edge of the elastic to the garment through all layers, using a long stitch and stretching the elastic. See Fig. 4-22.

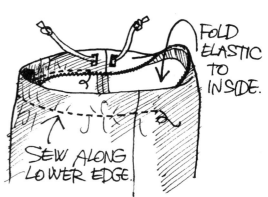

Fig. 4-22

For 1-1/2" and 2" elastic, stitch three more times, as shown in Fig. 4-23. Stitch close to the upper edge, just below that stitch line, and just above the first stitch line at the elastic lower edge.

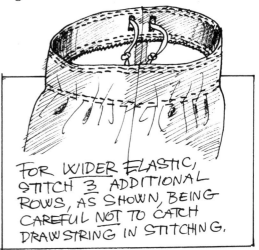

Fig. 4-23

11. Steam the elastic to return it to its original length.

Sources: Most fabric stores now carry drawstring elastic, but if you can't find it in your area, it can be ordered from these companies: Clotilde, Inc., Nancy's Notions, Ltd., The Perfect

Notion, Serge & Sew Notions, and Stretch & Sew Fabrics. (The addresses are listed in the Sew-by-Mail Directory," pages 160 – 173.)

Neat Waistbands

Trim, uncrumpled waistbands make you look trimmer. To stabilize waistbands and maintain a neat, wrinkle-free waistband for the life of the garment, try one of the firmly woven waistband stabilizers.

Ban-Rol®, Armoflexxx®, and RolControl® are available in several widths suitable for waistbands. RolControl® has a seam allowance with a stitching guide for easy, one-step application in applying the waistband to the garment.

Armoflexxx® and Ban-Rol® have no seam allowances and require a special application technique:

1. Cut the waistband with the un-notched edge on the selvage.

2. Cut the waistband stabilizer to fit the waistband length measurement, minus 1", so it will not be caught in the seam ends.

Fig. 4-24

3. Machine baste 5/8" from the long, notched edge of the waistband. Place one long edge of the stabilizer next to the basting so that the stabilizer is positioned within the 5/8" seam allowance on the wrong side. Using a ball- or universal-point needle, edgestitch it in place between the two end seam allowances (Fig. 4-24).

4. Apply the waistband following the pattern directions, stitching from the interfacing side, so that no interfacing is caught in the stitching.

Note: Slotted or perforated bands can also be used for stabilizing waistbands. See page 109 of Chapter 8, "Interfacing Update."

Sources: Most fabric stores carry at least one type of waistband stabilizer. Mail-order sources include Clotilde, Serge & Sew Notions, and The Perfect Notion (for addresses, see the "Sew-by-Mail Directory," pages 160 – 173).

Flattering Shorts From Favorite Slacks

Alas, you don't own a pair of shorts that are comfortable and flattering. But if you already have a pant pattern that fits, it can be easily adapted for shorts.

Full, flared, a-few-inches-above-the-knee shorts are ideal for camouflaging fuller thighs; cut shorts longer to cover

less-than-gorgeous knees. (However, watch for the more flattering 2/3:1/3 proportions—a slightly shorter short may create a longer illusion.) The classic trouser-style Bermuda is another fashionable, flattering option. Flatten your tummy by pressing the pleats toward the side seams (Fig. 4-25). Topstitch as shown.

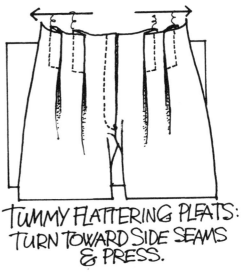

TUMMY FLATTERING PLEATS: TURN TOWARD SIDE SEAMS & PRESS.

Fig. 4-25

• **Make note of bottom leg widths.** Knee-length, flared shorts range from 25" – 29" (Misses 6 – 16), while trouser styles are in the 23"- 27"-width range for the same sizes. Have a pair you really like? Measure the width around the bottom as well as the finished length and use as a reference for pattern adjusting.

• **Alter the leg length and width.** (You've already adjusted your favorite pant pattern for fit.) First, decide on the finished length. Make sure that the shorts will cover the fullest part of your upper leg, without stopping there.

• **Draw a line on the pattern at the desired finished length,** perpendicular to the grainline. Add a 1-1/2" hem (Fig. 4-26). Determine the actual bottom width of the pattern by measuring the hemline width (do not include seam allowances). Compare to the desired finished width and adjust by adding to the side seams from just below the full hip (Fig. 4-27). Add 1" seam allowances just in case you want to add more width later.

DRAW THE SHORTS PATTERN

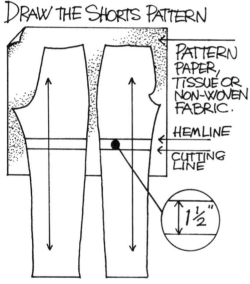

PATTERN PAPER, TISSUE OR NON-WOVEN FABRIC.

HEMLINE

CUTTING LINE

1½"

Fig. 4-26

☞ **Update tip:** This step is necessary because in current and more recent trouser patterns, legs are tapered. On most leg types (other than those very thin), trouser shorts are more slenderizing when cut fuller, making the leg appear smaller in proportion.

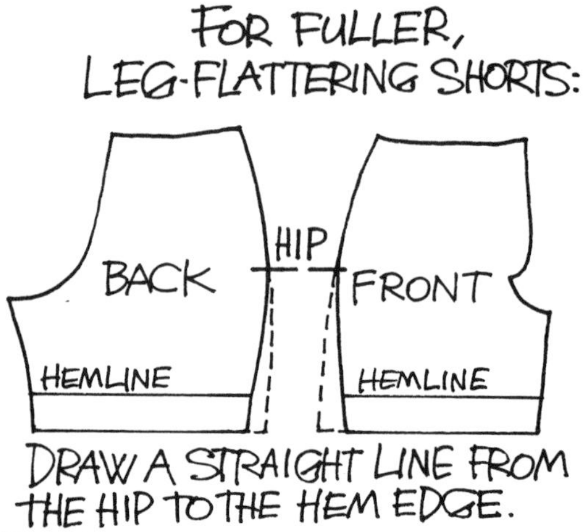

FOR FULLER, LEG-FLATTERING SHORTS:

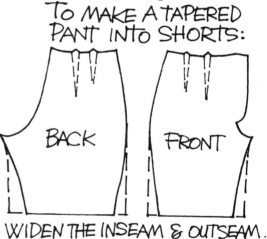

BACK   HIP   FRONT

HEMLINE   HEMLINE

DRAW A STRAIGHT LINE FROM THE HIP TO THE HEM EDGE.

Fig. 4-27

• **Add width as necessary to achieve the leg fit desired.** Tapered pants will require straightening of both the inseam and outseam (Fig. 4-28). For flared, skirt-like shorts, flare the outseam and straighten the inseam (Fig. 4-29). Again, allow at least 1" seam allowances as fitting insurance.

TO MAKE A TAPERED PANT INTO SHORTS:

BACK   FRONT

WIDEN THE INSEAM & OUTSEAM.

Fig. 4-28

FOR FLARED, SKIRT-LIKE SHORTS:

BACK   FRONT

FLARE THE OUTSEAM,
STRAIGHTEN THE INSEAM.

Fig. 4-29

Modifying Man-Tailored Slacks (for Women)

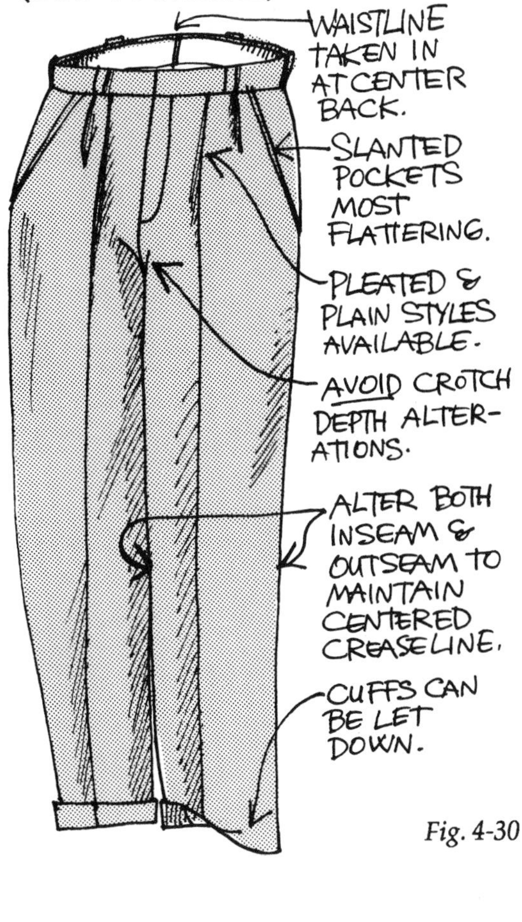

WAISTLINE TAKEN IN AT CENTER BACK.

SLANTED POCKETS MOST FLATTERING.

PLEATED & PLAIN STYLES AVAILABLE.

AVOID CROTCH DEPTH ALTERATIONS.

ALTER BOTH INSEAM & OUTSEAM TO MAINTAIN CENTERED CREASELINE.

CUFFS CAN BE LET DOWN.

Fig. 4-30

First, choose a style and size that flatters and will fit with quick alterations. For Gail's 29" – 30" waist, 39" hips, and 34" inseam, she's on the lookout for 32" (waist) LONG men's slacks. If you have shorter legs, you will find more slacks to fit. You'll soon discover that adaptable men's slacks are a real find, albeit a somewhat scarce breed; the majority are too short and wide. Keep in mind that men's slacks fit straighter figures best.

Some other helps: Slanted pockets are the most flattering and the crotch depth can be difficult to alter. Select accordingly. See Fig. 4-30.

• **Alter the waistline and upper hip through the center-back seam.** If the slacks have back pockets, they shouldn't be closer than 4" apart (or, if there's only one pocket, 2" from the center-back seam) after altering (Fig. 4-31). Also, taking in the center-back seam shouldn't obviously distort the side seams. After altering and checking the fit, blindstitch the curtained waistband (Figs. 4-32 and 4-33). *From the right side*, stitch-in-the-ditch of the waistband seam (Fig. 4-34).

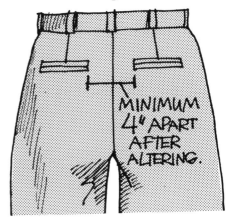

MINIMUM 4" APART AFTER ALTERING.

Fig. 4-31

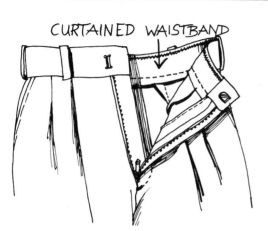

CURTAINED WAISTBAND

Fig. 4-32

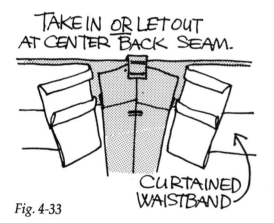

TAKE IN OR LET OUT AT CENTER BACK SEAM.

CURTAINED WAISTBAND

Fig. 4-33

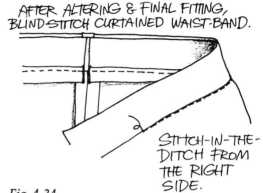

AFTER ALTERING & FINAL FITTING, BLIND-STITCH CURTAINED WAIST-BAND.

STITCH-IN-THE-DITCH FROM THE RIGHT SIDE.

Fig. 4-34

• **Take in or let out the inseam and outseam in equal amounts** to maintain the centered creaselines.

• For added length, **let cuffs down**. However, the fabric may be permanently worn along the cuff fold lines.

✎ **Note**: For altering men's jackets, also see "Restyling Menswear," pages 53 – 55.

5. Shortcuts

- *ThreadFuse*™ Ingenuity
- Fast Finishing from Nancy Kores
- Fast, Professional Darts
- Zipper Tips
- Quick Closures
- Better Buttonholes and Buttoning
- Fool-proof Gathering
- Automatically Eased Set-in Sleeves
- Double-bias Binding

Like all seamsters, we're constantly hungry for new sewing shortcuts, ways to make our sewing better, faster, and more professional. We've gathered some of our favorite "Why-didn't-I-think-of that?!" shortcuts, garnered from *Update* readers, writers, sample-makers, and our own experimentation.

ThreadFuse™ Ingenuity

Just when you thought nothing could be new in the world of thread, along comes an innovative new variety that could change the way you sew. *ThreadFuse*™, distributed by the mail-order specialist, The Perfect Notion (see page 164), is sure to become a must-have sewing aid. (It was introduced to us and our readers by *Update*'s "Notions News" columnist, Janet Klaer.)

Is it a thread or a fusible? It's both. Known generically as melt adhesive thread, it is a loosely twisted, two-ply polyester multifilament with a fusible component. The thread doesn't disappear. Only the fusible melts to form the bond, while the thread remains in the seam.

With melt adhesive thread, you can position a fine, precise line of fusible; simply stitch with melt adhesive thread along the line. It's easiest to use *ThreadFuse*™ in the bobbin, with all-purpose thread in the needle; loosen the bobbin tension slightly. For more fusing area, adjust for a zigzag stitch. Some *ThreadFuse*™ shortcuts:

- **Match plaids and stripes** (Fig. 5-1).

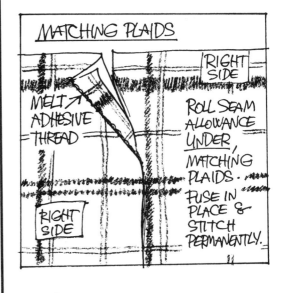

Fig. 5-1

- **Position fabric and lace appliqués** (see pages 93 – 94).

- **Secure seam allowances** flat or to one side (Fig. 5-2).

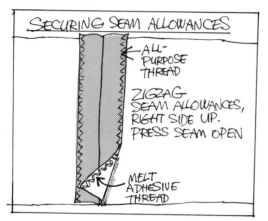

Fig. 5-2

- **Secure hem and facing edges.** With *Threadfuse*™ in the bobbin, zigzag from right side and press.

Fast Finishing from Nancy Kores

- **Topstitch edges, hems, facings, collars, and belts** for a flat, fast finish. (See fashion illustration, below.) Use the edge of your presser foot along the folded edge of the hem for straight, even topstitching.

- If topstitching isn't appropriate, **speed hemming time by using the blind-hem stitch** (and foot, if helpful) on your sewing machine. Test first on project scraps. Press the hem in place and pin near and parallel to the folded edge. The zigzag portion of the stitch just catches the fold of the hem. See Fig. 5-3.

Fig. 5-3

• **Eliminate facings** for faster sewing and breezier looks. Press under the seam allowance to the wrong side, clipping where necessary to make it lie flat. From the right side, stitch close to the edge fold with a short, narrow zigzag. Trim away the excess seam allowance close to the zigzagging. Or serge the seam, trimming off about 1/4". Press 3/8" to the wrong side. From the right side, topstitch 1/4" from the edge fold. See Fig. 5-4.

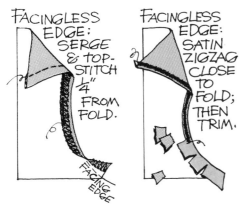

Fig. 5-4

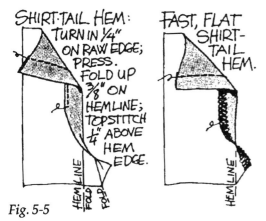

Fig. 5-5

• **Machine-stitch shirt-tail hems.** Press under the 5/8" hem to the wrong side. Fold the raw edge under about 1/4", as

shown, using the width of your presser foot to keep the stitching even. Or if you have a serger, serge the edge and press under 3/8" to the wrong side. Topstitch from the right side. See Fig. 5-5.

Fast, Professional Darts

Darts are back. They're crucial to fitted garments and require careful stitching for pucker-free points. Stitch toward the point, starting at the widest end. Shorten the stitch length for the last 1/2," stitching slowly while narrowing to the end. Catch only a thread of fabric at the point and stitch off the end several stitches to make a chain. Lift the presser foot, pull the dart toward you, and then lower the needle into the dart. Lock the stitches, stitching in place with the stitch length at almost 0. No knot to tie! See Fig. 5-6. Stitch double-pointed darts in two steps, sewing from the middle to each end point.

Fig. 5-6

Zipper Tips

• To support a long back zipper in a knit and prevent it from buckling, **stabilize the fabric** by fusing narrow strips of lightweight, fusible knit interfacing (see page 113) such as *Soft 'N Silky*™ or *Whisper Weft* to the wrong side of the placket seam allowances. Extend the interfacing 1" below the placket opening. Test on a scrap first. (The interfacing should support and not overpower the fabric.) See Fig. 5-7.

• **Use basting tape** (narrow, double-stick tape) to hold a zipper in place while stitching (Fig. 5-8). You'll find it in most notions departments and sewing mail-order catalogs.

• **Buy a zipper 1" – 2" longer than you need.** That way, the slider won't get in your way and cause crooked topstitching. Sew in, then unzip the zipper, sew waistband or facing over top, and cut off excess. See Fig. 5-9.

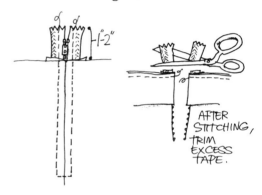

Fig. 5-9

• Remember, **invisible zippers, now making a fashion comeback, are perfect for** fitted fashions. The zipper teeth are hidden; only the small pull tab shows.

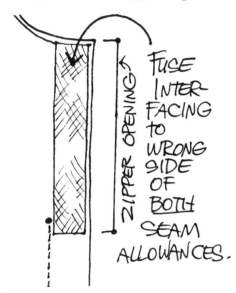

FUSE INTERFACING to WRONG SIDE OF BOTH SEAM ALLOWANCES.

ZIPPER OPENING

Fig. 5-7

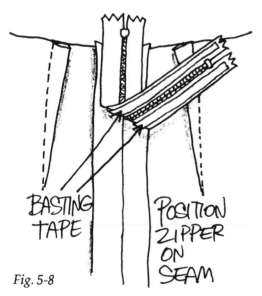

BASTING TAPE

POSITION ZIPPER ON SEAM

Fig. 5-8

• **Use the special zipper foot for easy application of invisible zippers**. The foot automatically guides the stitching alongside the coil. If you are using heavy or bulky fabrics, adjust the foot so that stitching is a little further away from the coil. See Fig. 5-10.

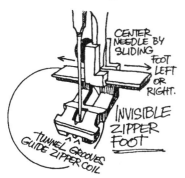

Fig. 5-10

☞ **Update tip**: Sewing pro Naomi Baker prefers using a standard zipper foot for application of invisible zippers. She says she has more control over and an unobstructed view of where the stitching line falls. Test both feet to determine your preference.

Quick Closures

• **Sew extended-snap closures** to blouse and dress center-back openings. No lap is necessary. Hand-stitch the ball half of the snap to the underside of the left corner. Position the socket half on the corresponding right edge; to secure to the edge, hand-stitch through only one of the holes. See Fig. 5-11.

Fig. 5-11

• **Create a loop/button back closure**, quickly. To make the loop cord, zigzag with a short, medium-width stitch over four thread strands (or one elastic thread strand). Thread the cord in a large-eyed needle and hand-sew to the top left neckline corner; the cord ends can be hidden inside the binding or facing. See Fig. 5-12.

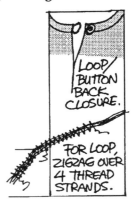

Fig. 5-12

Better Buttonholes and Buttoning

• **Use a *Simflex Gauge* to mark equidistant spacing of buttonholes** (Fig. 5-13). For the most accurate spacing, spread the gauge to its full expansion, then compress it to the desired spacing.

✎ **Note:** Some experts feel the Simflex Gauge is inaccurate; we haven't noticed problems, but always use a see-through ruler to double-check measurements between markings.

• **Cut a neat, fine line between the buttonhole stitching** using a chisel cutter and block, sold as a *Buttonhole Cutter Set.* For buttonholes that are shorter than the chisel, extend the stitching over the edge of the block, as shown (Fig. 5-14).

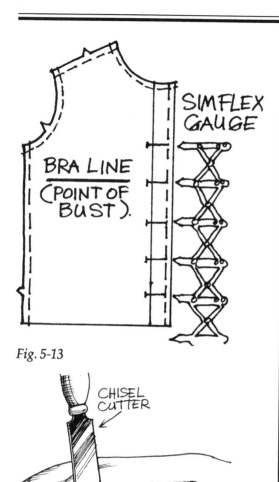

SIMFLEX GAUGE

BRA LINE (POINT OF BUST).

Fig. 5-13

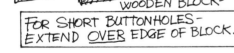

CHISEL CUTTER

WOODEN BLOCK

FOR SHORT BUTTONHOLES - EXTEND OVER EDGE OF BLOCK.

Fig. 5-14

• **Use your machine-stitched bartack to sew buttons in place.** (This method works for sew-through, not shank, buttons.) Test to adjust the width of the zigzag so that the needle clears the button and sews through holes. Position the button, secure with transpar-

ent tape (such as *Scotch™ Brand Magic™ Tape*) and bartack (Fig. 5-15).

BARTACK BUTTONS IN PLACE

TRANSPARENT TAPE

Fig. 5-15

If the thickness of your fabric calls for a thread shank, bartack over a special tailor tacking, fringing, or looping foot (Fig. 5-16). Or tape a needle or toothpick to the top of the button, between the holes.

MAKE A LONG BUTTON SHANK.

Fig. 5-16

• **Sew buttons on by hand—fast.** First, use thread that's wound on your machine bobbin. (It's straighter than thread taken from the spool because the curl was removed as it was wound on the bobbin.) Thread a large-eyed needle with two long strands of thread; when doubled up and knotted, you will be sewing with four strands of thread.

Fold back the edge of the fabric and sew through the fold. The farther the holes in the buttons are held from the edge of the fabric, the longer the thread shank. See Fig. 5-17.

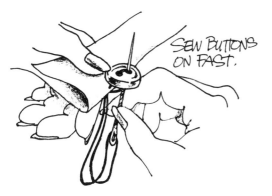

Fig. 5-17

Fool-proof Gathering

Put the fastest, most fool-proof gathering method to work. With a wide, medium-length zigzag, stitch over (but not catching) heavy thread like buttonhole twist. (In a pinch, we've even used string.) Secure one end and pull on the other to gather the edge. No more broken gathering threads! See Fig. 5-18.

Fig. 5-18

Automatically Eased Set-in Sleeves

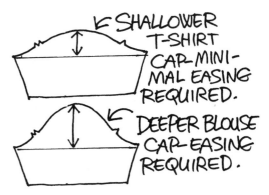

• **Set in shallow T-shirt sleeves** (that require minimal easing), *without pins or basting.* Allow the feed dogs to automatically ease; straight stitch the sleeve in place *with the bodice on top.* See Fig. 5-19.

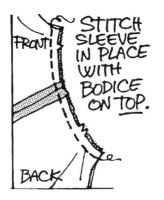

STITCH SLEEVE IN PLACE WITH BODICE ON TOP.

FRONT

BACK

Fig. 5-19

Double-bias Binding

Apply bias binding double layer to edges for a beautiful finish on sheer to lightweight fabrics.

1. Cut a bias strip of self fabric *six times the desired finished width* (about 3" for a 1/2" finished width) by the edge length plus 1-1/4".

2. Fold the bias strip *wrong sides together*.

3. Straight stitch the binding to the neckline; *the seam width determines the finished binding width*. (A 3/8"-wide allowance will form a 3/8"-wide binding.) Fold the ends in 1/2" before stitching. See Fig. 5-20.

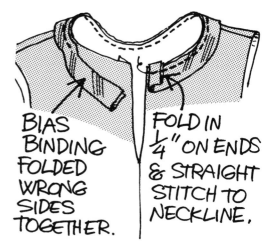

BIAS BINDING FOLDED WRONG SIDES TOGETHER.

FOLD IN 1/4" ON ENDS & STRAIGHT STITCH TO NECKLINE.

Fig. 5-20

☞ **Update tip:** Rather than folding the end of the binding as shown in Fig. 5-20, Gail wraps the binding around the edge end before straight stitching. (The raw seam allowance is then hidden in the wrap.)

4. Fold the binding to the wrong side and blindstitch by hand to the machine-stitching line (Fig. 5-21).

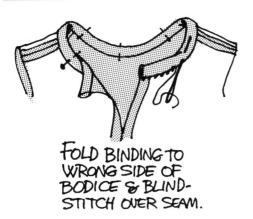

FOLD BINDING TO
WRONG SIDE OF
BODICE & BLIND-
STITCH OVER SEAM.

Fig. 5-21

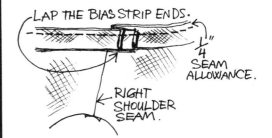

LAP THE BIAS STRIP ENDS.

¼" SEAM ALLOWANCE.

RIGHT SHOULDER SEAM.

Fig. 5-23

☞ **Update tip:** *Sewing Update* columnist Claire Shaeffer suggests steam shaping the binding before applying (Fig. 5-22). Also, for circular openings, Claire laps and staggers the bias strip ends, as shown in Fig. 5-23, to minimize bulk.

Sources: *ThreadFuse*™ is sold by Clotilde, Inc., Nancy's Notions, Ltd., The Perfect Notion, and YLI. Invisible zippers and the *Simflex Gauge* are carried by many fabric stores and by mail-order firms specializing in notions. (See all addresses on pages 160 – 173 of the "Sew-by-Mail Directory".)

Reference: Gail appears with Nancy Zieman on the video, *Share the Love of Sewing,* ©1989, Nancy's Notions, Ltd. In this 30-minute tape, Gail and Nancy share the best shortcut tips sent in by some of *"Sewing With Nancy"* TV show's 40 million viewers. (For the Nancy's Notions, Ltd., address, see the "Sew-by-Mail Directory," page 164.)

STEAM PRESS TO SHAPE BIAS TO NECKLINE CURVE.

STRETCH FOLD SLIGHTLY

Fig. 5-22

6. Genuine Fun:
Leather and Leather-likes

- **Sewing with Real Leather—Easier Than Ever**
- **Washable "Leather":** *Ultraleather®*

Take a creative departure from everyday sewing. Try leather or the new, incredibly leather-like (and washable) fakes. No, you won't need leather-sewing experience, a new machine, or equipment; just equip yourself with the different-but-definitely-not-difficult procedures described in this chapter. Soon you'll be marveling at the shortcuts made possible by these ravel-proof, durable "fabrics."

Sewing with Real Leather— Easier Than Ever

In the how-to video *Sewing with Leather*, Tandy's Jennifer Hurn claims, *"Anything that can be sewn in fabric can be sewn in leather."* She's right. The many skins now available to home-sewers (see our "Sources," "Real Leathers," pages 171 – 173) are softer and more pliable than ever, thanks to modern splitting, dyeing, and finishing processes. And lambsuede can replace velvet and faille as the ultimate choice for special-occasion dressing.

- **Pick an appropriate project.** Best bets are to begin with accessories or easy tops. In keeping with consumers' love of leather, some pattern companies have designed patterns especially for skins; the pattern's yardage charts even approximate suede or leather skin requirements. Some also include special guide sheets that cover all the basics—piecing, fitting, cutting out, sewing machine adjustments, stitching, and pressing.

If you're confident about your sewing skills (it's helpful to be familiar with *Ultrasuede®* techniques) and ready to make an investment in leather, graduate to a garment. You can't go wrong with a simple T-shirt that's minutes in the making.

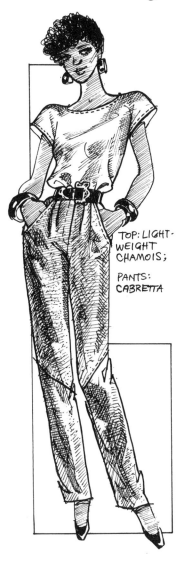

TOP: LIGHT-WEIGHT CHAMOIS;

PANTS: CABRETTA

• **Select the most suitable skin**. Remember, the more body-conforming the style, the more supple the leather should be. Let ready-to-wear be your guide. Most often, lightweight but durable and easy-to-wipe-off Cabretta (smooth-finished goatskin) is used for pants and skirts. Also, watch the weight, specified in ounces; sewable leathers range from 1-1/2 – 2-1/2 ounces (one ounce = 1/64" thickness).

Skin size may be a factor. Will the largest skin accommodate the largest pattern piece? If not, is piecing an option?

☞ **Update tips:** Remember, most (but not all) leathers call for special, and more costly, leather cleaning. Dramatically minimize those potential costs by buying darker shades of smooth, rather than sueded, skins. (Textured or patterned leathers can camouflage everyday soiling.) If possible, take extra care to protect the finished garment from body oils, greasy food stains, blood, and ink.

Sound like too much hassle? Then stick with real leather appliqués (see page 85) or accessories and sew garments from *Ultraleather®* (see pages 86 – 91), *Ultrasuede®*, *Facile®*, or *Caress™*.

• **Calculate the square footage required.** Leather is sold by the square foot, not by the yard. It's easy to convert yardage:

One yard of 45" fabric = 11 square feet of leather

One yard of 54" fabric = 13 square feet of leather

One yard of 60" fabric = 15 square feet of leather

Multiply the yardage requirement by the appropriate number of square feet, adding 15% – 20% for skin irregularities. For instance, if 2-1/2 yards of 54" fabric is required, multiply 2-1/2 by 13 = 42-1/2; add about 20% of 42-1/2 (5) to 42-1/2 to reach the total of 47-1/2 square feet.

Because dye lots vary, *buy plenty of skins for your project*. Don't worry—leftover leather is perfect for trim, yoke accents, belts, and fasteners. Friendly merchants will allow you to lay out your pattern on prospective skins before buying, a real bonus when trying to cut costs. (Make sure that the skins are large enough for your largest pattern pieces; if not, plan on piecing.)

✎ **Note**: Speaking of costs, most skins will range from $1.59 – $4.49/square foot. (At $2.79/square foot, pigskin is $30/yard, compared with a suggested retail of $55/yard for *Ultrasuede®*.)

• **Plan layouts and cut carefully.** The lengthwise "grainline" is the backbone of the skin's former wearer. Always lay out patterns single layer, making certain to cut a right and left side; create duplicate patterns out of tissue or butcher paper or nonwoven interfacing to facilitate easier layouts and cutting. See Fig. 6-1. Also, keep in mind that suedes must be laid out "with nap" (most pros prefer the nap running up).

By far the fastest way to secure pattern pieces is with movable transparent-type tape that will not leave a sticky residue on the leather. And need we remind you that of course you should fit the pattern first?

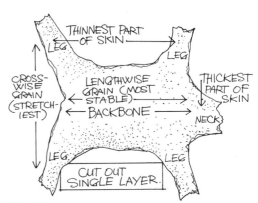

Fig. 6-1

• **Sew simple seams.** Set your machine on a long, straight stitch. Thicker leathers will require using a special triangular-pointed leather needle, but most lighter-weight leathers like lambsuedes and pigskins can be stitched trouble-free (and with less puncturing) using a universal point size 9/65 – 11/75 needle. Many experts stick with cotton-wrapped polyester thread, but we've found most 100% polyesters satisfactory. *Shy away from 100% cotton thread, however—it's simply not durable enough.*

After seaming with a standard 5/8" seam allowance, run a narrow line of rubber cement or *Clotilde's Sticky Stuff™* glue (see Sources, page 163) along the seamline. Finger-press the seam open after the cement becomes tacky. Then, flatten by pounding with a rubber/wood mallet or pressing block. Topstitching—after the cement is thoroughly dry—is optional.

☞ **Update tip:** Backstitching seam ends is a no-no. Tie off threads instead, to avoid damaging the leather.

• **Hem without sewing.** After carefully marking hem depth, glue up with rubber cement. Edge finishing is unnecessary and topstitching is optional.

• **Secure interfacings with rubber cement**. Collars, cuffs, and other areas of stress will require stabilizing. What better way to "pad-stitch" interfacings in place than with a light layer of rubber cement? Test interfacing weights and types (use sew-ins) on scraps before cementing to the garment pieces.

☞ **Update tip**: Judy Anton, of D'Anton leathers (see page 171), has experimented with using fusible interfacings on pigskin. She stresses, "Testing is a must—not all leathers can be fused." Place the leather right side down on a fluffy bath towel. Position the interfacing and fuse only as long as required to form the bond (not the full ten seconds recommended by most manufacturers). For durability, incorporate the fused interfacing into the garment seams.

• **Take creative departures**. Ravel-free, sturdy leather is a most versatile palette for creativity. Experiment first on scraps, then proceed with the fun of stenciling, beading, weaving, lacing, fringing, and appliquéing.

When fringing, here's a technique that will guarantee even-width fringe and smooth cutting: simply adhere sticky-back shelf paper, such as the Con-Tact® brand, to the wrong side of the fringe area. With nonsmear pencil, mark the fringe widths on the paper (unless you feel confident to eyeball even, parallel widths). Cut the fringe to the depth desired with sharp shears. After the fringing is completed, peel the paper away.

LEATHER FRINGE & CONCHO EMBELLISHMENT

When appliquéing, *leather how-to's differ little from those for fabric.* (See the "Appliqué Fast with Fusible Transfer Web" on page 92.) Keep the iron on a low wool setting and always use a press cloth. Test on leather scraps first. Any fusible transfer web works well—*Aleene's Hot Stitch*™ *Fusible Web, Fusible Film*™ *, Magic Fuse*™ *, Trans-Web*™ *,* or *Wonder-Under* ™—although *Wonder-Under*™ is the one we've used most frequently.

The leather appliqué can be fused to the garment or project. Using tearaway nonwoven or water-soluble stabilizer on the wrong side of the garment, stitch around the motif edges. Because the edges will not ravel (and to minimize bulk), zigzag stitches can be medium to long (8 – 12 per inch) or straight stitching will suffice. To prevent puckering and pulling, use an even-feed or roller foot—see page 142).

LEATHER APPLIQUÉS

☞ **Update tips:** Try the sticky-back shelf paper trick (see fringing, on the previous page) when cutting out appliqués without the help of fusible transfer web. Apply the sticky side to the wrong side of the leather, draw the appliqué shape, cut out, and then remove the paper. When appliquéing leather to leather, use rubber cement or *Sticky Stuff*™ to hold the motif in place.

Notions specialist Clotilde has another tip for leather appliqués: use pressure-sensitive *Sticky Stuff*™ glue to temporarily adhere the appliqués to garments, so they can be removed when laundering is required. (The *Sticky Stuff*™ makes the appliqués behave like *Post-it*™ brand notes.)

Apply the *Sticky Stuff*™ to the back of the leather motif, let it dry until tacky, then press the appliqué in place on the garment. When it's time for washing or dry-cleaning, just peel off the appliqué. Reapply the appliqué easily—simply press into position. (If, after a few removals, more stickiness is needed, reapply the *Sticky Stuff*™ to the appliqué.)

Sources: Refer to "Real Leathers," in the "Sew-by-Mail Directory," pages 171 – 172. Also, look in the Yellow Pages under "Leather Retailers." Order *Sticky Stuff* and *Trans-Web*™ from Clotilde, Inc., *Fusible Film*™ from Speed Stitch, and *Wonder-Under*™ from Nancy's Notions (see pages 160 – 173 of the "Sew-by-Mail Directory").

References: *Leathers and Suedes*, a videotape produced by Nancy's Notions, Ltd., © 1988, and *Sewing with Leather*, a videotape produced by The Tandy Leather Corp., © 1986 (see company addresses and catalog information in the "Sew-by-Mail Directory," pages 160 – 173).

Washable "Leather" : *Ultraleather*®

Ultraleather® is the exciting new fabric from Skinner that looks and feels like natural leather skins but has the launderability, sewability, and resiliency of a knit. It is the smooth synthetic leather-like in the Skinner family of suede-like fabrics: feather-weight *Caress*™, lightweight *Facile*®, and jacket-weight *Ultrasuede*® .

• **Take advantage of the stretch qualities.** *Ultraleather®* stretches lengthwise and crosswise but has 100% recovery. It doesn't lose its shape or bag out. (Susan Jones, designer of *Patterns-by-the-Yard™*, often chooses *Ultraleather®* for her sleek pull-on stirrup pants.)

• **For pattern ideas, look to ready-to-wear.** Because of its stretchability, *Ultraleather®* can be used with patterns designed for fabrics which have up to 25% stretch (check the back of the pattern envelope), as well as those suitable for wovens or leathers. The illustration shown here is an excellent example of a pattern that combines this faux leather with wovens.

Sew the straight skirt from the *Ultraleather®* and trim the jacket with leftover strips, as shown. (Also see the unconstructed wool crepe jacket shown on the front cover of this book; it is trimmed and belted in *Ultraleather®*, eliminating the weight and bulk of facings and interfacings.)

Ultraleather® is 48" wide and usually sells for more than $50 a yard, although several retailers offer everyday discounts up to 30% off the suggested retail price; watch for sales at fabric stores in your area and refer to the "Sources" listed on pages 172 – 173.

Careful planning will save you money too; *at $50 per yard, buying 1/4 yard less can save you $12.50.* For maximum use of the fabric, either measure the pattern to determine the exact yardage or actually lay out the pattern pieces. (Leftover fabric isn't wasted, however—use it for appliqués, binding, accessories, and patchwork.)

• **Wash, dry-clean, or wipe away soil.** *Ultraleather®* is the epitome of cleaning versatility. Because it's machine-washable (or dry-cleanable), costly leather cleaning bills can be eliminated. This leather-like fabric does shrink in both width and length—up to 1/2" per yard—so pretreat it before cutting. To preshrink and care for the finished garment, machine wash in warm water with a mild detergent. Tumble dry on low heat.

Ultraleather® is water repellent, so a garment may also be wiped clean of spills. And it's wrinkle free—a boon for travelers.

When using a pattern for knits, lay out the pattern so that the greatest amount of stretch (crosswise grain) will go around the body.

☞ **Update tip:** For patterns other than those designed for knits, the pieces may be placed in any direction because *Ultraleather®* does not have a nap—a savings on yardage if the stretch is not needed.

• **Consider lining *Ultraleather®* skirts and jackets.** The rayon/nylon-blend knit backing is comfortable worn next to the skin, but the backing doesn't allow slipping the garment off and on smoothly. So for fitted jackets, full or partial lining is suggested. A lining can also prevent stretching, although we've found most stretching-out to be minimal and cured by hanging the garment overnight. Choose a lining fabric compatible with the care you will give your *Ultraleather®* garment.

✎ **Note:** Clotilde, of sewing notion's fame, avoids lining *Ultraleather®* because of the additional weight and restriction of stretchability. Gail agrees.

☞ **Update tip:** Rub the lining and the wrong side of the *Ultraleather®* together to simulate the rustling sound that will be made as you walk. (Some linings will be noisier than others.)

• **Go ahead—fuse interfacings to *Ultraleather®*.** Place the interfacing fusible side down on the wrong side of the fabric. Cover with a damp press cloth. Steam generously with an iron set on wool. For light- to medium-weight stabilization, try *Stacy® Quick Knit™*, *Easy-Knit®*, *Fusi-Knit™*, *Knit Fuze™*, or *SFR®*, *Stretch-Ease™*. For jackets and waistbands, a fusible weft-insertion interfacing, such as *Suitmaker™* or *Tailor Fuse™*, works well.

• **To avoid pin holes, lay out pattern pieces using weights;** use those specially designed for sewing or small, heavy objects. (Gail anchors the tissue with gourmet pet food cans.)

If you do use pins, use the finest available—pleating or extra-fine pleating (small pin holes are self healing).

• **Stitch *Ultraleather®* conventionally.** Use all-purpose thread and universal point needles, size 11/75 or 12/80. (Special leather-sewing needles make too-large stitching holes and may tear the fabric.) If stitches are skipping, loosen the needle tension slightly or change to a larger size needle. Sew with a longer stitch length—about 10/inch. Topstitch with a long stitch—from 5 – 8/inch.

Use conventional seaming, placing right sides together. (Lapped seaming, so popular in *Ultrasuede®* construction, is not recommended because the knit backing will show along the lapped edge.)

Stitching can leave holes when removed, so fit before sewing. (Most needle marks will heal when steamed and in time.) If you need to pin, use long sharp pins, sparingly, within the seam allowances.

Press the seams open, using a press cloth, with the iron set on the wool temperature.

• **Topstitch seams.** To keep the seam allowances flat, topstitch using one of the following methods:

Option A: Press the seam open and topstitch 1/4" away from each side of the seamline (Fig. 6-2).

Option B: Press the seam allowances to one side. Trim the underlying seam allowance and topstitch 1/4" away from the seamline through all layers. See Fig. 6-3.

Option C: Press the seam open and, using a wide (3 – 4mm) twin needle, topstitch over the seamline, as shown. Trim the seam allowances to 3/8". See Fig. 6-4.

PRESS SEAM OPEN. TOPSTITCH WITH WIDE TWIN NEEDLE. TRIM SEAM ALLOWANCES TO 3/8" AS SHOWN.

Fig. 6-4

When topstitching parallel rows, stitch all rows in the same direction to avoid pulling the fabric.

✎ **Note:** Because the presser foot tends to stick to the fabric and stretch the upper layer, hold both layers of the fabric taut while topstitching. To eliminate this sticking problem, several different presser feet are available: the walking foot, roller foot, or *Teflon®* foot. A silicone lubricant, such as *Sewers Aid* or *Needle Lube®*, is another remedy; rub on the underside of the presser foot and on the needle.

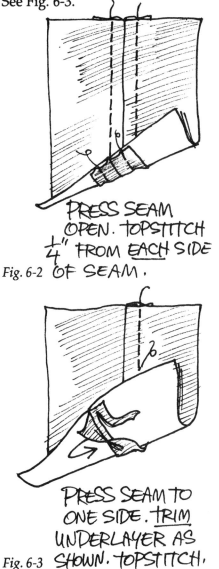

PRESS SEAM OPEN. TOPSTITCH 1/4" FROM EACH SIDE OF SEAM.

Fig. 6-2

PRESS SEAM TO ONE SIDE. TRIM UNDERLAYER AS SHOWN. TOPSTITCH.

Fig. 6-3

• **Use centered applications for zippers:**

1. Lightly press both seam allowances to the wrong side.

2. Working from the right side, butt the seamline together. Secure with movable transparent or masking tape. **Caution**: *Avoid other types of tape that can damage the Ultraleather® surface when pulled off.* If you're not sure what you have, test first.

3. From the wrong side, center the zipper right side down over the seam; tape into place. (It's easier if you use a zipper *at least 1" longer than the opening*—see Chapter 5, "Shortcuts," page 76, Fig. 5-9.)

4. From the right side, topstitch the zipper in place. Stitch both rows directionally, from the bottom to the top, to prevent pulling. Remove the tape.

☞ **Update tip:** Invisible zippers are practical and attractive in *Ultraleather®* garments because they're fast to apply and there's no need for topstitching. For application and source information, see pages 76 – 77 and 172 – 173.

• **Bind jacket lapels, necklines, hems, and pockets with *Ultraleather®*.** You can economize on fabric — the binding strips can be cut in any direction on the *Ultraleather®*.

1. Cut the binding strip *three times wider than the finished binding, plus 1/2".* (A finished width of 1" or less is easiest to apply, especially on curved edges.) The length should be the length of the opening, edge, or hem, plus two seam allowances or about 1".

2. Place the garment and facing wrong sides together. Machine baste 1/8" away from the seamline, as shown. Trim the seam allowance to the basting. See Fig. 6-5.

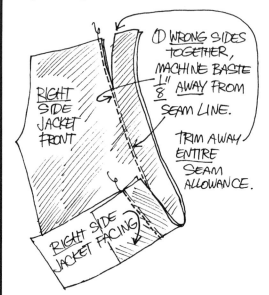

Fig. 6-5

✎ **Note:** For a softer binding, skip Step 2 and *bind the edge without facings.*

3. Right sides together, straight stitch the binding to the edge. *The seam allowance should equal the finished width of the trim.* Stretch slightly around inside curves and ease around outside curves. See Fig. 6-6.

4. Fold the binding over the seam to the wrong side. *Carefully* stitch-in-the-ditch to hold the binding in place. (Finger-press the seam flat as you stitch-in-the-ditch; when the fabric relaxes, the stitching will be hidden in the well of the seam.) Trim close to the stitching on the wrong side. See Fig. 6-7.

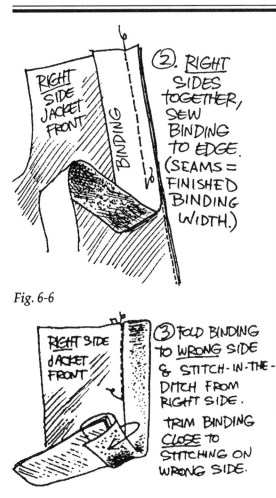

Fig. 6-6

② RIGHT SIDES TOGETHER, SEW BINDING TO EDGE. (SEAMS = FINISHED BINDING WIDTH.)

③ FOLD BINDING TO WRONG SIDE & STITCH-IN-THE-DITCH FROM RIGHT SIDE.

TRIM BINDING CLOSE TO STITCHING ON WRONG SIDE.

Fig. 6-7

TO MAKE BELT LOOP: FOLD 1¼" WIDE STRIP IN THIRDS. EDGESTITCH LONG SIDES OF STRIP.

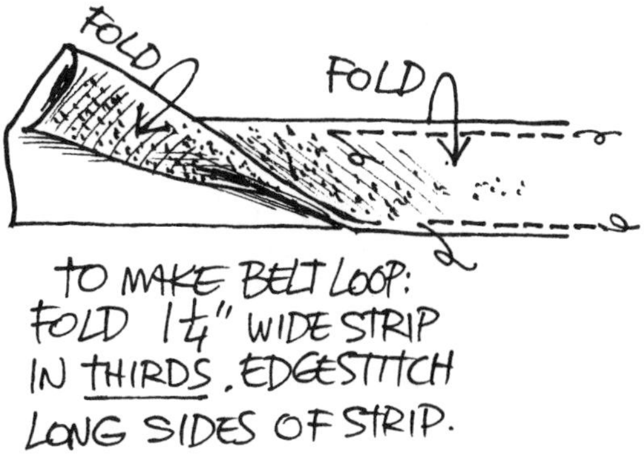

Fig. 6-8

and facing layers of fabric. Straight stitch a 1/8"-wide rectangle and cut through its center, being careful not to cut through the stitching. See Fig. 6-9.

TO MAKE BUTTONHOLE: STRAIGHT-STITCH A ⅛" WIDE RECTANGLE. CAREFULLY CUT THROUGH CENTER OF RECTANGLE BEING SURE NOT TO CUT THROUGH ENDS STITCHING.

SLICE

Fig. 6-9

• **Finish hems by fusing or hand-stitching,** catching the stitches to the backing only. Hems can also be top-stitched with one or more rows of stitching.

Sources: Ask for *Ultraleather®* at your local fabric stores. Also, refer to "Leather-likes: *Ultrasuedes®, Ultraleathers®, Etc.,*" on pages 172 – 173 of the "Sew-by-Mail Directory."

References: *Claire Shaeffer's Fabric Sewing Guide,* by Claire Shaeffer (see "References," page 174), and *Sewing with Leather* videotape (available at Tandy stores or through their catalog—see the "Sew-by-Mail Directory," page 172).

• **Make speedy fold-and-stitch belt loops.** Cut a long 1-1/4"-wide strip of *Ultraleather®;* allow at least 3" in length for each belt loop. Fold the width into thirds, as shown, and edgestitch along both long edges to secure. Cut individual loops into the lengths desired. See Fig. 6-8.

• **Sew easy buttonholes.** Stabilize the buttonhole area by fusing a piece of interfacing on the wrong side of front

7. Easy Embellishments

- **Appliqué Fast with Fusible Transfer Web**
- **Position Appliqués with *ThreadFuse*™**
- **Quick! Painted-on Appliqués**
- **Double Needles: Double Your Options**
- **Couching: Age-Old but Up-to-date**

Embellishing makes good sewing and fashion sense—you sew a simple, flattering silhouette and enhance it to your heart's delight. The results copy the ready-to-wear rage for appliqué and couching, but your custom-mades are definitely a cut above—better-quality materials, more durable and launderable, and, of course, the embellishment scheme is uniquely yours.

Appliqué Fast with Fusible Transfer Web

Every appliquér has a pet method for applying his or her fabric embellishments. However, the fastest method for fused-on appliqués is using fusible transfer web, like Aleene's *Hot Stitch Fusible Web*, HTC's *Trans-Web*™, J & R's *Magic Fuse*™, Pellon's *Wonder-Under*™, Speed Stitch's *Fusible Film*™, or Thermo Web's *Heat N Bond*.

✎ **Note:** Fusible transfer webs are not created equally. Test to compare ease of use, bulk, adherence (especially after laundering), and price.

1. **Trace** the appliqué design(s) on the paper side of the fusible transfer web. If the image must be "readable" left to right, flip the design before you trace it.

2. **Press** the fusible transfer web to the fabric. Allow to dry and cool. See Fig. 7-1.

3. **Cut** the appliqué out of the fabric.

4. **Peel** the paper backing off the design. The appliqué is now ready to be fused to the project.

5. **Fuse** the appliqué(s) to the project. Use tearaway nonwoven or water-

Fig. 7-1

soluble stabilizer *on the wrong side* of the project. Stitch to the project using a satin stitch—a close, narrow- to medium-width zigzag.

References: *Appliqué the Kwik-Sew Way*, by Kerstin Martensson, and *Country Style Appliqués*, by Mary Mulari. (Addresses and ordering information are included in "Sewing Book Favorites," under "References," pages 174 – 177.)

Position Appliqués with *ThreadFuse*™

With melt adhesive thread, you can exactly position a fine, precise line of fusible. Stitch with *ThreadFuse*™ along the line where you want to fuse. For permanent fusing, the fusible bond is soft and pliable, yet it holds extremely well (especially when zigzagged in

place). So it's perfect for positioning appliqués, readying for satin-stitching (Fig. 7-2); the resulting appliqués are softer than those completely fused in

APPLIQUÉ

ALL PURPOSE THREAD ON RIGHT SIDE OF APPLIQUÉ.

SEW AROUND MOTIF, FUSE IN PLACE, THEN SATIN-STITCH EDGES.

MELT ADHESIVE THREAD ON WRONG SIDE OF APPLIQUÉ.

Fig. 7-2

place with fusible transfer web (see pages 92 – 93).

• Use *ThreadFuse*™ in the needle of your machine and all-purpose thread in the bobbin. Loosen the bobbin tension slightly.

• For fuse-basting, use a slightly longer-than-normal straight stitch.

• *Wrong side up*, straight stitch around the appliqué, close to the edge.

• Change to machine-embroidery thread. Fuse the appliqué in place, then satin-stitch the edges.

Sources: For *ThreadFuse*™, contact Clotilde, Inc., Nancy's Notions, Ltd., Serge & Sew Notions, The Perfect Notion, and YLI. (For addresses, see the "Sew-by-Mail Directory," pages 160 – 173.)

Reference: Also see *"ThreadFuse*™ Ingenuity,"* on pages 73 – 74 of Chapter 5.

Quick! Painted-on Appliqués

Barb Griffin, an accomplished craft designer and the author of *Petite Pizzazz*, passed on these neat tips for painting on appliqués. Perfect for or by kids.

• **Prewash and dry** the garment fabric or the finished garment.

• **Fuse** all appliqué pieces to the project following the "Appliqué Fast with Fusible Transfer Web" instructions on pages 92 – 93.

• **Place** a sheet of waxed paper under the project to prevent excess paint from oozing through to the reverse side.

Fig. 7-3

• **Draw** with fabric paints around the appliqué edges. Don't limit yourself to simple outlining; add splashes of paint, as shown in Fig. 7-3. Allow four hours for the paint to dry completely.

• **Wait** at least one week before laundering. You're done.

• **Wash** the finished project with care. Turn inside-out and enclose in a large laundry bag or pillow case. If the painted area stiffens, add fabric softener to the wash cycle.

☞ **Update tip:** A brand-new product, *Liquid Web*, makes another appliqué method possible. As the name implies, the solution is applied wet; upon drying the appliqué is fusible and can be ironed on at any time. Look for it in fabric and craft stores, or order it through mail-order suppliers such as Clotilde (see addresses in the "Sew-by-Mail Directory," pages 163 – 165).

Double Needles: Double Your Options

If you have a zigzag sewing machine, you can create attractive parallel stitching with a double or twin needle. The rows of stitching are sewn simultaneously, saving time and producing very professional-looking accents.

The two top threads combined with the single bobbin thread result in a zigzag on the underside (Fig. 7-4). Hence, the stitch is more flexible than single straight-stitching and well-suited to both decorative and knit sewing.

✎ **Note:** Also see "Twin-needle Sewing," on pages 32 – 34.

Machine specialist Ann Price (she writes the "Machines in Motion: Sewing Machines" column for *Sew News*) has compiled the following tips to ensure first-rate double-needle stitching:

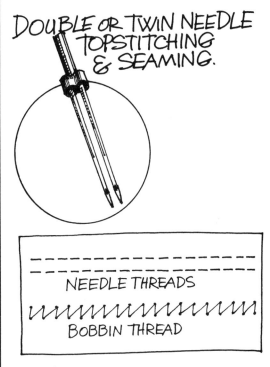

DOUBLE OR TWIN NEEDLE TOPSTITCHING & SEAMING.

NEEDLE THREADS

BOBBIN THREAD

Fig. 7-4

• **Topstitch a hem.** It's faster, easier, and more durable than other methods. Double-stitching also prevents hem and facing edges from rolling, helpful for fabrics like terrycloth. Plus, the double row of stitching adds a design detail, unified by repeating the stitching elsewhere on the garment or project. On sheer knits, such as lingerie tricot, trim to the stitching; the hem edge will disappear under the bobbin stitching. Experiment with stitches other than the straight stitch, for an individual touch. See Fig. 7-5.

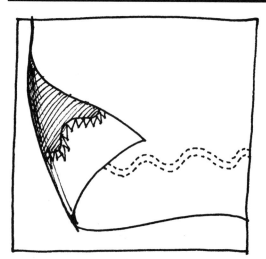

Fig. 7-5

• **Double the versatility of your machine.** Any stitch can be sewn with a double needle for a different look. Even utilitarian stitches take on a decorative quality (Fig. 7-6). The "new" stitches will vary in suitability depending on fabric, stitch length, and width. Try graduated shades of one color thread or two contrasting colors for interesting variations.

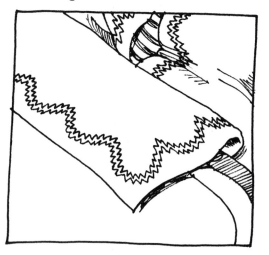

Fig. 7-6

Threading

To prevent the two threads from tangling when sewing, *place the spools so that they unwind in opposite directions.* Place the left spool so that the thread unwinds from behind the spool; the right thread will unwind from the front of the spool. See Fig. 7-7. Make sure threads run smoothly, without twisting, from the take-up lever to the needles.

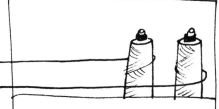

Fig. 7-7

Stitch-Width Limitations

For straight stitching, the machine's stitch width is always set at 0. For any other stitch, however, allow for the distance between the needles when setting the width. This distance determines the size of the double needle, measured by the distance between the needles. The 2.0mm size is the most common, but needles are available in sizes from 1.6mm to 4.0mm. *If the stitch width is set too wide, the needles will break as they hit the presser foot or needle plate.*

So limit your machine's stitch width according to the following formula:

Machine's maximum
stitch width .... _____

Minus the needle size............... (-) _____

Maximum usable
stitch width .... (=) _____

For example, if the machine's maximum stitch width is 4.0mm and you are using a 2.0mm double needle, the stitch width must be limited to 2.0mm.

Caution: Before sewing, turn the handwheel manually to be sure the needles clear the presser foot and needle plate. Stitch length can vary depending on the look desired. Always test on a scrap of the same fabric before starting on the actual project.

☞ **Update tip:** The latest computerized sewing machines have double-needle width indicators. The machine automatically narrows the stitch width when you've told the machine you're using a double needle; you avoid breaking the needle and damaging the foot or plate. Refer to "Update: Computerized Sewing Machines," pages 145 – 154.

Corner Strategies

Curves are easier to stitch than corners, but it is possible to sew a right angle with a double needle.

One-step pivot method: When you reach the corner, stop with the needles out of the fabric. Pivot the fabric, then lower the inside needle into the same corner point and continue sewing. One large stitch will cross the corner of the outside row of stitching. See Fig. 7-8.

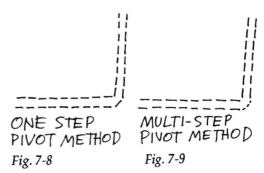

ONE STEP
PIVOT METHOD
Fig. 7-8

MULTI-STEP
PIVOT METHOD
Fig. 7-9

Multistep pivot method: You can avoid the large outside stitch by taking two or more stitches to turn the corner. Manually turn the handwheel to take one stitch at a time, pivoting the fabric just a fraction with each stitch. *The inside needle must be placed into the same pivot point each time until the corner is completely turned.* The outside corner will be slightly rounded. See Fig. 7-9.

Couching: Age-Old but Up-to-date

Although it's the latest designer craze, couching is an age-old technique. (Barbara Weiland reports: for centuries, it has been used to decorate church vestments, outlining with heavy metallic threads, braids, and yarns.) Also known as *passementerie* (pronounced PASS-MEN-TREE) and scrollwork, couching is your ticket to copying fashion's favorite toreador looks, elegantly accented blouses, and lavishly embellished sweaters.

• **Materials:** Use any flexible yarn, heavy thread, trim, or braid. The curvier your design, the more flexible the couching material must be. Try two or more strands together—fuzzy yarns

Couching!!

ALSO CALLED SCROLLWORK OR PASSEMENTERIE

like chenille or mohair, bead strand trim, even narrow strips of real or synthetic leather. The classic is soutache braid. Add coordinating tassels, beads, or appliqués to enhance the scheme.

• **Methods: Traditional couching** is worked by placing the couching material on the design lines, then stitching through it with a straight stitch (called piercing) or over it with a simple zigzag stitch. See Fig. 7-10. Matching, contrasting, or invisible thread can be used.

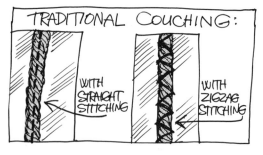

TRADITIONAL COUCHING:

WITH STRAIGHT STITCHING

WITH ZIGZAG STITCHING

Fig. 7-10

Experiment with the many decorative machine stitches. Pierce the couching material, or set the stitch width wide enough to just catch or completely clear the material edges. Worked in a contrasting thread, the trimotion rick-rack stitch is one of our favorites. Or use the blindhem stitch to barely catch one side of the material. See Fig. 7-11. On fabric scraps, test couching material and stitch possibilities before proceeding to embellish your project.

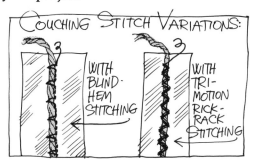

Couching Stitch Variations:

WITH BLIND-HEM STITCHING

WITH TRI-MOTION RICK-RACK STITCHING

Fig. 7-11

Traditional Couching

✎ **Note:** For your first attempt, accent a pocket, collar, yoke, belt, hemline, or pillow, then graduate to larger projects. Choose a simple garment, with dart- and seam-free expanses; to facilitate continuous couching, stitch the shoulder seam first. Also consider ready-made sweaters and sweatshirts, although keep in mind that, because they are seamed, sewing will not be in the easier flat construction order. For a unified look, carry the scrolling to the back of the garment.

1. **Transfer the design lines** to the right side of the fabric with erasable marking pen. Or mark with an iron-on transfer pencil; draw or trace the design on

paper or the pattern tissue and press it onto the fabric (it will be a mirror image).

2. **Make any necessary foot adjustments.** Reduce the pressure (consult your manual) so that the foot will ride smoothly over the couching material. Most regular zigzag feet work well, but you can change to a special-purpose foot that's slotted for braid, yarn, or heavy thread applications.

3. **Set the stitch.** With all-purpose thread in the bobbin, and contrasting, matching, or invisible thread on top, position the couching material between the presser foot toes (Fig. 7-12). Start with a 1/2" tail extending behind the foot. Guide the couching material along the design lines, stitching it in place. *Don't stretch the couching material as you sew*—this can cause ugly puckering.

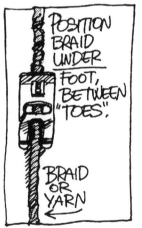

Fig. 7-12

☞ **Update tip:** Machine expert Jackie Dodson suggests substituting a hemming or invisible zipper applicator foot if you don't have a cording foot (Fig. 7-13). Both of these feet have grooves that will accommodate the

couching material. Two new feet handy for couching applications are the *Pearl 'n Piping™* and the *Sequin, Ribbon 'n Ric Rac™* feet manufactured by C. J. Enterprises: the *Pearls 'n Piping™* foot was used to apply the *Cross-Locked Glass Bead Trim* shown on the color pages.

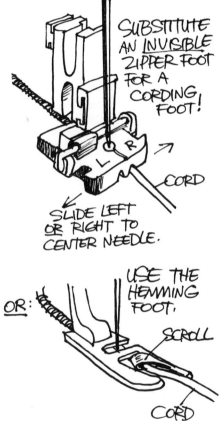

Fig. 7-13

✎ **Note:** For dramatic color splashes, the foot can be removed and the couching material laid down side-by-side and sewn in place free-form embroidery style.

4. **Draw the couching material tails to the wrong side** with a tapestry needle.

Bobbin Couching

Bobbin couching, also known as cable stitching, can simulate traditional couching. Heavier thread, ribbon floss, pearl cotton, crochet thread, and even 4-ply knitting yarn can be wound on the bobbin, slowly and carefully by machine or by hand.

To enable these heavier threads to feed smoothly through the bobbin, loosen the tension; do so incrementally, turning the tension screw counter-clockwise.

☞ **Update tip:** Rather than tamper with the tension on their bobbin case, some sewing pros we know purchase a second bobbin case and use it exclusively for decorative purposes, such as bobbin couching.

1. **Transfer the scrollwork outlines** to water-soluble stabilizer, such as *Wash-Away Plastic Stabilizer* or *Solvy*. Position over the wrong side of the fabric (the bobbin couching will show on the right side). Put both layers into an embroidery hoop.

2. **Set the machine** for a long, wide zigzag or long straight stitch. Change to an embroidery foot. Lower the foot. Carefully draw up the bobbin thread; if necessary, *you can use a large hand needle to work the couching material through.* Sew a few inches, then turn the fabric over to check the couching. The top tension must be loose enough not to pull the couching material through the fabric, but it must be tight enough to secure the couching material. See Fig. 7-14. Stitch slowly.

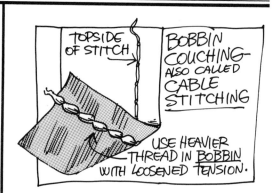

Fig. 7-14

3. Finally, **remove the water-soluble stabilizer** by spritzing with water.

Sources: Inquire first at your local fabric store or machine dealership about the products listed in this chapter. *For mail-order supplies of fusible transfer web, tearaway nonwoven, and water-soluble stabilizer*—Aardvark Adventures, Clotilde, Inc., Nancy's Notions, Ltd., Sew-Art International, SewCraft, Speed Stitch, and Treadleart. *For special sewing machine feet*—C. J. Enterprises, Clotilde, Inc., Nancy's Notions, Ltd., Sewing Emporium, and Treadleart. (For addresses, see the "Sew-by-Mail Directory," pages 160 – 173.)

References: *Beyond Straight Stitching*, by Barbara Weiland O'Connell, ©1988 Update Newsletters, *The Complete Book of Machine Embroidery*, by Robbie and Tony Fanning, ©1986 Chilton Book Company, *Know Your Sewing Machine* by Jackie Dodson, ©1988 Chilton Book Company. (For information, see "References," pages 174 – 178.)

8. Interfacing Update

If your pockets droop, necklines stretch, and waistbands roll, chances are the right interfacing is missing—it's an important key to the success of your sewing project. Nearly everything you sew requires some type of inner support. Interfacing adds shape, strength, stability, and crispness where needed. Use it between the garment and the facing to reinforce wear-intensive areas—collars, cuffs, pockets, front edges, hems, and buttonholes.

As you survey the wide array of interfacings available, choosing the right one may seem complicated. Rely on the updated information in this chapter to guide your selection. As you utilize the timesaving tips here, the choices will become clearer and you will develop favorites suited to the fabrics and items you sew most. Soon you will not only know which interfacing to choose, but you will learn how to use it to achieve the optimum results.

☞ **Update tip:** There have been significant changes in the wholesale interfacing business, including the closure of Stacy Fabrics Corporation, Pellon's adoption of Stacy's best-sellers, and the debut of Dritz, Handler Textile Corporation, and J & R Interfacing products. The information in this chapter, researched by *Update* writers Barbara Weiland and Leslie Wood, reflects the changes you'll see in store inventories and brand names.

Overview of Types Available

Manufacturers spend lots of time and money developing interfacings to meet the special needs of clothing manufacturers; home-sewers reap the rewards of this research by the extensive selection of interfacings available. The three main categories are woven, nonwoven, and weft- or warp-insertion. Within those categories, you have a choice of traditional sew-ins or ravel-free fusibles:

✎ **Note:** For brand-name examples of the interfacing types, refer to the "Interfacing Selection Guide," on pages 112 – 113.

• **Woven interfacings** are available in several weights and finishes. They are especially suited to woven fabrics and any knits you want to stabilize to prevent stretching. Cutting woven interfacings on the bias gives them more drape and flexibility for softer shaping and support.

Woven fashion fabrics work well as interfacings in special situations. Consider interfacing sheer fabrics with a layer of the same fabric, organdy, or organza when traditional interfacing would show. Where color is a concern, batiste, preshrunk muslin, and lightweight broadcloth offer a wider color range than is available in standard interfacings.

• **Nonwoven interfacings** are soft, flexible, and ravel-free. They're available in a variety of weights and constructions in both sew-in and fusible versions. Unlike their paper-like predecessors of the 1950's, they're easy to use and offer a variety of options.

Stable nonwovens have little or no give in any direction, so it is NOT necessary to follow grainline direction during layout. Recommended for detail areas like waistbands, or for use in craft items.

Stretch nonwovens have stability in the lengthwise direction and a considerable amount of stretch in the crosswise direction. Recommended for knits and stretch-wovens.

All-bias nonwovens have some stretch in all directions. Grainline is NOT a consideration. Used in areas like collars and cuffs that turn or roll back on themselves and wrap around the neck or wrist.

☞ **Update tip:** All-bias interfacing is not recommended for stabilizing buttonholes; use a more stable interfacing for these areas.

• **Knit and weft-insertion interfacings** are specialty interfacings constructed differently than standard wovens or nonwovens. Available only as fusibles, they provide supple shaping for fashion fabrics.

Selection Factors

Consult the pattern envelope for guidance when selecting an interfacing. (Some patterns also include a comprehensive interfacing chart on their guide sheets.)

• **Manufacturer's instructions:** Read the description on the bolt for use recommendations. "Crisp" interfacings add body and preserve shape; "soft" interfacings add body without stiffness. Interfacing should not overpower the fashion fabric, but allow it to retain its original texture, drape, and color.

• **Color:** If show-through is a problem in sheer and lightweight fabrics, use a lightweight, flesh-colored interfacing or one designed specifically for sheers. Or try a layer of self-fabric.

• **Fabric characteristics:** If a fabric is sensitive to the steam needed to apply fusibles (some silks, metallics, sequined fabrics), sew-ins are the best choice. For knits, select an interfacing that will stretch and recover with the knit—unless the goal is to stabilize a particular area, such as a buttonhole or waistband. For puckered or napped fabrics, like seersucker or velvet, use a sew-in because the pressure and steam needed to apply a fusible would flatten their surfaces.

Laundering compatibility: Both the interfacing and the fashion fabric should have the same care requirements.

Sew-in Interfacings

Selection: To select the best sew-in woven or nonwoven interfacing for your sewing project, sandwich each possible choice between two layers of the fashion fabric to check weight and body. Roll the layers over your hand to determine how flexible the interfacing is, then fold the layers to simulate the roll of a collar. Look for a soft roll without points or breaks in the curve. See Fig. 8-1.

How to apply:

1. Prelaunder the interfacing as you will the finished garment. (Either machine-wash and -dry or steam dry-cleanables—at home or professionally—to ensure against residual shrinkage.)

FEEL INTERFACING BETWEEN 2 LAYERS OF FASHION FABRIC.

Fig. 8-1

2. Cut the interfacing following pattern directions. Baste in place 1/2" from the raw edge by hand or machine. Or use dots of fabric glue, such as Slomon's *Sobo*, placed close to the raw edge; allow to dry. (The glue will be trimmed away after seaming.) See Fig. 8-2.

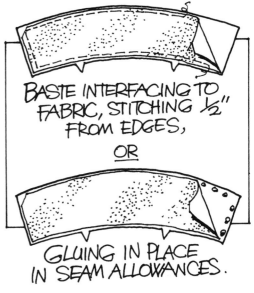

BASTE INTERFACING TO FABRIC, STITCHING ½" FROM EDGES,

OR

GLUING IN PLACE IN SEAM ALLOWANCES.

Fig. 8-2

Note: Sew-in interfacings do not need to be pretrimmed; trim after stitching seams.

3. Complete the garment following pattern instructions. On enclosed seams, trim interfacing close to the stitching to reduce bulk.

Fusible Interfacings

Fusible interfacings have a heat-activated resin on one side, applied in a random pattern of flakes or dots. When the correct amount of heat, pressure, and moisture is applied with an iron and press cloth for the specified time, the fusible resin melts and creates a bond between the interfacing and the fashion fabric. Fusibles are time-savers, eliminating the hand or machine work required with sew-ins; when applied correctly, they provide the long-term support your garment requires.

Fusibles should not be used on fabrics damaged by prolonged heat, pressure, and moisture. And they may not fuse permanently to heavily textured fabrics or to those with slick, glazed surfaces. Water-repellent and stain-resistant finishes may also resist fusibles.

Each type of fusible has distinct characteristics. *No matter which you choose, remember that the end result with a fusible will be slightly crisper than with a similar-weight, sew-in interfacing.* TEST-FUSING is essential to making a good choice.

Woven and nonwoven fusibles are available in a wide range of weights and colors appropriate for every project. Because of the variety, it helps to read all available information on the bolt in order to make the best selection.

Fusible knits (*Stacy® Easy-Knit®, Knit Fuze™, Fusi-Knit™, Quick-Knit™*) are made of 100% nylon tricot and provide soft and supple shaping. Knits are prone to higher shrinkage than wovens, so it is essential to preshrink fusible knits and the fashion fabric prior to cutting to eliminate any differential shrinkage problems.

Fusible knits are appropriate for shaping both knit and woven fabrics. Knit fusibles can also reinforce areas subject to strain, such as jacket elbows and pant knees. And they're great for backing scratchy fabrics and stabilizing machine-knitted, hand-woven, or loosely woven fabrics. (For easy handling, fuse the knit to the fabric before cutting out the garment sections.)

Weft- and warp-insertion interfacings (*Armo® Weft, Suitmaker™, Tailor Fuse™*) are tricot knits with a crosswise or lengthwise yarn woven in and out of the knit stitches. They drape like a knit but, like wovens, are stable in the lengthwise and crosswise directions and stretch on the bias. Available in two weights, they give firm yet supple shaping to dresses, jackets, and coats. The lighter-weight versions (*Whisper Weft, Soft 'N Silky™*) are alternatives to fusible knit. Preshrink the fashion fabric and weft-insertion interfacings before cutting.

Specially textured fusible nonwovens (*Pel-Aire®, Shape-Up ™ Suitweight*) adhere to more heavily textured tailoring fabrics. Very stable, crisp fusibles (*ShirTailor®, Armo® Shirt-Shaper™,*

Shirt Maker™, _Shirt Bond™_) make it possible to duplicate ready-to-wear crispness in the collar, front band, and cuffs of tailored shirts.

Nonwoven fusibles for crafts and decorating (_Style-A-Shade®_, _Decor-Bond®_, _Craft-Bond™_, _Create a Shade™_, _Shade Maker™_, _CRAF-T-BACK™_) add crispness and stability.

Preshrinking Fusibles

Although some fusibles are labeled "preshrunk," it's still a good idea to preshrink them. All fabrics, whether woven, knit, or nonwoven, are held under tension on the bolt. Most will relax and shrink in size with the first laundering, dry cleaning, or steam pressing. Because most fusing requires more steam pressing than normal, there's a higher chance of shrinkage in both the interfacing and the fabric.

Important—Do not preshrink fusibles in the washer and dryer! The adhesive resin may flake off. Follow these preshrinking instructions carefully:

• **Preshrinking by immersion**—use this method for fusible woven, knit, and weft-insertion interfacings.

1. Fill the sink or bathtub with hot tap water. Let the interfacing form soft accordion folds as you gently place it in the water. Allow it to rest, without agitation, until the water is cool. Drain the water and allow the interfacing to rest for an additional 5 to 10 minutes as excess water drains away.

2. Carefully remove the interfacing from the sink and roll it in an absor-

bent towel to remove any excess moisture. Drape the damp interfacing over a towel rod or shower rod until dry. Before storing, attach a notation to the interfacing that it has been preshrunk.

• **Steam-shrink knit and nonwoven fusibles.** Due to fiber content and structure, knit and nonwoven fusible interfacings can shrink from excessive heat during the fusing process. To prevent this, steam-shrink them after cutting, just prior to fusing.

✎ **Note:** _Do not preshrink nonwoven fusible interfacings by immersing in water._ Because knit fusibles have a tendency to shrink more than wovens, they should be steam-shrunk in addition to being preshrunk by immersion in water.

1. Press the fashion fabric where the interfacing will be applied. Then position the interfacing resin side down.

2. Hold the steam iron an inch above the interfacing and steam for a few seconds. Use the burst-of-steam feature on your iron if you have it. See Fig. 8-3.

STEAM SHRINK KNIT & NON WOVEN FUSIBLES: HOLD IRON ABOVE INTER-FACING, GIVE SHOT OF STEAM. BRING IRON _CLOSER_ TO FABRIC—1" ABOVE IT.

Fig. 8-3

You can often see the edges of the interfacing draw up slightly as you steam; the slight change in size due to shrinking does not affect the finished product.

Test to Select the Right Fusible

Test, Test, Test! Every fabric responds differently to each type of fusible interfacing, and fusibles change the character of the fabrics to which they are fused. Test-fuse several interfacing types and weights to select the most appropriate one and to determine the correct amount of heat, pressure, moisture, and time needed for a permanent bond. Always test fusible interfacings on the actual fabric.

Good news: You'll only have to test once for a specific fabric type and fiber. Make note of the best interfacing and use it again when sewing the same type of fabric.

1. For each interfacing to be tested, cut a 4" square from scraps of your fashion fabric. If possible, for easier comparison, cut a long 4"-wide strip to accommodate all of the test interfacings (Fig. 8-4). Cut 2" squares of each test interfacing and pink one edge of each. Press the fashion fabric to warm it, making it more receptive to fusing. **Place each interfacing square on the fashion fabric, resin side down,** with one straight raw edge next to the edge of the fabric.

2. Cover the interfacing sample with a dampened press cloth. **Fuse,** using the iron setting and fusing time recom-

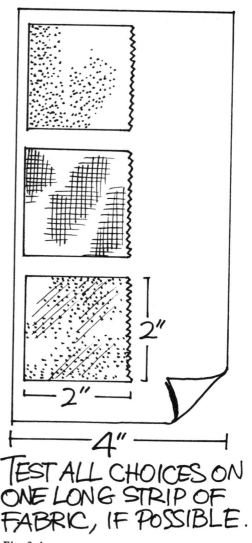

TEST ALL CHOICES ON ONE LONG STRIP OF FABRIC, IF POSSIBLE.

Fig. 8-4

mended by the interfacing manufacturer.

3. Turn the fabric strip to the right side and **repeat the fusing process.** This draws the fusing resins deeper into the fabric structure and guarantees a strong, permanent bond. Because most iron heat is concentrated near the steam vents, the second pressing also

ensures that all areas are thoroughly fused. Allow the sample to cool completely.

4. **Examine and evaluate** each sample as follows:

- **Check for a permanent bond.** If the interfacing peels away from the fabric, try fusing again with more heat, time, and pressure. If fusible interfacings won't adhere securely, choose a sew-in interfacing instead.

- **Look for puckers or bubbles** in the fabric surface; it should be smooth and pucker-free. If not, try fusing longer with increased pressure. Puckers may also indicate that the interfacing is too heavy for the fashion fabric or that the heat and moisture used for fusing caused the fabric to shrink.

    If the surface of the interfacing bubbles, the iron is too hot. Lower the iron temperature and fuse longer, if necessary, for a smooth, pucker-free bond.

- **Examine the right side of the fabric.** *Is there any noticeable color change? Is there an obvious ridge on the right side, indicating the cut edge of the interfacing? Does the pinked edge show through?* If straight or pinked edges show, the interfacing may be too heavy for the fashion fabric.

- **Check for strike-through.** Heavy dots of fusible resin may fuse through and show on the right side of the fabric. Sometimes this doesn't show up until the finished garment is laundered and pressed. When testing dot-type fusibles, wash and press test samples, especially those on smooth-surfaced, solid-colored fabrics like silks and silky synthetics. If there's a problem, substitute a flake-type fusible or a sew-in interfacing. Another option is to use the dot interfacing on the garment in areas where it won't show (on the undercollar instead of the upper collar, or on the underside of a front band or cuff rather than the outer side).

- **Decide how each interfacing will shape the garment.** Fold the test sample in half lengthwise to cover the interfacing samples and simulate the actual layers in the garment where the interfacing will be used. *Are you happy with the drape, hand, and appearance? Is the finished sample too crisp or too soft? Is it too heavy or not heavy enough for the look you wish to create?* If one test is too light and the second too heavy, always choose the lighter weight. *Too soft is better than too stiff.*

- **Fold each interfacing sample against itself.** Look for a smooth roll with a slightly rounded edge. Cracks in the fold mean the interfacing is too heavy or too crisp for the fashion fabric.

- **Launder test samples** to double-check compatibility and permanency of the bond.

What If the Directions Are Missing?

✎ **Note:** Fusible interfacing manufacturers usually recommend trimming away 1/2" of the interfacing seam allowance before fusing. However, *pretrimming is optional on all but the bulkiest fabrics.* Including the interfacing in the seam allowances allows for closer trimming to reduce bulk in enclosed seams. It also prevents raveling of the trimmed seam edges.

Once you have selected the appropriate interfacing, fuse to the garment following the manufacturer's recommendations and your test results. The following steps can be used as general directions when the instructions for fusing the interfacing are missing:

1. Preheat the iron to the wool setting in the steam range. Warm and remove any wrinkles in each fashion fabric piece by steam pressing.

2. Position the interfacing, resin side down, and smooth it into place on the fashion fabric. Steam-shrink (see page 105).

3. Cover with a press cloth and dampen with a liberal misting from a spray bottle, even when using a steam iron. More moisture ensures a good bond.

4. Begin to fuse at the center of large or long pieces of interfacing. Work from the center to each end. Use an up/down motion to move the iron to the next location (Fig. 8-5). Do not slide the iron from one position to the next; this can disturb or move the softened resin. To ensure complete fusing, overlap iron positions.

5. Use both hands on the iron to increase pressure and force the melted fusing resin into the fabric structure for a secure bond. Adjust the ironing board lower than normal so you can exert more pressure while fusing. Fuse for the time recommended—10 to 15 seconds for most fusible interfacings.

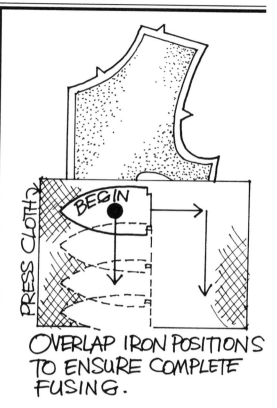

OVERLAP IRON POSITIONS TO ENSURE COMPLETE FUSING.

Fig. 8-5

Otherwise, the bond will not be permanent and will eventually pull away from the fabric. *Watch the second hand on your watch for accurate timing.*

6. Always repeat the fusing process on the right side, using a press cloth to protect the fabric surface.

7. *Do not handle or work with fused pieces until they are thoroughly cool and dry; fusing resins are easily reshaped or distorted while warm.*

Specialty Interfacings

In addition to the standard interfacings described in the "Interfacing Selection Guide," pages 112 – 113, there is a growing array of interfacing products designed for special purposes:

• **Perforated strips or slotted bands** of fusible interfacing (*Pellon® Waist Shaper®, Fold-a-Band™ For Waistbands, For Blouse & Shirt Plackets* or *For Facings and Hems, Perfect Waist Maker, Pero-Fuse™, Waist Magic™*) were created for easy application in hemlines, vents, front bands, pocket edges, and waistbands. Perforations create a stitching guideline and ensure a smooth, evenly folded edge. See Fig. 8-6. As with any fusible, test first on fashion fabric scraps for suitability.

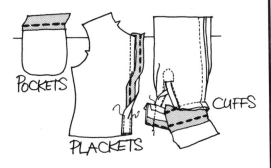

Fig. 8-6

• **Woven waistband stabilizers** (*Ban-Rol, Armoflexxx®, Rol-Control*) are available in several widths suitable for waistbands. See "Neat Waistbands," pages 68 – 69 of Chapter 4, "Simply Flattering Slacks."

• **Tearaway stabilizers** (*Pellon® Stitch-n-Tear®, Armo® Tear-Away™*) can be used on the right or wrong side of the fabric. Machine-embroidery enthusiasts love stabilizers because they help maintain the stitch width and float the thread on the fabric surface. Also, they minimize puckering and stretching of the fabric, or pulling of lightweight fabric through the machine throat

plate. Clear "plastic" stabilizers (*Solvy* and *Wash Away*) are water-soluble; after stitching, simply spray the stabilizer away. Also see Chapter 7, "Easy Embellishments," pages 92 – 100.

• **Fleeces** (*Pellon® Fleece, Craft-T-Fleece™, Ultra-Fleece™, HTC-Fleece™, Big Fleece™*) are popular for crafts, quilting, and sleeve heads in tailored jackets. They're 100% polyester and needlepunched for durability and easy handling. New on the market are fusible fleeces (*Fusible Craft-T-Fleece™*).

Interfacing Tips From the Pros

Here are some tricks of the trade that will speed up your sewing and produce superior results:

• **Before you cut, consider the purpose of the interfacing** and take advantage of built-in characteristics. For example, cut the collar interfacing so the give will go around the neck and help shape the neck curve. Cut front interfacings for blouses and dresses so the stable direction of the interfacing (usually lengthwise) is the same as the direction of the buttonhole. This will prevent stretching in the buttonhole area. See Fig. 8-7.

• **With sheers, interface and clean-finish the facing edges all-in-one** with the faced-facing technique: Cut the interfacing from self fabric using the facing patterns. Stitch and press the shoulder seams in each set of facings, then sew sets together along the outer edge. For conventional seaming, stitch right sides together using a 1/4" seam; stitch again a scant 1/8" away. Turn

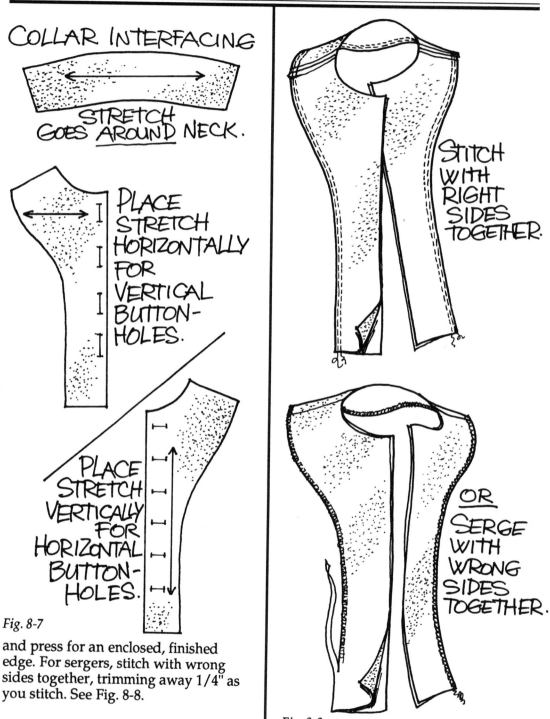

COLLAR INTERFACING

STRETCH GOES AROUND NECK.

PLACE STRETCH HORIZONTALLY FOR VERTICAL BUTTON-HOLES.

PLACE STRETCH VERTICALLY FOR HORIZONTAL BUTTON-HOLES.

Fig. 8-7

STITCH WITH RIGHT SIDES TOGETHER.

OR SERGE WITH WRONG SIDES TOGETHER.

Fig. 8-8

and press for an enclosed, finished edge. For sergers, stitch with wrong sides together, trimming away 1/4" as you stitch. See Fig. 8-8.

• **Eliminate a step with cut-on interfacings** in blouses and dresses. Interface straight-cut facings with self fabric by cutting on an extra width to turn back on itself. See Fig. 8-9.

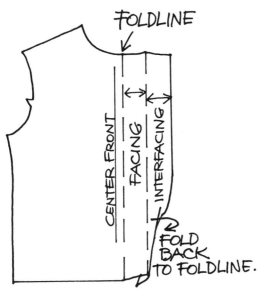

USING SELF-FABRIC: CUT AN EXTRA WIDTH AT FRONT EDGE EQUAL TO THE WIDTH OF THE FACING.

Fig. 8-9

• **Pink the inner edge of front fusible interfacings.** Pinking creates a "buffer" so the interfacing is less likely to leave a ridge on the right side of the finished garment (Fig. 8-10). If the pinked edge shows on your test sample but the interfacing is not too heavy for the fabric, apply the interfacing to the entire front, or fuse to the facing rather than to the garment.

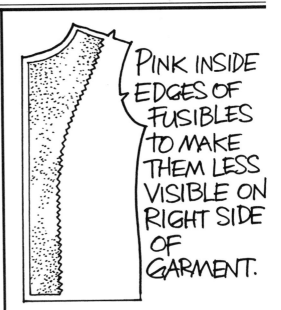

PINK INSIDE EDGES OF FUSIBLES TO MAKE THEM LESS VISIBLE ON RIGHT SIDE OF GARMENT.

Fig. 8-10

• **Protect nonwoven interfacings with facings or linings** to prevent abrasion during wear and cleaning. Without a protective covering, these interfacings will eventually shred away.

✎ Note: Interfacing tips for coats and jackets are covered in "Time-saving Tailoring: Better, Faster Jackets and Coats," pages 35 – 55.

Sources: Most of the products carried in this chapter will be carried by your local retailer. For mail-order, contact Clotilde, Inc., Nancy's Notions, Ltd., and Sew/Fit Co. (For addresses, see the "Sew-by-Mail Directory," pages 160 – 173.)

Interfacing Selection Guide

These charts contain a comprehensive list of the most widely available interfacings from the major suppliers — Pellon, J & R Interfacing, Handler Textile Corp. (HTC), and Dritz. You may find comparable interfacings not listed from these and other companies. Use the charts as a general guide in making selections for your sewing projects. Interfacings are grouped in two categories (sew-ins and fusibles), by weight (sheer, light, medium, heavy, and tailoring), and by type (woven, nonwoven, knit, weft-insertion, and warp-insertion). Because many similar interfacings are interchangeable, you'll need only one or two from each category.

Key: W = Woven
      N = Nonwoven

Sew-in Interfacings

Weight	Type	Supplier	Interfacing	Colors	Comments
Sheer	N	HTC	Armo® Sheer-Shape™ Sew-in	White	Soft and drapable for extra sheer and very lightweight fabrics: voile, gauze, chiffon, crepe de chine; little or no crosswise stretch; lengthwise stability.
	N	Pellon	#905 (Sew-in)	White, Beige	
Light	N	HTC	Armo® Intra-Face™ Bias Featherweight	White	For lightweight knits and wovens needing give; has some stretch in all directions.
	N	Pellon	#910 Featherweight	White	Little crosswise give; stable lengthwise; for light- and medium-weight durable press wovens.
	N	HTC	Sew Shape™ Featherweight	White	For soft, drapable, gentle control in lightest weight knits and wovens; flexible.
	W	HTC	Armo Press® Soft	White	Durable press; for soft shaping in lightweight wovens.
	W	Pellon	Shapewell® (#70)	White	100% cotton; crisp shaping for light- and medium-weight dress and blouse fabrics: oxford cloth, poplin, calico.
	W	Dritz	Shape Maker™	White, Black	
Medium	N	Pellon	#930 (Sew-in)	White	For firm to very firm shaping medium- to heavy-weight knits and wovens.
	W	HTC	Armo Press® Firm	White	
	W	HTC	Sta-Form™ Durable Press	White, Black	Durable press; crisp shaping in medium-weight wovens, stable knits; use for back stay in tailored jackets and coats.
	W	HTC	Veri-Shape™ Durable Press	White, Black	
	W	Dritz	Sew-in DuraPress™	White	
	W	J & R	Woven Form™	White	
Heavy & Tailoring Weight	W	HTC	Acro	Natural	Washable hair canvas for medium to heavy tailoring fabrics: 52% rayon/ 43% polyester/ 5% goathair.
	W	HTC	Fino II	Natural	Luxury hair canvas for fine couture tailoring: 35% wool/ 35% rayon/ 15% polyester/15% goathair; high wool content provides easy collar and lapel shaping.
	W	HTC	P-26 Red Edge	Natural	Economy hair canvas for tailoring medium- to heavy-weight wovens: 57% cotton/ 32% rayon/ 11% goathair.
	W	Pellon	Sewer's Choice™ (#90H)	Natural	Traditional hair canvas for tailoring medium- and heavy-weight coat and suit fabrics: 43% cotton/ 36% rayon/ 21% goathair.

Pellon® and Stacy® are registered trademarks of The Pellon Company, a division of Freudenberg Nonwovens Limited Partnership. The Stacy® products listed were purchased by Pellon when Stacy Industries went out of business.

Armo® is a registered trademark of Crown Textile Company; Handler Textile Corporation (HTC) sells Armo® products to the home-sewing market.

Interfacing Selection Guide

Key: W = Woven   WI = Weft-insertion
N = Nonwoven   WA = Warp-insertion
K = Knit

Fusible Interfacings

Weight	Type	Supplier	Interfacing	Colors	Comments
Sheer	N	Pellon*	Sheerweight Fusible (#906F)	White, Beige, Charcoal	Crosswise give; soft and drapable; use for lightweight sheers and extra-sheer fabrics: batiste, chiffon, gauze, voile, crepe de chine.
	N	HTC	Sheer D'Light™ Featherweight	White, Charcoal	
Light	K	Pellon	Stacy Easy-Knit®	White, Beige, Black	Nylon tricot knits with excellent crosswise stretch and lengthwise stability; supple, drapable; support without stiffness; use in light- and medium-weight knits and wovens.
	K	Dritz	Knit Fuze™	White, Beige, Black	
	K	HTC	Fusi-Knit™	White, Ivory, Black, Grey	
	K	J & R	Quick Knit™	White, Beige, Black, Grey	
	WI	HTC	Whisper Weft	White, Beige, Grey	Excellent lengthwise and crosswise stability with bias give like a woven; soft drape like a knit; for lightweight tailoring.
	WA	J & R	Soft 'N Silky™	White, Bone, Black	
	N	Pellon	Sof-Shape® (#880F)	White, Charcoal	All bias; suitable for a range of fabric weights, from light to heavy; suitable for lightweight tailoring.
	N	HTC	Armo® Uni-Stretch® Lightweight	White	Exceptional crosswise give, stretch, and recovery; especially suited to knits, stretch-wovens, and bias-cut wovens.
	N	Pellon	#911 FF(MVP) (Featherweight Fusible)	White, Grey	Soft, supple shaping for light- and medium-weight knits and wovens.
	N	HTC	Sheer D'Light™ Lightweight	White, Charcoal	
Medium	W	Pellon	Shapewell® (#70F)	White	100% cotton; use in lightweight wovens for soft shaping.
	W	Pellon	Stacy Shape-Flex® All Purpose	White, Black	100% cotton; use in lightweight wovens for crisp support.
	W	HTC	FormFlex™ All Purpose	White, Black	
	W	J & R	Classic Woven™	White	
	WI	Dritz	Suitmaker™	Natural	Excellent lengthwise and crosswise stability and bias give like a woven; has the drape of a knit; use in medium to heavy tailoring fabrics.
	WI	J & R	Tailor Fuse™	White, Black	
	N	Pellon	Easy-Shaper®	White, Charcoal	Soft, supple, controlled shaping for light- and medium-weight knits and wovens.
	N	Dritz	Shape-Up Lightweight™	White, Charcoal	
	N	HTC	Sheer D'Light™ Medium Weight	White, Charcoal	
	N	J & R	Stretch 'N Shape™	White, Black	
	N	Pellon	Sof-Shape® (#880F)	White, Charcoal	Crosswise give; suitable for a range of fabrics, from light to heavy; good for corduroy.
	N	HTC	SRF™®	White, Charcoal	Offer stretch and recovery for medium-weight knits, wovens, and stretch-wovens.
	N	Pellon	Stretch-Ease™ (#921F)	White, Charcoal	
	N	HTC	Armo® Uni-Stretch® Suitweight	White	Excellent recovery; good for collars, lapels, cuffs. Grid on suitweight retards abrasion.
	N	Pellon	ShirTailor® (#950F)	White	For shirt collars, cuffs, and other details where firmness is desirable for crisp, tailored look.
	N	HTC	Armo® Shirt-Shaper™	White	
	N	Dritz	Shirt Maker™	White	
	N	J & R	Shirt Bond™	White, Black	
Heavy & Tailoring Weight	W	HTC	Fusible Acro	Natural	A machine-washable, fusible hair canvas; gives very firm, crisp shape: 52% rayon/43% polyester/5% goathair.
	WI	HTC	Armo® Weft	White, Beige, Black, Grey	Lengthwise and crosswise stability with bias give like a woven.
	N	Pellon	#931 TD Midweight (MVF)	White	For firm support in medium-weight knits, wovens, and stretch wovens; good for active sportswear: chino, poplin.
	N	Dritz	Shape-Up™ Suitweight	White, Charcoal	Textured surfaces and heavier adhesive coating to provide better adhesion to suit- and coat-weight fabrics for tailoring.
	N	Pellon	Pel-Aire® (#881F)	Natural, Grey	

* Pellon is the only manufacturing supplier.

9. Dramatic Fabric Decorating

- **Decorating Essential:
  Never-Miss Miters**
- **Napkins: Sew Fast Without Serging**
- **Quickest Tablecloths**
- **Tension Rod Remedies**
- **Grace Your Home with Lace**

- **With Just One (or Two?) Sheets:
  Transform a Room**
- **Really Easy Ruching**
- **Dramatic Holiday Decorating
  for Hurried Seamsters**

We never have enough time or money to re-create, detail for detail, pages out of *House Beautiful*. But we can fake it pretty well, with the help of fabric. You can decorate in minutes, without painting, wallpapering, carpeting, or carpentry. Create some drama around your house—just borrow some of our favorite techniques and projects.

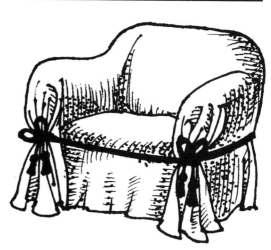

☞ **Update tip:** If you've got absolutely no time but guests are on the way, remember that fabric, or sheets, can camouflage a multitude of decorating disasters. Drape the fabric over a worn couch, an uncovered table (you'll have hidden storage underneath), a naked window, or an unpainted wall. To secure it, tack, tape, tie, or glue in place. Turn under the unsewn edges (selvages are OK), and you're done.

Decorating Essential: Never-Miss Miters

Because so many decorating projects require mitering—table linens, draperies, bedspreads—we included this method in this chapter. (Although it's nifty for fashions too.) Every seamster has a pet mitering method, but we've never been shown one easier or one that produces better results than this never-miss miter.

1. Mark the hemline corner point (where the two hemlines intersect). *Important*: make sure the intersecting hemlines are the same depth. See Fig. 9-1.

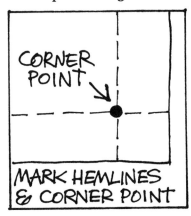

Fig. 9-1

☞ **Update Tip:** If you will not be turning under the hem edges, it's best to finish them now with pinking, zigzagging, overlock stitching, or serging.

2. Fold the corner rights side together so that the two raw edges meet (Fig. 9-2).

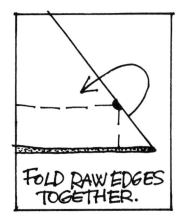

Fig. 9-2

3. Fold the corner again, as shown in Fig. 9-3, from the corner point. Match all the raw edges.

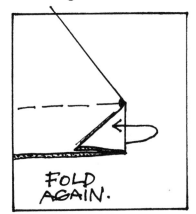

Fig. 9-3

4. Using the diagonal foldline as a guide, straight stitch next to (but not catching) the fold. Stitch to within 3/8" of the raw edges. Backstitch at both ends of the seam. Trim the seam, tapering at the corner to minimize bulk. See Fig. 9-4.

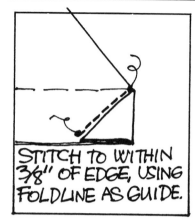

Fig. 9-4

5. Press open the trimmed seam (Fig. 9-5). Then turn right side out. Align the miter in the middle of the corner and press again from the right side (Fig. 9-6).

Fig. 9-5

6. If you've already finished the hemline edge (or if finishing is unnecessary), simply topstitch the hem (Fig. 9-6). On ravel-prone fabrics or for particular projects (like the napkins below), turn under the raw edges 3/8" and edgestitch.

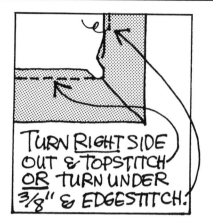

Fig. 9-6

Napkins: Sew Fast Without Serging

Use the goof-proof mitering method when you want to make napkins fast, without serging. Serger expert Naomi Baker actually favors this method over serging when working with ravelly or textured fabric that resists rolled-edge finishing.

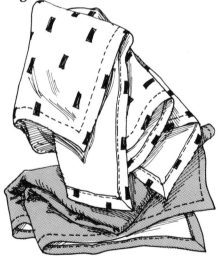

Medium-weight yarn-dyed or solid-colored fabrics, such as linens, damasks, and beefy cotton textures, are best made single layer. Lighter-weight, single-sided prints and solids, such as broadcloth and gingham, are perfect for the double-sided napkins; the unprinted side is hidden inside and the contrasting side is beautifully framed by the mitered edging. Production for either napkin style—single or double layer—is efficient: one napkin can easily be finished in fifteen minutes. Great for hostess or holiday gifts and best-sellers at bazaars.

For single-layer napkins: Cut 16 – 17" squares of medium-weight fabric. Mark corner points using 1" hemlines. Miter as described in "Decorating Essential: Never-Miss Miters," pages 115 – 116, finishing by turning under the raw edges and edgestitching.

For double-layer (lined) napkins: Cut 17" squares of the fabric (that will be the right side of the napkin). Mark the corner points using 1" hemlines. Miter as described in "Decorating Essentials: Never-Miss Miters," pages 115 – 116. Before finishing, place a 16" square of the lining fabric, *wrong sides together,* under the mitered edges of the fabric. Pin to secure. Turn under the raw edges and edgestitch as shown in Fig. 9-6, sewing the lining and mitered hems in place.

Quickest Tablecloths

Tablecloths are godsends during seasons of less sewing and more houseguests—holidays and summer, in particular. But shopping for them can be exasperating; ready-mades are often spendy, never the right size and shape, and constructed of cheap fabrics in weird colors or prints. Luckily, creating your own table coverups is a quick, painless project. It pays off in dramatic decorating that doubles as clever camouflage for marginal furniture and under-the-table storage.

TABLE TOPPINGS

• **Estimate the yardage necessary** by determining the unhemmed tablecloth length and width. For most average to larger-sized tables or full-length cloths, you will need two or more lengths of fabric. Custom calculate this way:

✎ **Note:** Except when using large-motif decorator fabrics or plaids, print matching is unnecessary.

1. **Measure the length and width of the table.** Differentiate between the two measurements with an "L" and a "W."

2. **Determine the desired drop**—the amount that hangs down from the edge of the table. Usually, for casual cloths, the drop is 10 – 12", or about 1" – 2" above the chair seat. Formal cloths have 16 – 24" drops, and full-length cloths reach the floor (about

29 – 30", or longer, if you want the "puddled" look).

3. **Calculate the total length required:**

a. Measure the table length (A) = ____.

b. Add the drop length (B) = ____.

c. Multiply the drop (B) by 2 = ____(C).

d. Add (A) + (C) + hem allowances (a total of 4" for rectangular cloths, 2" for all others) + one design repeat (the distance between matching motifs) if using a print that must be matched =____(D) — **the total length required.**

4. **Calculate the total width required:**

a. Measure the table width =____(E).

b. Add (E) + (C) + hem allowances (same as for the length — see D, above) = ____(F).

c. Add (F) + seam allowances (a total of 3") = ____(G) — **the total width required.**

5. **Compute the number of fabric lengths required:**

a. Measure the width of the fabric = ____(H).

b. Divide the total width required (G) by (H) = ____(I).

c. If (I) is a decimal, round up to the next largest whole number = ____(J)— **the total number of lengths required.**

6. **Calculate the yardage required:**

a. Multiply (J — the total number of lengths) by (D — the total length required) = (K) — the total inches required.

b. Divide (K) by 36 (the number of inches in a yard) = ____(L)—**the total yards required.**

☞ **Update tip:** Remember, wider-width fabrics and flat sheets will reduce piecing and yardage requirements. For instance, a full-length tablecloth for a 48" round table requires 8 yards of 45"-wide fabric, but only 5-3/8 yards of a 60"-width (or just one king-size flat sheet).

• **Bypass prewashing;** laundering reduces stain-protective finishes and demands too much pressing time. Because you're not fitting a body, shrinkage is seldom a problem.

• **Cut the fabric into the total number of lengths required (J),** allowing for print-matching, if necessary (it seldom is).

• **Piece as shown,** to avoid a seam running down the center of the cloth and table, using 1/2" seams. (See Fig. 9-7.) Whenever possible, seam along the finished selvage edges, and hem the raw edges of the half widths.

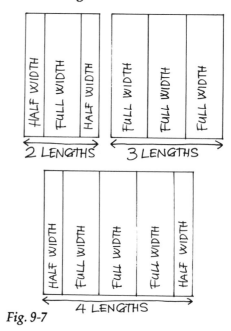

Fig. 9-7

• **Trim to the unhemmed length and width dimensions (D and G)**, allowing 2" hems for squares and rectangles, and only 1" hems for ovals and rounds.

To make a round cloth from the pieced fabric: carefully fold the fabric in half, with the fold running parallel to the piecing seams. Find the exact center of the fold, then pivot a measuring tape half the unhemmed length from this point; mark and trim.

To make an oval cloth from the pieced fabric: center the cloth wrong side down on the oval table. Mark the edge of the table on this cloth with tailor's chalk or washable marker. Take the cloth off the table; from the table-edge marking, add the desired drop plus a 1" hem.

☞ **Update tip:** In a big hurry? Finish the hem edge with seam sealant, and glue the hem in place. (Be sure to use glue that's permanent and washable, such as *Glu-N-Wash*™.) Or, if you're making a full-length cloth, allow a 6" hem, pink the edge, and puddle the hem on the floor; before washing or cleaning, turn up and machine stitch the pinked hems.

• **Finish hems really fast.** Gail avoids any technique that calls for stitching the hem more than once. *For square and rectangular cloths*, hem and miter as shown on pages 115 – 116. *For round and oval cloths*, fold under the 1" hem; from the right side of the cloth, stitch 1/2" (or so) from the hem fold (the allowance underneath will be automatically eased in place). Then, with sharp scissors, trim to the stitching.

☞ **Update tips**: To update everyday cloths, **top or layer with smaller cloths**. A full-length round tablecloth can be topped with a 44" square; only 1-1/4 yards of 44/45"-wide fabric is required. Or layer a lace cloth over a solid cloth.

Consider protecting the cloth and the table surface with glass custom-cut to the table-top shape. You'll launder the cloth less, while creating a surface that's really better for writing, drawing, and eating. Call your local glass supplier for prices and recommended thicknesses for your particular table and its uses.

Source: For *Glu-N-Wash*™, look in the Clotilde, Inc., catalog (see "Sources," page 163 for the address and information).

Tension Rod Remedies

Without hammering or drilling, you can install curtains, room dividers, and canopies. Do it with fabric-covered tension rods, spring-loaded to fit instantly. Soft furnishings can be effortlessly revamped and relocated. Take it from us: tension rod projects are as elementary as they look.

Functional Favorites

Pick your project; then get set for instant results.

• **Shower curtains.** Use the permanent rod (or another tension rod) to hang an inexpensive liner. (Hang two liners, side by side for better protection against shower leakage.) Install another tension rod outside and above the liner for the decorator curtain. See Fig. 9-8. Add a third rod inside the bath to drip-dry prewashed fabrics and hand washables.

SHOWER CURTAIN:
FABRIC DRAPED OVER ROD.
↙FOLD↘

TENSION RODS↗

2-2½ TIMES THIS LENGTH

LINING LAYER

├─┤ FABRIC WIDTH├─┤

Fig. 9-8

• **Window covers.** Simply install one or more rods inside the frame. Not only is this installation fast, but the covers are also energy-efficient. With two rods, the fabric can be stretched inside the frame, allowing you to move the rods up and down as desired for light and privacy. See Fig. 9-9.

• **Fabric walls.** This is the perfect method for curtaining alcoves and making pass-throughs less public. Simply install tension rods between walls to divide a room, create a closet or dressing area, or add a bed canopy. See Fig. 9-10.

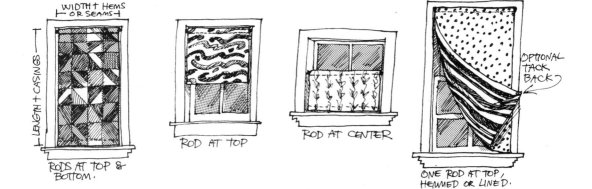

WIDTH + HEMS OR SEAMS

LENGTH + CASINGS

RODS AT TOP & BOTTOM.

ROD AT TOP

ROD AT CENTER

OPTIONAL TACK BACK

ONE ROD AT TOP, HEMMED OR LINED.

Fig. 9-9

Fast furnishings—scarf-print floor cushion, a tie-on pillow cover, and a metallic-accented runner. The oblong cushion was wrapped in batting, recovered with a Ralph Lauren sheet, and finished with ruched piping. See Chapter 9.

Cross-locked Glass Bead Trim *echoes the V neckline of this wool jersey top. To anchor the beads before zigzagging in place, the strands were fused first to ThreadFuse™, basted along the stitching lines (see inset). See Chapter 7. Paired with Ultraleather® stirrup pants, shirred at the waistband. See Chapters 5 and 6.*

Semi-lined rather than fully lined, this tweed jacket has extended facings, lined sleeves, and edges bound with bias strips of the contrasting-color lining. See Chapter 3. The reverse side of the tweed was used for the lapel facings.

Dramatic splashes of holiday color—no-sew fabric gift wraps, quick-finished bias-cut napkins. Notice the curled ribbon: fabric was fused to giftwrap, then cut into strips and curled. See Chapter 9.

• **Soft closet doors.** Replace clunky conventional or louvered closet doors with fabric curtains. After removing the door(s), adjust a heavy-duty rod inside the top of the closet frame. See Fig. 9-10. With this inviting access, kids (and Dad?) might hang up their clothes.

The Right Tension Rod

After deciding on your project, select the tension rod(s) carefully. For heavy fabric, find one that's hefty, at least 1" in diameter and 6" or more longer than the expanse. (The overlap of the unused length inside the rod adds tensile strength.)

Fabric, decorating, hardware, and discount stores carry tension rods in a variety of colors, diameters, and lengths. In isolated areas, your best sources may be the Sears and J. C. Penney catalogs. However, you'll spend more for these than closet or curtain rods not spring-loaded; a heavy-duty 39" to 74" length sells for about $12, lighter-weight 28" to 48" and 48" to 84" lengths, about $5 and $8, respectively. The larger 1" diameter 40" to 60" sizes are also being marketed in dozens of shades as shower curtain rods, but you can use them throughout the house.

Suspension Savvy

Finally, decide how you're going to suspend your fabric on your carefully chosen tension rod(s).

• **Draping** is a no-sew method. Just drape the fabric over the rod, arranging the fullness. When you've got gobs of fabric and only minutes to spare, draping's the ticket. (Gail's

houseguests rave about the shower curtain she made by throwing 4 yards of lace over a tension rod.)

Drape folds are soft and lavish when there's almost twice the length of fabric to hang behind, weight, and self-line the front layer. For a divided curtain or covering, drape one full width of fabric at each end of the rod. The excess length can fall onto the floor in an unhemmed puddle, the latest decorating craze and the epitome of casual elegance. See Fig. 9-8.

• **Shirring** calls for basic straight stitching to form the rod casing and hems. First, calculate the fabric required. Remember, for a smooth-feeding casing, *the stitching lines should be twice the rod diameter apart*. A double layer hem will minimize billowing; allow twice the hem depth, press up half the hem allowance, twice, and topstitch. See Fig. 9-10.

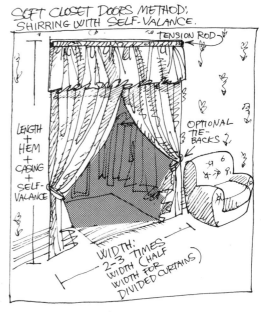

Fig. 9-10

Add a top ruffle or self-valance by allowing the extra length desired; stitch the casing the width of the ruffle or valance from the top edge or fold.

☞ **Update tip:** Give the popular balloon or cloud look to gathered valances by tying them into swags with ribbons or edge-finished fabric strips. Make some soft bows or rosettes and pin them at the peaks of the swags. See Fig. 9-11.

Fig. 9-11

☞ **Update tip:** Fabric can also be suspended from the rod, straight across, with no shirring (Fig. 9-12). You'll need the same length estimate calculated for the shirred method, but only the width plus hem or seam allowances. The sewing's the same, too, although lining flat fabric is recommended for extra body. When stretching fabric rod to rod, *add enough length for both casings.*

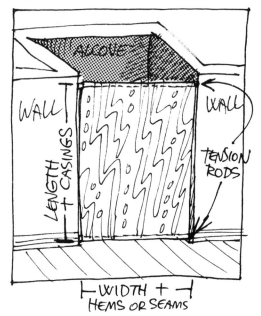

FABRIC WALL: STRETCHED BETWEEN RODS.

Fig. 9-12

Grace Your Home with Lace

Lace can put on all sorts of decorating faces—romantic, Victorian, or country. Undoubtedly there's a place for lace in your home, no matter what your decorating preferences. All you need are designer Barb Griffin's quick project ideas, a short sewing session, and, of course, lace.

Napkin Table Topper

Your local discount department store or linen outlet is a likely treasure trove of Battenburg lace or crocheted

A ROMANTIC ACCENT!

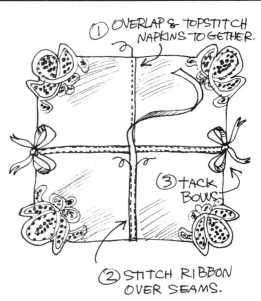

① OVERLAP & TOPSTITCH NAPKINS TOGETHER.

② STITCH RIBBON OVER SEAMS.

③ TACK BOWS.

Fig. 9-13

3. Tie four bows out of 18"-long pieces of the ribbon, cutting the ends into inverted "V's." Hand-tack or glue one bow to each end of the ribbon trim.

Tablecloth Curtains

HANG HALF TABLE CLOTH OVER ROD.

FINGER-PLEAT FULL-NESS.

DRAPE ENDS EVENLY.

Fig. 9-14

napkins at reasonable prices. To make a lovely kerchief cloth, purchase a set of four of your favorite napkins.

1. Open the napkins and press using spray starch. Arrange the napkins into a square, *with the most decorative corners forming the corners of the kerchief*. Seam them together by overlapping the edges 1/4" and topstitching. See Fig. 9-13.

2. Use 1"- to 2-wide grosgrain or satin ribbon to cover the seams. Place the ribbon over the seams and turn the raw ribbon ends under. Topstitch along both sides and the ends (Fig. 9-13).

Add personality to narrow windows (up to 28" wide) by transforming a round lace tablecloth into two swag valances. (See Fig. 9-14.) To determine the approximate diameter of the tablecloth needed, measure the window height and add the window width; for a 40" by 28" window, you'll need a 68" or larger diameter cloth.

1. Cut the tablecloth into two equal half-circles. Finish the straight edges by turning 1/4" under twice and edge-stitching. On loosely woven lace, stabilize the edges by fusing narrow strips of *Easy-Knit®* to the wrong side. Each semicircle will make one swag. See Fig. 9-15.

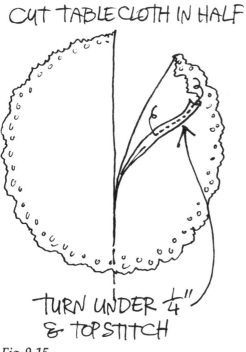

CUT TABLECLOTH IN HALF

TURN UNDER $\frac{1}{4}$"
& TOPSTITCH

Fig. 9-15

2. For even more romance, sew lace trim to the curved edge of the tablecloth.

3. Hang each swag over a curtain rod, draping the ends over the rod to the back side; adjust the ends evenly and finger-pleat the fullness for a decorator look.

☞ **Update tip:** A delicate curtain or valance can be quickly fashioned from a 36" – 45" square Battenburg lace tablecloth—*without sewing*. Fold the cloth diagonally over the rod, so that two corner points hang in the center of the window. Tack or pin to secure the position and drapes.

With Just One (or Two?) Sheets: Transform a Room

We agree with decorating specialist Judy Lindahl—even the most expensive sheet is a bargain when you calculate its decorating mileage.

• Use some graph paper and a calculator when sketching possible layouts. Measure and study your sheet. Look at the design and ponder layout schemes.

• Get the most decorating mileage from nondirectional, all-over prints. If necessary, let out sheet hems for additional width and length.

• Visualize the possibilities by making a list of all the items you need. Next, see how many items you can get out of the sheet.

• Maximize the number of projects you can make from the sheet by using narrow seams and hems and substituting other fabric for the underside of cushions or placemats. Also, you can reduce some of the fullness ratio in ruffles and curtains—from 3:1 to 2:1,

Transform A Room with Sheets

for instance, and cut valances shallower—12" rather than 14", for instance. Using ribbons and trims for tie-backs and edge-finishing will economize too.

• **Consider the bathroom**. Careful planning can yield over a dozen decorating items from one king-size flat sheet. Here are some projects that maximize the sheet yardage (Fig. 9-16):

A. Shower curtain. (The deep hem of the sheet can be the casing or the hem of the shower curtain.) Don't need a shower curtain? Then more sheet "fabric" will be available; use for a wall or window covering.

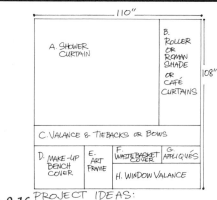

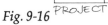

Fig. 9-16 PROJECT IDEAS:

B. Roller or Roman shade. (Add 2" in width for the Roman shade side hems.) This piece could also be cut in half to yield two **café curtains.**

C. Valance and the tie-backs or bows for the shower curtain.

D. Bench, toilet seat, and/or tank lid covers.

E. Picture frame covers, stretcher bar, or embroidery hoop art.

F. Wastebasket cover. (Glue fabric directly to the basket or use an elastic casing top and bottom for a slipcover.)

G. *Optional*: **Window valance.**

H. Design strips and appliqués for towels.

Really Easy Ruching

Welting, or piping, is commonly used as a decorative finish for pillows and cushions. This traditional fabric-covered cording trim also stabilizes pillow and cushion edges.

Materials Needed

• **Cording:** Ruching may be delicate or bold, depending on the size of cording

GREAT GATHERED WELTING.

that is used as a filler. Welt cording is a twisted cotton or polyester cable cord, found in various sizes in most fabric stores. The most common size for pillow ruching is 1/4" in diameter, sometimes labeled 8/32".

• **Fabric:** Select a fabric that matches or contrasts with the pillow. For best results, choose one that is light- to medium-weight; heavy fabrics are too bulky when gathered.

Cutting Directions

Your fabric must be cut in strips to cover the cording. Fabric may be cut on the straight or bias grain; *for the most economical use of the fabric, cut the strips on the crosswise grain* (Fig. 9-17).

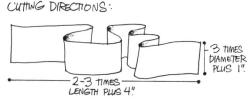

CUTTING DIRECTIONS:

3 TIMES DIAMETER PLUS 1".

2-3 TIMES LENGTH PLUS 4"

Fig. 9-17

• **Determine the width of the fabric strip.** Measure three times the diameter of the cording plus 1" for seam allowances. For 1/4" cording, cut the strip of fabric 1-3/4" wide. (**Note:** A 1/2" seam allowance is most commonly used in home decorating.) (See Fig. 9-17.)

• **Determine the amount of ruched welting**. Measure the pillow or cushion circumference. Add 4" for the cording length. Multiply by two or three for the total length of fabric strip needed (Fig. 9-17); piece short strips together in 1/4" seams and press the seams open. Lighter-weight fabric will require more gathering.

Make the Ruching

1. Center the cord on the wrong side of the fabric strip. Fold the strip over the cord and match the cut edges (Fig. 9-18).

WRAP CORDING WITH FABRIC.

STRAIGHT-STITCH END to SECURE.

Fig. 9-18

2. Secure the cord inside the casing by stitching across the covered cording 1/2" from the end (Fig. 9-18).

3. Using a zipper foot and a long stitch length, stitch close to the cord for 6" – 8". *Be careful not to stitch too close to the cording*—leave room for the fabric to gather. See Fig. 9-19.

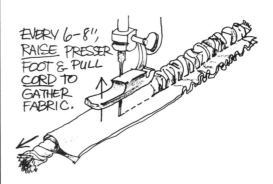

EVERY 6-8", RAISE PRESSER FOOT & PULL CORD TO GATHER FABRIC.

Fig. 9-19

4. *With the needle in the fabric*, raise the presser foot. Gently pull the cord until the fabric behind the needle is tightly gathered. Experiment to see how much fullness looks best with the fabric.

5. Repeat until the entire length has been gathered and approximately 4" of the cording remains uncovered. Pin through the end of the strip to prevent the cording from sliding back into the casing.

Apply the Ruching

1. Pin the ruching to the right side of the edge, matching the cut edges and the stitching line of the ruching to the seamline (Fig. 9-20).

2. Beginning 1" from the end of the covered cording, stitch over the original stitching line of the ruching. Continue stitching around the pillow to within 1" of the first welt end (Fig. 9-20).

☞ **Update tip:** When applying the ruching to the corners, round the corners slightly for ease in maneuvering.

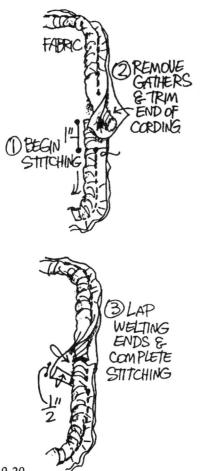

FABRIC

② REMOVE
GATHERS
& TRIM
END OF
CORDING

① BEGIN
STITCHING
1"

③ LAP
WELTING
ENDS &
COMPLETE
STITCHING

1/2"

Fig. 9-20

3. Join the ruching ends: Remove approximately 1" of stitching from one end of the ruching. Cut the cording so it will butt against its other end. Fold under 1/2" of the unstitched casing and lap it around the first end. Refold the strip, encasing the cord. Complete stitching the ruching to the seam line. See Fig. 9-20.

Complete the cover by placing the right sides of the top and bottom cover together. *Stitch directly over the stitching line of the ruching*, leaving an opening for turning.

Dramatic Holiday Decorating for Hurried Seamsters

Addressing Christmas cards. Entertaining Auntie Bertha. Cooking Santa cookies. Wrapping presents. Sharing yuletide cheer. All these activities add up to another holiday happening: no time to sew. What's a frustrated seamster to do? Plenty. Lavish your home with dramatic splashes of fabric and forget the time-consuming techniques.

✎ **Note:** Be on the lookout for red, green, and white solid and print fabrics suitable for decorating. We often buy them at bargain prices during post-season sales. You cannot buy too much holiday fabric (ten yards minimum of a color or print). *The more material you have, the more quickly you can transform a room.* No fabric on hand now? Dig through discounted fabrics in search of less obvious but perfectly adaptable choices—red-and-white candy stripes, red acetate satin, even bright green pinwale corduroy.

• **Staple a holiday pin-up board**. Great for displaying cards, photos, and calendar reminders. The size and shape are up to you. (Tammy, a space-conscious San Franciscan, cuts hers to fit inside a print frame that hangs on her wall year-round; no extra wall space is required.) If you don't have space to store the board for next season, it can be quickly recovered for everyday use.

For the board base, use lightweight *FoamCore*, found in most art supply stores. *FoamCore* isn't cheap (a 4' by 8' sheet can cost $16.00, a 3' by 4' sheet about $8.00), but we haven't discovered an alternative that's as lightweight, easy-to-cut, or versatile. Cut the *FoamCore* to the size and shape desired, using an X-acto knife or straight-edge cutter. Inquire where you purchase the *FoamCore*; they may cut it for you free of charge.

Then, using the *FoamCore* as a pattern, cut a piece of polyester fleece about 1/2" wider on all sides. Sparingly glue the fleece to the foam core. Center the fleece-covered board on the wrong side of the fabric. Alternating from side to side, staple the fabric to the board snugly. (Use the lightest-weight staple gun and staples.) Cover the fabric raw edges on the back with wide cloth tape. Hang it up on the wall or door with inconspicuous brads (small-headed nails); if you mount it in a picture frame or over a mirror, use double-sided rug tape. Buy matching "map pins" (available at office supply stores) for sticking up your mail and mementos. See Fig. 9-21.

• **Tie chair throws.** Cut 45" – 54" squares of the covering fabric. Fringe, clean-finish, serge, or just pink the edges. Hang the square on the chair with the corner points in front, back, and on the sides. Tie the side points in a square knot in the back. *Optional:* Use push pins to secure any other loose ends and to prevent slippage. See Fig. 9-22.

A PADDED BULLETIN BOARD FOR A HOLIDAY DOOR.

Fig. 9-21

Fig. 9-22

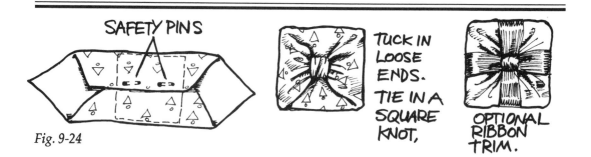

SAFETY PINS

Fig. 9-24

TUCK IN LOOSE ENDS. TIE IN A SQUARE KNOT,

OPTIONAL RIBBON TRIM.

Fig. 9-23

• **Gift-wrap pillows or presents with fabric.** The box or pillow to be covered should be squarish and the fabric covering light- to medium-weight and tightly woven. Yardage required will range from 1-1/4 yards of 45" width for a 14" – 16" square box or pillow to 2 yards for a 30" square box or pillow. Remember, all fabric wrapping is recyclable.

Center the box or pillow on the wrong side of the fabric. Bring one corner up and over the box. Fold in the opposite corner and bring the folded edge up to the center of the box. Secure with two safety pins, making sure the fit is tight. Neatly fold the other two opposite points and tie in a square knot. Tuck in the loose ends. Adorn with ribbon ties, lace trim, or appliqués. See Fig. 9-23.

• **Accent your home with fabric swags.** Cut 45"-wide fabric in half, lengthwise, yielding 22-1/2"-wide swag strips. Lengthwise edges needn't be finished if you use pinking shears. Or cut and finish simultaneously with a serger.

Drape the lengths around a staircase guardrail (piece with seaming as necessary), above the fireplace, or along a window frame or table's edge. Secure with ribbon ties and/or push pins. Embellish with dried flowers, pine bows, and ornaments. See Fig. 9-24.

• **Make instant ornaments.** Wrap inexpensive plastic foam balls with exciting holiday fabric like lamé, velveteen, your favorite color, or print.

Pink, serge, or use seam sealant or glue under the edges to finish. Attach an ornament hanger (available wherever tree ornaments are sold) with a pretty ribbon. Make several of one color or print for the most dramatic overall effect on your tree. See Fig. 9-25.

• **Make ribbon out of fabric.** Using fusible transfer web, fuse the wrong side of a holiday fabric to the wrong side of a coordinating gift wrap. The paper-backed fabric can be cut into ribbon strips and curled (from the paper side) as you do paper ribbon (see the color pages).

Fig. 9-25

10. Making the Most of Your Machine

- From Sewing Pros: Favorite Machine Tips
- New, Innovative Notions
- Machine Troubleshooting with Gale Grigg Hazen
- Feet Smarts: A Pictorial Guide

This chapter is a collection of innovative machine-use tips from people who, because of their professions and enthusiasm for sewing, work with sewing machines nearly every day. To make the most of your machine (no matter what the vintage or brand), glean a few secrets from these sewing journalists, dealers, and machine-company representatives. Try utilizing a tip or two the next time you sew. You'll discover—if you haven't already—that the better you know your machine, the better you sew.

From Sewing Pros: Favorite Machine Tips

"What are some of your best sewing machine tips?" When polled by well-known writer Barbara Weiland, these sewing professionals shared their favorites.

Know More, Sew Better

All those Barbara polled also suggested taking a class specific to your machine. If your dealer doesn't offer one, use your machine manual as a guide or purchase a workbook. Make samples of the stitches, note the procedures, and keep them in a small notebook or the workbook for reference.

Learn how each presser foot works and with which stitches. Make a habit of checking with your dealer about new feet and accessories. Special generic machine attachments like rufflers and buttonholers may also help expand your machine's capabilities.

Experiment! Improvise!

Some of the most innovative sewing machine tricks come from experimenting with utility stitches and presser feet. Many have multiple functions. For example, try these special techniques, inspired by tips from the professionals surveyed:

• **Use your machine's sew-on button foot for snaps and hooks and eyes,** as well as for the plastic rings on Roman shades. A dab of glue stick or a tiny piece of water-soluble basting tape will hold the item in place while you stitch. Also, use this foot with nylon monofilament thread to invisibly machine stitch jewels and sequins. See Fig. 10-1.

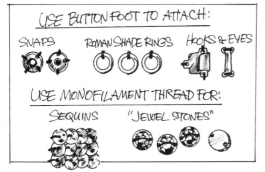

Fig. 10-1

• For better visibility, **use your machine's zipper foot to stitch-in-the-ditch** when completing waistbands and cuffs. The long toe on the Viking buttonhole foot can also be used in the same manner. See Fig. 10-2.

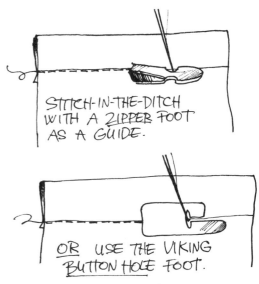

Fig. 10-2

• If you don't have double or triple needles on hand, **take advantage of the varying needle positions of some** zigzag machines to stitch multiple rows of perfectly parallel topstitching. See Fig. 10-3.

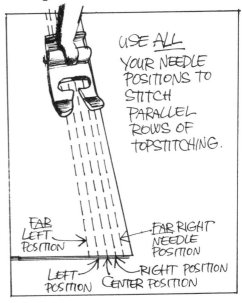

Fig. 10-3

• The quilting foot and guide can be used as a topstitching guide, too. Sue Bagley **recommends using it for a seam guide if you have trouble seeing the markings on the throat plate**—a great idea for those with more "mature eyesight." See Fig. 10-4.

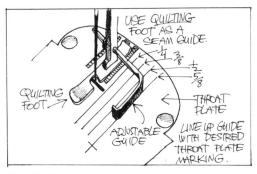

Fig. 10-4

• Instead of using transparent tape, *Sew News* editor Linda Griepentrog **ties a piece of narrow elastic around the free arm of her sewing machine as an adjustable stitch-width gauge** (Fig. 10-5). It's handy for machine-stitched hems and sure beats peeling sticky tape residue from the machine.

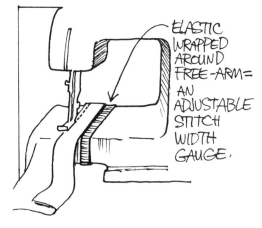

Fig. 10-5

• Sewing author Ann Marie Soto and Pfaff Educational Manager Louise Gerigk **suggest using a double or twin needle to topstitch knit hems** (Fig. 10-6). It adds a nice detail and clean-finishes the raw edge in one easy step. (Also, see "Twin-needle Sewing," pages 32 – 34, and "Double Needles: Double Your Options," pages 95 – 97.)

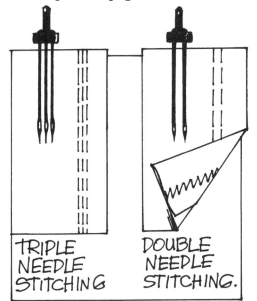

Fig. 10-6

• Karen Dillon, a Tacony sewing consultant (and coauthor, with Gail, of *Sew a Beautiful Wedding*), loves to **use the new extra-long basting setting for marking buttonhole placement.** Set the machine for the longest stitch possible and mark the buttonhole length with two rows of equally spaced stitching, as shown. This basting/marking method keeps all the layers from shifting while making the buttonholes. See Fig. 10-7.

• For perfect edgestitching, notions authority and *Sewing Update* columnist Janet Klaer **loves the convenience of**

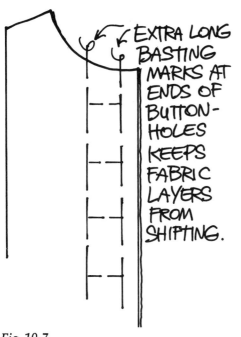

EXTRA LONG BASTING MARKS AT ENDS OF BUTTON-HOLES KEEPS FABRIC LAYERS FROM SHIFTING.

Fig. 10-7

needle positions on her zigzag machine. By adjusting the needle to the left or right after positioning the garment under the foot, you can get very close to an edge but still have the control of the presser foot on the fabric (Fig. 10-8). Remember to re-center the needle when you're finished.

• Janet also **suggests using an even-feed device or attachment** on your machine all the time. "With so little time to sew," she says, "who needs to stop and rip seams that have slipped or bunched while stitching? With even feeding, those problems never occur."

• Another favorite of Barbara's is to **thread slippery threads, such as rayon machine embroidery thread, from the spool on one spool pin through the hole in the second pin** to keep the thread from sliding off the spool. (See Fig. 10-9.) If your pin doesn't have a

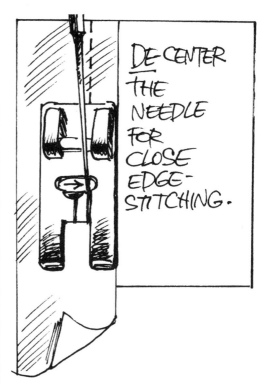

DE-CENTER THE NEEDLE FOR CLOSE EDGE-STITCHING.

Fig. 10-8

hole, try this slick trick Barbara learned from her favorite expert, her mom (who learned it in a class by quilting pro Harriet Hargrave): Tape a #1 safety pin—loop end up—to one spool pin (Fig. 10-10).

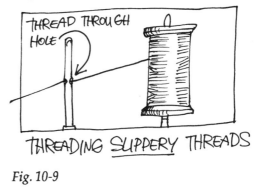

THREAD THROUGH HOLE

THREADING SLIPPERY THREADS

Fig. 10-9

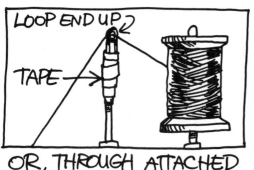

LOOP END UP

TAPE

OR, THROUGH ATTACHED #1 SAFETY PIN PROVIDING HOLE.

Fig. 10-10

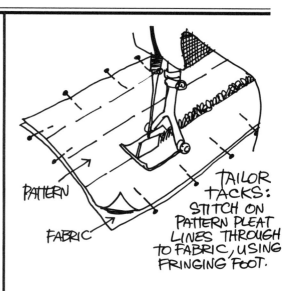

PATTERN

FABRIC

TAILOR TACKS: STITCH ON PATTERN PLEAT LINES THROUGH TO FABRIC, USING FRINGING FOOT.

• Another tip from Barbara's mom, a sewing enthusiast: When using cross-wound monofilament nylon thread, **put the thread tube in a small, empty jar behind the machine, then thread up through the safety pin or the spool pin.** If you don't own a cone thread stand, try this trick with serger cone thread, too. It keeps the cone from bouncing around on the sewing table while you sew.

• Author Jan Saunders **uses machine tailor tacks to mark pleat lines.** This requires a fringing or looping foot. Check with your dealer to see if there's one to fit your machine. Loosen the upper tension and place the fabric, still pinned to the pattern piece, under the foot. Set the machine for a wide (4mm) zigzag of medium length (2 – 3mm) and stitch on any lines to be marked. Remove the tissue and pull the two fabric layers apart. Clip the threads between the layers. See Fig. 10-11.

• Author and *Sew News* columnist Ann Hesse Price **emphasizes that the blind-hem stitch is not just for hemming.** It's ideal for applying patch pockets

PULL TWO LAYERS OF FABRIC APART & CLIP THREADS.

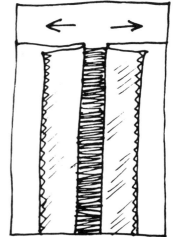

Fig. 10-11

quickly by machine, yet with the refined good looks of handstitching. Ready the pocket for application by lining or turning under hems and seam allowances. Position the pocket on the garment with pins, basting, or narrow strips of fusible web.

Set your sewing machine on a narrow blindhem stitch (test on scraps first). Using an open-toe or transparent presser foot for the best visibility, sew around edges of the pocket. The left swing of the narrow zigzag should barely catch the edge of the pocket, while the straight stitches are hidden in the "ditch" between pocket edge and garment. A shorter stitch length ensures more durability because the pocket is caught by more zigzags. See Fig. 10-12.

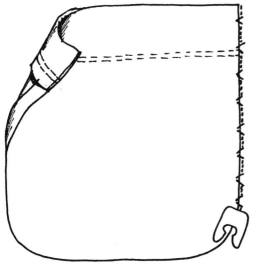

Fig. 10-12

Ann adds that you may prefer this "blind" pocket application even when the design calls for topstitching. Topstitch the pocket first, then apply to the garment using the blindhem method. It will be easier to topstitch a straighter, more even line on the pocket alone rather than the pocket and the garment. Also, you can use this blindhem technique for appliqué.

Care for Your Investment

The experts concur on one paramount concern: basic machine maintenance. Having the machine cleaned, oiled, and adjusted by a dealer yearly is high on everyone's list, especially for frequently used machines.

The machine specialists are also adamant about needles and thread: Close-out thread and "grocery-store" needles are no-nos. The consensus on needles: Use the correct needle for the fabric type you're using and throw it away when the project is completed.

New, Innovative Notions

Janet Klaer, formerly Education Director at Coats and Clark and now a busy free-lance writer, keeps *Sewing Update* readers posted on the latest notions in her column, "Notions News." The following are some of her most recent finds for enhancing machine sewing.

Little Foot

Invented by Lynn Graves, *Little Foot* was designed for piecing fabric for patchwork. However, it's a natural anytime you're sewing narrow seams (1/8" or 1/4") or topstitching.

Little Foot has a flat bottom and round hole for straight stitching. The space from the needle to the right outside edge of the foot is 1/4" wide; to the left inside is 1/8" wide. The foot is marked on both sides with three easy-to-see guidelines. See Fig. 10-13. The center line marks the needle position;

the forward and back lines are 1/4"
from the needle mark. This enables you
to start or stop stitching precisely 1/4"
in from the edge of the fabric, making
this foot an ideal guide when mitering
or pivoting at corners or piecing quilts.
See Fig. 10-14.

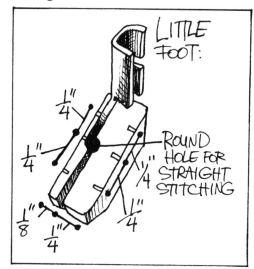

Fig. 10-13

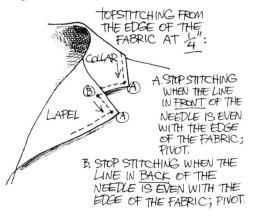

Fig. 10-14

Because the left side of *Little Foot* is
narrow, it is not likely to interfere with
the bulk of a seam allowance from
previous stitching. And when easing

one layer of fabric to another, there is
less chance of a pleat or pucker
forming. *Little Foot* can also be useful as
an 1/8" sewing guide (Fig. 10-15). Use
it when topstitching, sewing double-
stitched or French seams, or making a
Hong Kong finish.

✎ **Note:** When using the 1/8" side as
a guide, it may be necessary to place
the bulk of the fabric to the right of the
needle and to train your eye to use the
left side of the presser foot as a guide.

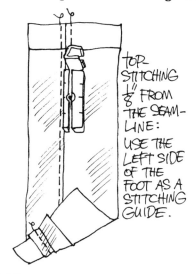

Fig. 10-15

Currently available in a style to fit
most low-shank machines, soon *Little
Foot* will be available to fit both high-
shank and slant-needle machines.
(**Note:** For the Bernina, you will need
their special adapter.)

Sources: Ask for *Little Foot* at your
local sewing machine dealer. If not
available locally, it can be ordered from
Clotilde, Inc. (See the "Sew-by-Mail
Directory," pages 160 – 173.)

Hump Jumper

It's happened to all of us: all of a sudden you come to a bulky seam and the presser foot tilts upward, so the stitches get shorter or skipped. The reason? With the presser foot at an angle, it's not possible for the fabric to feed evenly.

A new sewing tool, the *Hump Jumper* by SN Designs, levels the presser foot in these troublesome areas. It's available in two thicknesses, 1/16" and 1/8"; use the two together for 3/16".

To use the *Hump Jumper:*

• Select the height which most closely corresponds to the thickness of your fabric.

• When the presser foot just touches the seam, stop the machine with the needle in the fabric.

• Lift the presser foot; slip the *Hump Jumper* under the back (Fig. 10-16).

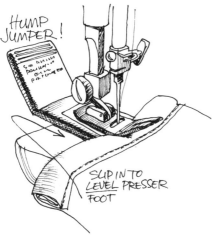

Fig. 10-16

• Lower the presser foot and continue stitching. The *Hump Jumper* will slide out from under the presser foot as you sew.

The *Hump Jumper* is also useful when attaching belt loops or stitching any thick fabric; or slip it under a sew-through button to create a thread shank.

☞ **Update tip:** Simulate the *Hump Jumper* action by slipping a piece of cardboard (the thickness necessary) under the back of the foot. Also, look for similar products available from other companies; another one we've seen is the *Jean-a-ma-jig.*

Sources: The *Hump Jumper* should be available soon at your local fabric store. It can also be ordered through The Perfect Notion. *Jean-a-ma-jig* is also sold in fabric stores and through mail-order suppliers, such as Serge & Sew Notions. (See the "Sew-by-Mail Directory," pages 160 – 173.)

Trim As You Stitch

Many *Update* readers have asked us about "serging" attachments advertised in *Sew News, Threads,* and other sewing publications. These compact attachments trim the fabric edge while

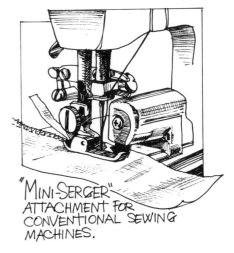

Fig. 10-17

you sew. Available for low-, high-, and slant-shank model zigzag machines, they replace the standard presser foot (Fig. 10-17).

Recommended stitches to use in combination with cutting attachments include overcasting, multiple-stitch zigzagging (also known as serpentine stitching), and a knit stitch (Fig. 10-18). Regular zigzagging also works, but is more prone to tunneling.

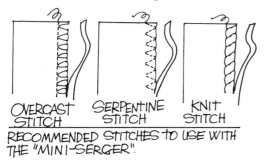

RECOMMENDED STITCHES TO USE WITH THE "MINI-SERGER".

Fig. 10-18

Cutting attachments do not speed the sewing rate (about half that of a serger) or change the stitch to duplicate overlocking. But in light of the low price (from $40 – 80) and easy operation, this attachment is worthy of consideration.

Sources: Ask your dealer about a cutting attachment to fit your machine. (Both Tacony and Bernina distribute cutting attachments; there's probably one to fit your machine. Or write to *Micro-serger*™ USA, 1800 Stumpf Blvd., Suite #9, Gretna, LA 70056.)

Machine Troubleshooting with Gale Grigg Hazen

Though small and seemingly simple, the sewing machine needle serves a mighty function; it can be at the root of your sewing problem or the secret of your success. That's why knowing the size and type of needle to use, as well as which thread to use with it, is so essential. Gale Grigg Hazen, sewing-school owner and sewing-machine expert, is the author of the *Owner's Guide to Sewing Machines, Sergers, and Knitting Machines*. Here she answers commonly asked special-needle questions to help you on the road to trouble-free sewing.

✎ **Note:** All needle sizes are given with European sizes first, American sizes second.

Q. "How can I reduce pulling and puckering on slippery silk and synthetic silkies?"

A. Fine, lightweight fabrics have very thin fibers packed close together. To make the seams lie smooth and flat, use the smallest needle possible—the size will vary with thread weight (Fig. 10-19). For the best results, use a 60/8 H needle (the "H" stands for "all-purpose"). This size may require extra-fine thread, sometimes called lingerie

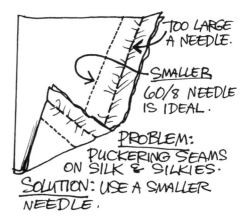

TOO LARGE A NEEDLE.

SMALLER 60/8 NEEDLE IS IDEAL.

PROBLEM: PUCKERING SEAMS ON SILK & SILKIES.

SOLUTION: USE A SMALLER NEEDLE.

Fig. 10-19

or fine machine-embroidery weight, to fit through the eye. Use cotton thread for sewing on silk and silkies; its softness and flexibility yield the most invisible seam. If fine thread is unavailable, use a 70/10 needle with all-purpose thread.

Q. "Should I use ballpoint needles on all knits?"

A. Although ballpoint needles will prevent skipped stitches on knits, they can also cause small holes along the seamline (Fig. 10-20). The best needle choice is an H-S—a newer type made especially for knits by Schmetz, a leader in specialty needles. H-S needles come in two sizes: 75/11 or 90/14. The 75/11 H-S is great for tricot and dress-weight knits, while the larger 90/14 is best for pant-weight fabrics and heavy, knit-backed pile fabrics.

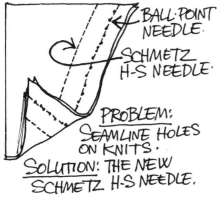

Fig. 10-20

Q. "When I topstitch with special thread, the stitching looks irregular and uneven and loops form on the bottom side. How can I remedy this?"

A. Thread called "topstitching thread" or "buttonhole twist" used to highlight decorative sewing, such as flat-felled

seams on jeans, is much heavier and thicker than normal thread. This can mean the hole in a standard needle is too small for the thread to slide through easily, which causes your thread problem. See Fig. 10-21.

Schmetz makes needles with an oversized eye to accommodate this thread. Classified as N needles, they are available in several sizes: light- to medium-weight fabrics use an 80/12 N; heavy-weight fabrics, as well as extra-thick thread, require a 90/14 N.

To use this heavy thread in the bobbin, reduce the lower tension. If this isn't possible, use a normal-weight thread in the bobbin.

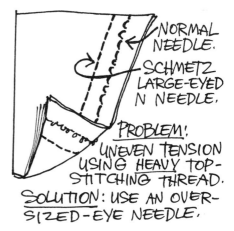

Fig. 10-21

References: *Owner's Guide to Sewing Machines, Sergers, and Knitting Machines*, by Gale Grigg Hazen, ©1989, Chilton Book Company (see "References," page 175). Also, *The Best Needle Kit: A Guide and Sample Kit*, by Gale Grigg Hazen, available from The Sewing Place, 18870 Cox Ave., San Jose, CA 95070, for $19.50 postpaid.

Feet Smarts:
A Pictorial Guide

Jackie Dodson, author of Chilton's *Know Your Sewing Machine* series, does indeed know more about sewing machines and their accessories than anyone we know. We've made a collage of her foot identification hints and their creative applications. You can't help but be inspired. (For information on Jackie's books, see page 175 of "References.")

STRAIGHT STITCH FOOT:

SMALL HOLE HELPS KEEP SILKY FABRICS ABOVE STITCH PLATE.

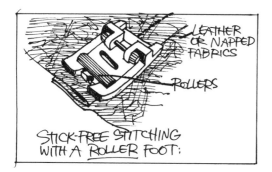

STICK-FREE STITCHING WITH A ROLLER FOOT:

LEATHER OR NAPPED FABRICS

ROLLERS

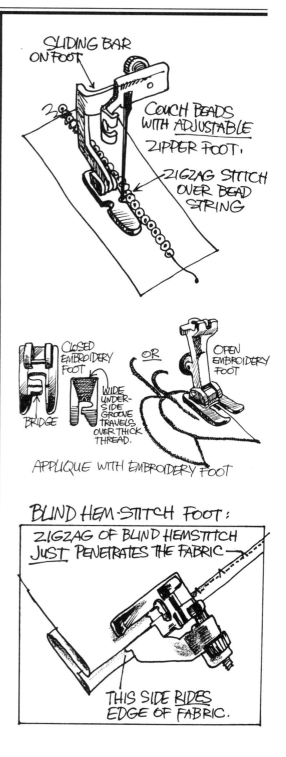

SLIDING BAR ON FOOT

COUCH BEADS WITH ADJUSTABLE ZIPPER FOOT.

ZIGZAG STITCH OVER BEAD STRING

CLOSED EMBROIDERY FOOT

BRIDGE

WIDE UNDERSIDE GROOVE TRAVELS OVER THICK THREAD.

OR

OPEN EMBROIDERY FOOT

APPLIQUE WITH EMBROIDERY FOOT

BLIND HEM-STITCH FOOT:

ZIGZAG OF BLIND HEMSTITCH JUST PENETRATES THE FABRIC

THIS SIDE RIDES EDGE OF FABRIC.

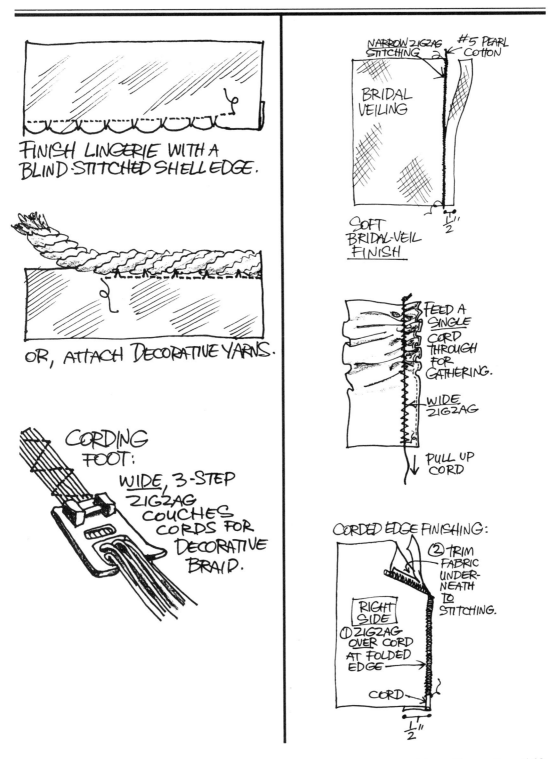

FINISH LINGERIE WITH A BLIND-STITCHED SHELL EDGE.

OR, ATTACH DECORATIVE YARNS.

CORDING FOOT: WIDE, 3-STEP ZIGZAG COUCHES CORDS FOR DECORATIVE BRAID.

NARROW ZIGZAG STITCHING #5 PEARL COTTON

BRIDAL VEILING

SOFT BRIDAL-VEIL FINISH

$\frac{1}{2}$"

FEED A SINGLE CORD THROUGH FOR GATHERING.

WIDE ZIGZAG

PULL UP CORD

CORDED EDGE FINISHING:

② TRIM FABRIC UNDERNEATH TO STITCHING.

RIGHT SIDE

① ZIGZAG OVER CORD AT FOLDED EDGE

CORD

$\frac{1}{2}$"

Thread Reference Chart

Thread Type	Fiber Content	Uses
All-purpose sewing	Cotton-covered polyester	Wovens: medium- to heavy-weight, all fibers Knits: medium- to heavy-weight, all fibers
All-purpose sewing	Polyester	Wovens: medium- to heavy-weight, all fibers Knits: medium- to heavy-weight, all fibers
All-purpose sewing	Long-fiber polyester	Wovens: light- to medium-weight, all fibers Knits: medium- to heavy-weight, all fibers
All-purpose sewing	Cotton	Wovens: light- to medium-weight, natural fibers only Knits: Not recommended
Extra-fine lingerie	Cotton-covered polyester	Wovens: light- to medium-weight, all fibers Knits: light- to medium-weight, all fibers
Extra-fine embroidery	Cotton or long-fiber cotton	Wovens: light- to medium-weight, natural fibers only, and only for decorative machine embroidery Knits: not recommended
All-purpose serger	Cotton-wrapped polyester	Wovens: light- to medium-weight, all fibers Knits: light- to heavy-weight, all fibers
All-purpose serger	Polyester	Wovens: light- to heavy-weight, all fibers Knits: light- to heavy-weight, all fibers
All-purpose serger	Long-fiber polyester	Wovens: light- to heavy-weight, all fibers Knits: light- to heavy-weight, all fibers
Serger, fine cotton	Cotton or long-fiber cotton	Wovens: light- to medium-weight, natural fibers only Knits: not recommended
Serger, specialty	Multifilament stretchy nylon	Wovens: for decorative serging Knits: light- to heavy-weight, all fibers

- Thread size and strength should be compatible with the fabric. Exceptions would be to use polyester or cotton-wrapped polyester (because of its stretchability) for any fiber which is knitted or to use fine polyester, cotton-wrapped polyester, or cotton for woven silks (due to the scarcity of silk thread).

- Some thread size guidelines: in cotton, size 50 is an all-purpose thread; the larger the number, the finer the thread. Silk thread, if you find it, is sized by letter, from A to D; size A is fine, size D is for topstitching. Coned threads can be the most confusing, commonly labeled 100/3, for instance; again, the larger the top number, the finer the thread. The bottom number refers to the number of plies twisted to make the thread.

- Test threads if uncertain about use on a certain fabric. Then study stitch quality, stretchability (on knits), size suitability, and color match. Remember, when finishing seams that will never be seen publicly, the thread needn't match at all.

11. Update: Computerized Sewing Machines

- **Computer Expertise Unnecessary**
- **Will You Pay More for a Computerized Machine?**
- **Time to Upgrade?**
- **Know the Language of Feature Options**
- **Shop Smart (for Any Machine)**
- **Special Care for Computer Machines**
- **Conclusion: Is Computerized Sewing Worth Your Investment?**

Have you ever wished for one-step buttonholes, all identically sized? Automatic tying-off of stitches? Stitching control at any speed, and through multiple layers of fabric? Super-wide (to nearly 3/8") satin stitching? Stitches preset to the "right" width and length? Now, thanks to innovative electronics and computer-sewing technology, these features (and more) are realities.

Computer Expertise Unnecessary

Be reassured that computer knowledge is not a prerequisite for computer sewing. If you can operate a sewing machine, you can operate a computerized sewing machine. (Actually, many computer functions are easier and faster to use than comparable mechanical functions.)

As the name implies, computer machines utilize a minicomputer to control the movement of the needle and the feed dogs, whereas a mechanical machine uses levers and gears. Immediately noticeable is the lack of knobs and dials on computer machines; most commands are push-button (a wonderful advancement for those with arthritic or otherwise disabled hands).

Computerization allows creation, memorization, storage, and retrieval of stitch-structure information, plus ultra-precise feeding—features never before possible with mechanical machines. In addition, because of their ability to store stitch-structure data in a small space, computerized machines can offer the widest selection of stitch patterns.

✎ **Note:** *The terms "electronic" and "computerized" are not universally interchangeable.* All computer and some mechanical machines are electronic, that is, made with some type of electronic circuitry. (For more refined speed control, many mechanical machines have foot pedals that are electronic.)

Will You Pay More for a Computerized Machine?

Generally, yes. However, the price disparity (at the time of publication) is notable—from $500 to $2400—on top-of-the-line models (all computerized). Whether or not you can justify a higher price depends completely on the type and amount of sewing you do.

Prioritize the features and then weigh them against the price. Also keep in mind the amount of time you spend (or would like to spend) sewing; chances are, in relation to other pastimes like golf, tennis, or shopping, the money you spend per hour sewing is lower. Plus, while reveling in the satisfying process, you've produced a wearable or craft as well.

Will you have to buy more features than you'll actually use? Probably. It's similar to when you buy a top-of-the-line washing machine for its load capacity but never use its special tub and cycle for delicates. You may base your decision primarily on the variety and ease of making buttonholes, but only occasionally use the decorative stitches.

Still, you'll have the other features at your disposal, ready if you expand your sewing repertoire. And before you write off any other-than-straight stitching, consider the creative potential of your option—monogramming for fashions and furnishings, decorative edge-finishing for table linens, and stretch stitching for seaming stretch knits.

Time to Upgrade?

You may be satisfied with your twenty-year-old machine. Or your current machine may be the source of constant frustration (and the reason why you're not sewing regularly). But even if only mildly curious, you owe it to yourself (and your sewing) to check out the new computer machines.

If you're not yet compelled to shop, peruse the features defined in "Know the Language," below, that appear in "The Feature-by-Feature Checklist," pages 153 – 154. Stitch variety and "memorized" buttonholes are just two of the many computer features even confirmed traditionalists can't resist.

Know the Language of Feature Options

Simplify comparison shopping by learning the language—the terms and features associated with this new kind of sewing. You'll better understand how this language translates into faster, more efficient techniques and expanded sewing capabilities. Not all the terms are exclusive to computerized sewing, but most are common to the computer machines currently on the market.

✎ **Note**: "The Feature-by-Feature Checklist,"on pages 153 – 154, relates these terms to the top-of-the-line computer machines. They are listed below in order of appearance (left to right) on the chart; those with obvious meanings aren't defined. If you have any questions or need more information, consult your local sewing machine dealer.

Preprogrammed stitches are the number of utility, stretch, and decorative stitches programmed into the machine.

Alphabet and numeral styles are the different ways you can write alphabetically and numerically. For example, some machines can write in both block (Fig. 11-1) and script lettering and numbers. (TV host Nancy Zieman recently suggested machine stitching the pattern number on your garment hem for handy reference.)

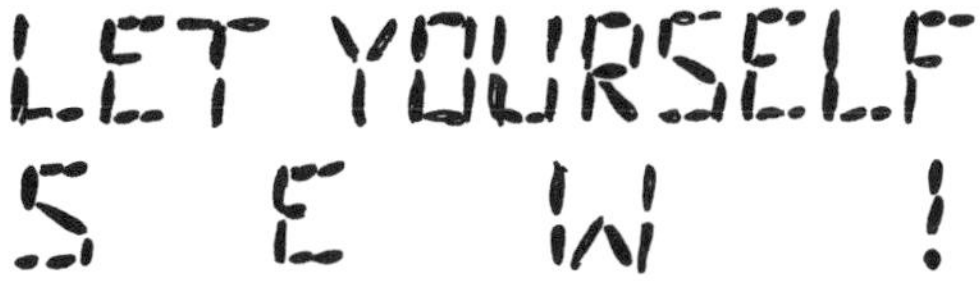

LET YOURSELF SEW !

Fig. 11-1

Programmable stitch selection allows the stringing together of several motifs to create a custom design.

Light-emitting diode (LED) or liquid crystal display (LCD) are the two different ways that the machine information can be displayed. Company representatives argue about the brightness advantages of one over the other. Some machines have both. Comparison-shop to determine the importance of the display mode as a selection factor for you.

Preprogrammed width and length with override: The machine automatically adjusts for the recommended width and length of the stitch. With override, these adjustments can be altered.

Double-needle width indicator automatically narrows the stitch width when you've told the machine you're using a double needle. Thus, you avoid breaking the needle and perhaps damaging the foot or the plate. (Using double needles for any stitch pattern instantly doubles the imagery.)

Single pattern selection: A single motif of a stitch pattern can be isolated.

Automatic tie-off: With the push of a button, threads are tied off by stitching several times in one place.

Stitch elongation is elongating the motif image while maintaining the stitch density. Usually this feature is described as a multiple; for example, "5X" means that the stitch can be elongated five times its original length while maintaining the original stitch density.

Automatic one-step buttonhole and number of styles: All the computer machines on "The Feature-by-Feature Checklist" automatically make buttonholes. The buttonhole lives up to its name; additional steps, such as pivoting the fabric or readjusting the stitch, have been eliminated. After you've made one, the machine memorizes the size and shape; to make identical buttonholes, just stitch again.

Undoubtedly one of the main attractions to computerized sewing, the buttonholes beautifully simulate the best seen in ready-to-wear. (Keyhole shapes look incredibly like tailor-handworked buttonholes.) See Fig. 11-2.

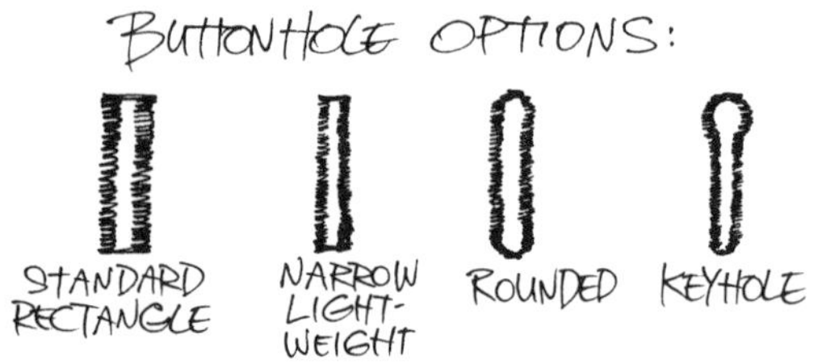

BUTTONHOLE OPTIONS:

STANDARD RECTANGLE — NARROW LIGHT-WEIGHT — ROUNDED — KEYHOLE

Fig. 11-2

Audio feedback: A bleep, bell, or digitalized human voice talks to you about a necessary procedure or caution.

Updatable cartridges or cassettes: Although this isn't a new concept, being able to update your machine makes sense. To add stitches, buy a cartridge or cassette, rather than an entire machine.

Mirror imaging: The machine is capable of creating a mirror image of the stitch or motif, important for centering or for symmetrical designs. Mirror imaging can be horizontal or can also include vertical imaging.

Stitch memory bank retained: After the machine is turned off, the memory of the stitch settings is retained.

Memory: After combining stitches, the machine remembers the combination.

Needle up/needle down: The needle can be controlled to stop in the up position for easy removal of the fabric, or in the down position for pivoting.

Variable speed or "cruise control": The sewing speed can be preset, so that when accuracy is crucial, acceleration surges are eliminated.

Automatic basting is straight stitching longer than the longest stitch-length setting—usually 6mm or longer for effortless removal of the stitches.

Oscillating or rotary hook: Oscillating hooks move the shuttle back and forth; rotary hooks rotate the shuttle a full 360 degrees. The debate persists about the advantages and disadvantages of each. In this price range, however, the differences in performance should be minimal.

Presser foot indicator specifies which foot is prescribed for the stitch selection made.

Create-your-own or "free programming" is free-form motif designing. You plot the motif—a logo, for instance—then program the stitch components necessary to create the motif. Programming methods vary from machine to machine.

Automatic or universal tension: The tension is adjusted automatically for any weight or texture fabric. To test this feature, layer a variety of fabric types in a row; then, stitch through the center. The tension should have automatically adjusted for the variances, maintaining a balanced stitch that's pucker-free.

Horizontal or vertical thread delivery are the two ways in which the thread can feed off the spool. Several machines offer both, although some are limited to one delivery option. Because there's less drag when thread feeds horizontally from the top of a spool, some proponents argue that horizontal feeding is best. But due to the horizontal configuration, the size and shape of the spool are necessarily limited. Keep in mind that thread, especially large cones, can always be placed on cone stands at the back of the machine, then fed through the guides.

Instant and continuous reverse: Instant reverse is push-button backstitching (a straight stitch), whereas continuous reverse repeats the stitch shape, width, and length in reverse. Some seamsters find continuous reverse indispensable, particularly when removing the fabric from under the foot is awkward, such as when mending a jean leg over a free arm.

Droppable feed: The feed dogs can be dropped, useful when darning, for free-form stitchery, and when removing fabric jams.

Knee lift serves as a presser foot lever. When the knee lift is pushed, the presser foot is raised, freeing both hands for manipulating the fabric.

Direct-winding bobbin: When the bobbin is wound from the needle thread, no unthreading of the needle is required. All you do is resume sewing.

Walking foot is a foot, either built-in or an accessory, that feeds the fabric on top, so that the top and bottom layers feed more evenly. Applications that benefit from even feeding include quilting, matching plaids, and seaming extra-long seams.

Shop Smart (for Any Machine)

• **Study the terms and features before shopping.** Look over the "Know the Language of Feature Options" (pages

147 – 154) and "The Feature-by-Feature Checklist" (pages 153 – 154). The more you know, the better prepared you'll be to ask pertinent questions. If you have time, sewing machine companies welcome your written inquiries; you'll be sent dealer referrals for your area and product brochures. (Find sewing machine company addresses on "Sources," page 159.)

• **Buy a dealer, then a machine.** Remember, reliable service and ongoing education are essential to maximizing your investment and enjoyment. Ask about after-purchase lessons, sewing machine owners' clubs, and special workshops and lessons.

Understand the service policy, plus warranty periods and limitations. Where will the machine be serviced? How long will it take? Do they have loaner machines to use during service periods? What exactly is, and is not, covered by the warranty?

Ask for customer referrals. When spending up to $2400, you deserve to hear testimonials—about the machine's performance and the dealer's service— from other customers. (However, most seamsters converted to sewing by computer would never go back to sewing without it.)

Find out about trade-in values on your current and the prospective machine. What is the machine you now own worth toward the purchase? (It's a good idea to keep it as a second machine if it still runs well and the trade-in value is relatively low). Also pose the question, "When a newer model of the same brand is released, what will be the trade-in value of the machine I'm considering buying?"

• **Test-sew on a wide variety of fabrics.** Bring samples of a wide range of fabrics—e.g., wovens (sheers to heavy-weights), knits (stable double-knits, stretchy interlocks, and sweater-knits, Lycra® blends), leather-likes, such as Ultrasuede® and Ultraleather®, and slippery silks and silklikes. Thoroughly investigate the stitches, button-holes, and tension on all the fabrics. (Testing on the dealer's heavily starched batiste doesn't give you a fair assessment of stitching performance.)

Also, if mending is required for your family's wardrobe, bring in an unfinished project; darning capabilities are highly touted by all the sewing machine companies.

• **Determine if, and how easily, you can override stitch programming.** For instance, if stitch width and length are preprogrammed, how difficult is it to alter the default settings?

• **If you stitch decoratively (or would like to), bring decorative threads to your test-sewing session.** A good challenge for any machine is slippery rayon thread. Stitchery pros also suggest bringing a machine-embroidery hoop.

• **Allow *at least* an hour for test-sewing.** Operate the machine yourself.

• **Look at the manual.** Is it thorough and easy-to-follow? During popular sewing times—late at night and early in the morning—the manual is your only guide.

• **Inspect the full range of models and prices.** Compare the top-of-the-line computer machine with the top-of-the-line mechanical/electronic machine. Then investigate the models in other price levels. Are the extra features priorities for you? Enough to justify the extra cost?

☞ **Update tip:** Used machines can be great values, and are often overlooked; once reconditioned, they perform like new. As more computerized models are introduced, more will be available used. But there are a surprising number of dependable, used mechanical and electronic models at most dealerships now. Inquire about them, even if you don't see used machines displayed.

• **If available, view the video** that demonstrates the machine's use and creative capabilities. Just about every company has produced a brand-specific videotape. Dealers often play them in-store and make them available for loan or rent.

• **Shop comparatively.** If you're lucky enough to have more than one dealer in your area, shop them all. Brand loyalty is strong among sewing enthusiasts, but don't prejudge, thereby limiting your search. (As a courtesy, inform dealers you are comparison shopping and test-sew during slow-traffic periods.)

Special Care for Computer Machines

• **Carefully follow the manufacturer's guidelines** for oiling, or *not oiling*.

• **Keep the machine dust- and lint-free**, both enemies of any computer. Simply fluff out your lint brush and use it to remove a majority of the fuzz.

Machine expert Gale Grigg Hazen, author of the *Owner's Guide to Sewing Machines, Sergers, and Knitting Machines* (see page 175), warns against forced-air propellants ("the cold air can coagulate oil and actually damage metal parts"). Instead, to remove lint, she uses a hair dryer (on the lowest setting) or a special computer vacuum. Gail says the best dust protection is covering your machine when it's not in use.

• **Invest in a surge protector** if power surges plague your area. According to *Sew, Serge, Press* author Jan Saunders, you may save stitch memory in progress or stored in the memory bank. Surge protectors are sold at electronics, hardware, and computer stores.

• **Ask your dealer about adhering magnets**, such as *Grabbit®* magnet pin cushions, directly to the machine. The magnetic pull may scramble stored stitch information. A magnet sitting next to the machine, however, shouldn't be a problem.

• **"Don't expose your computerized machine to airport X-ray security."** So says our editor, well-known sewing journalist and publisher, Robbie Fanning.

Conclusion: Is Computerized Sewing Worth Your Investment?

Like all the other household appliances that have streamlined our lives—microwave ovens, touch-tone telephones, remote-control televisions—computer machines are here to stay. *Is computerized sewing for everyone? No. But is it worthy of consideration by any sewing enthusiast?* Definitely.

At the least, shopping for machines will clarify what's possible (technically and creatively), what's available (computerized or otherwise), and at what price. And, if you do buy, that new machine should help you savor sewing that's easier, faster, and more professional than ever.

Sources: For sewing machine accessories—Clotilde, Inc., Nancy's Notions, Ltd., Sew-Art International, Sew/Fit Co., Sewing Emporium, and Treadleart. For addresses, see the "Sew-by-Mail Directory," pages 160 – 173.

References: *Beyond Straight Stitching, The Basics of Creative Machine Stitchery,* by Barbara Weiland O'Connell; *Feet Smarts, Using Presser Feet to Make the Most of Your Sewing Machine; Know Your Sewing Machine,* both by Jackie Dodson (also ask about the brand-specific *Know Your...* books coauthored by Dodson); *Owner's Guide to Sewing Machines, Sergers, and Knitting Machines,* by Gale Grigg Hazen; *Sew News* (specifically, the column "Machines in Motion: Sewing Machines," by Ann Price); *Sew, Serge, Press: Speed Tailoring in the Ultimate Sewing Center,* by Jan Saunders; *The Complete Computer Sewing Book,* by Myra Coles, ©1987, William Heinemann Ltd. Distributed in the United States by David & Charles, Inc., North Pomfret, VT 05053, $19.95 postpaid; and *The Complete Book of Machine Embroidery,* by Robbie and Tony Fanning. All addresses not listed here are included in "References," pages 174 – 178.

Computerized Sewing Machines Feature-by-Feature Checklist	Baby Lock	Bernina	Brother	Elna	Necchi	New Home	Pfaff	Riccar	Sears (Kenmore)	Simplicity	Singer	Sonata Compu-Sew	Viking	White
Number of preprogrammed stitches														
Alphabet styles														
Numeral styles														
Programmable stitch selection														
Light-emitting diode (LED) display														
Liquid Crystal Display for info. and/or program														
Preprogrammed width and length with over-ride														
Maximum stitch width (in mm)														
Double-needle width indicator														
Single-pattern selection														
Automatic tie-off at end of stitch pattern/program														
Stitch elongation														
Automatic one-step buttonhole														
Number of buttonhole styles														
Audio feedback														
Updatable stitch cartridges/cassettes														
Mirror imaging														
Stitch memory band retained when machine off														
Memory														
Low-bobbin thread indicator														
Needle up/needle down														
Variable speed control/cruise control														
Automatic basting														
Oscillating hook														
Rotary hook														
Presser-foot indicator														

Computerized Sewing Machines Feature-by-Feature Checklist	Baby Lock	Bernina	Brother	Elna	Necchi	New Home	Pfaff	Riccar	Sears (Kenmore)	Simplicity	Singer	Sonata Compu-Sew	Viking	White
Built-in needle threader														
Built-in instruction guide														
Create your own ("free") programming														
Retractable power cord														
Automatic or universal tension														
Automatic darning														
Horizontal thread delivery														
Vertical thread delivery														
Instant reverse														
Continuous reverse														
Variable needle position(s)														
Built-in light(s)														
Adjustable foot pressure														
Extension table														
Free-arm														
Snap-on feet														
Droppable feed														
Knee lift														
Thread cutter(s)														
Top drop-in bobbin														
Self-stopping bobbin winder														
Direct-winding bobbin														
Walking foot (dual feeder)														
Oiling requirements														
Other features														

12. Finding the Time and Space to Sew

- Time-to-Sew Strategies
- Tailor Any Space to Suit Your Sewing Needs
- Get Organized!
- Fabric Stashing

You can't use any of the new techniques in this book unless you first put the strategies in this chapter to work. Neither of us has unlimited time to sew. But without these time and space efficiency guides, we could easily become nonsewers. Let us know if these tips help and what you do to sew more (and more enjoyably); write us in care of *The Sewing Update*, 2269 Chestnut, #269, San Francisco, CA 94123.

Time-to-Sew Strategies

No time to sew? Perhaps it's time to rethink your daily priorities and schedule. Here are some strategies we use:

1. **Have a "sew-in."** Divide project tasks and share a babysitter with other busy sewing enthusiasts.

2. **Leave your machine out, near or in the hub of family activities.** For most, the kitchen, dining, or TV-watching areas are productive.

3. **Sew during brief intervals,** as short as 15 minutes. To do so, it's a must that your machine and projects be left out. Waiting for two-hour stretches may mean never sewing!

4. **Buy extra-long phone extension cords** (coiled cords are available up to 25 feet). Pin, cut out, or hand sew while talking with long-winded friends and family. Stitch by machine as you talk, if you dare (we do, and some time-conscious dressmakers we know do, without apology).

5. **Do handwork on the bus, train, in the car, or while watching TV.**

6. **Study pattern guide sheets and sewing while commuting.** (Please, not if you're the driver—Gail resists that temptation and her passengers thank her.)

7. **Have-machine-will-travel.** Cut out and interface all project pieces before leaving. Then organize all related ingredients in small plastic bags. Pack your machine on a luggage carry-all and you're ready for sewing on the road. Our editor, Robbie Fanning, says there's a well-kept secret every sewing fanatic should be privy to—the one electrical outlet available on most

commercial planes. Ask that you be seated next to it on your next flight, then sew rather than eat Mystery-meat Tetrazzini.

8. Resolve NOT to do everything. Recruit your spouse and children to help with grocery shopping, dishes, laundry, and tidying. If your budget allows, hiring a housekeeper—regularly or even occasionally—can free up precious hours for sewing. Your improved disposition may justify the dollar trade-off.

References: *The Busy Woman's Sewing Book,* by Nancy Zieman, ©1988 (for more information, see page 176) and *Get It All Done and Still Be Human,* by Robbie and Tony Fanning, ©1990 Open Chain Publishing, available for $11.95 postpaid from Open Chain Publishing, P.O. Box 2634, Menlo Park, CA 94026, and *Share the Love of Sewing,* a video collection of time-saving tips, featuring Gail and Nancy Zieman, ©1989 by Nancy's Notions, Ltd. (see page 164 of the "Sew-by-Mail Directory").

Tailor Any Space to Suit Your Sewing Needs

Most of us can't afford the luxury of a room reserved exclusively for sewing, but through clever space utilization, can carve a productive niche practically anywhere. Rearranging or creating a sewing space usually inspires more sewing. Get inspiration from some of these favorite organizational schemes.

Get Organized!

Store items together according to their use and within reach of the particular work area—cutting, pressing, and sewing.

Convert a closet to a sewing room!

Folding screens "camouflage" fabrics, books, notions & shelves behind sitting-room bookshelves.

Divide a large room to create an area.

Use mobile storage systems.

Turn a short wall into a sewing area!

Keep tools handy with wall-mounted hooks & racks.

Fabric Stashing

To plan your future sewing projects more efficiently, organize your fabrics by color, fiber type, or end-use. (Gail groups fabrics by color for easier wardrobe coordination.) At a glance, you should be able to see everything in your stash (gulp).

☞ **Update tip:** Consider donating to a charity or less fortunate friend any fabric you've stored for over three years. You probably won't use it. (Because you continue to buy more fabric, right?) You'll shed a ton of guilt, help a good cause—and, of course, make room for more purchases!

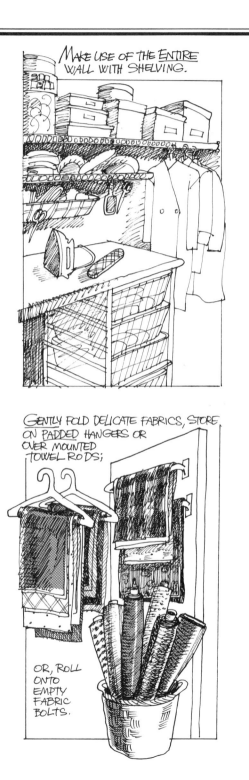

MAKE USE OF THE _ENTIRE_ WALL WITH SHELVING.

GENTLY FOLD DELICATE FABRICS, STORE ON _PADDED_ HANGERS OR OVER MOUNTED TOWEL RODS;

OR, ROLL ONTO EMPTY FABRIC BOLTS.

CONVERT AN ARMOIRE TO A SEWING CENTER!

Sources

- Sewing Machine Companies
- Sew-by-Mail Directory

Sewing Machine Companies

If you're in the market for a sewing machine, write to the following companies for dealer referrals and promotional brochures. (Brand names are in parentheses following each company name.)

Allyn International, Inc. (*Necchi*)
1075 Santa Fe Drive
Denver, CO 80204

Bernina of America (*Bernina*)
534 West Chestnut
Hinsdale, IL 60521

Brother International Corporation
(*Brother*)
8 Corporate Place
Piscataway, NJ 08854

Elna, Inc. (*Elna* and *Elnita*)
7642 Washington Ave. South
Eden Prairie, MN 55344

Fabri-Centers of America
(*Sonata Compu-Sew*)
23550 Commerce Road
Cleveland, OH 44122

New Home Sewing Machine Company (*New Home*)
100 Hollister Road
Teterboro, NJ 07608

Pfaff American Sales Corporation
(*Pfaff*)
610 Winters Ave.
Paramus, NJ 07653

Riccar America (*Riccar*)
14281 Franklin Ave.
Tustin, CA 92680

Sears Roebuck Company (*Kenmore*)
Sears Tower
Chicago, IL 60684

Simplicity Sewing Machines
(*Simplicity*)
P.O. Box 56
Carlstadt, NJ 07072

Singer Sewing Company (*Singer*)
North American Sewing Products Division
135 Raritan Center Parkway
Edison, NJ 08837

Tacony Corporation (*Baby Lock*)
Babylock U.S.A.
P.O. Box 730
St. Louis, MO 63026

Viking Sewing Machine Company
(*Viking*)
11750 Berea Road
Cleveland, OH 44111

White Sewing Machine Company
(*White*)
11750 Berea Road
Cleveland, OH 44111

Sew-by-Mail Directory

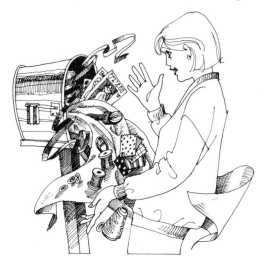

We recommend that every sewing enthusiast develop a special relationship with his or her local dealers and retailers for convenient advice and inspiration, plus the ease of coordinating purchases. However, when specialty items cannot be found locally or when a home sewer lives several miles from a sewing retailer, mail-order specialists are the best alternative.

☞ **Update tip:** Chances are, nearby retailers will welcome your phone order. Just ask. If you're busy, it may allow you to shop locally without leaving the house.

The following list will make your search for these resources a breeze. Each company is listed under just one or two categories—the major product concentrations—although the company may offer other merchandise or services. *Our list is for reference only and does not carry our endorsement or guaran-*

tee. (We have not knowingly included any questionable items or firms.) Enjoy.

☞ **Update tip:** To streamline information gathering, be specific even when simply requesting samples or specific product brochures. Let the company know exactly what you are looking for—which may include color, fiber, texture, or size.

Risk-free Mail Order

• **Before you buy:** Read catalog descriptions carefully to make sure the product is what you want. Is there a guarantee? What is the policy for returns?

• **Placing your order:** Fill out the order form carefully and make a copy of both order and payment for future reference. Never send cash. When ordering by phone, complete the order form first to prevent mistakes. If possible, keep a record of the date of your phone order, as well as the name of the salesperson.

• **If there is a problem with your order:** Contact the company right away, by phone or by mail. If you contact by phone, be sure to record the time and date of your call, as well as the name of the contact person. Follow up in writing, describing the problem and outlining any solution reached during the phone call. Send copies of your order and payment record. Get a return receipt from the shipper when returning merchandise.

• **The "30-Day Rule":** If a delivery date isn't given in a company's materials, it must ship within 30 days of receiving your order (COD orders excepted), according to the Federal Trade Commission's Mail Order Merchandise Rule. If you place an order using a credit card, your account shouldn't be billed until shipment is made. If you send payment with your order and your order doesn't arrive when promised, you may cancel the order and get a full refund.

👉 **Update tip:** In today's volatile business climate, any mail-order source list will change frequently. Please send your comments on any out-of-business notifications or unsatisfactory service to *Update Newsletters*, 2269 Chestnut, Suite 269, San Francisco, CA 94123.

Key to Abbreviations and Symbols:

SASE = Self-addressed, stamped (first class) envelope with your request.

L-SASE = Large SASE (2-oz. first class postage) with your request.

(Check with your postmaster regarding Canadian mail.)

* = refundable with order.

= for information, brochure or catalog.

✎ **Note:** If you're familiar with the "Serge-by-Mail Directory" in our companion book, *Innovative Serging*, you'll notice that several of the source listings are the same. (Most mail-order merchants sell both sewing and serging supplies, not one or the other exclusively.) However, the list has been updated, with new categories; those that carry only serging supplies have been deleted. If you want a complete reference to mail-order serger supplies, consult *Innovative Serging* (see page 175).

Hard-to-Find Patterns and Designs

✎ **Note:** Patterns from the major companies (Butterick, McCall's, New Look, Simplicity, and Vogue) are readily available from your local fabric stores.

Campbell's, R.D.I. Box 1444, Herndon, PA 17830. Vintage-look patterns. $4#.

Fabric Fancies, 501 Evans Ave., Reno, NV 89512, 702/323-0117. Historic frontier garment patterns. $2#.

Ghee's, 106 E. Kings Highway, Suite 205, Shreveport, LA 71104, 318/868-1154. Patterns and notions for making handbags. $1#.

Great Copy Patterns, Stretch & Sew Fabrics, P.O. Box 85329, Racine, WI 53408, 414/632-2660. One-size-fits-all pattern styling for knits. L-SASE#.

Great Fit Patterns, 221 S.E. 197th, Portland, OR 97233, 503/665-3125. Fashionable styles created exclusively for the large figure, sizes 38-60. $1#.

Jean Hardy Patterns, 2151 La Cuesta Dr., Santa Ana, CA 92705. Patterns for riding, cheerleading, skating, and square dancing. $1#.

Kids Can Sew, P.O. Box 1710, St. George, UT 84771-1710, 800/I-MADE-IT. Patterns for kids' clothes, plus teach-kids-to-sew training materials. Free#.

Kwik-Sew Pattern Co., Inc., 3000 Washington Ave., N., Minneapolis, MN 55411, 612/521-7651. Kwik-Sew Patterns (Canada), Ltd., 5035 Timberlea Blvd., Unit #7, Mississauga, Ontario L4W 2W9 Canada, 416/625-0135. Easy-to-sew fashions for the whole family. Choose from 800 patterns. $3.50# ($4 in Canada).

Logan Kits, Route 3, Box 380, Double Springs, AL 35553, 205/486-7732. Lingerie and activewear kits for men, women, and children. $1 and L-SASE#.

Peg's Fabric and Yarn Closet, 4110 Callfield Road, Wichita Falls, TX 76308. Peg's Pieces patterns. SASE#.

Picks Fine Handwovens, 3316 Circle Hill Rd., Alexandria, VA 22305. Hand-woven silk skirt lengths and matching sweater yarns packaged with lining, notions, and sewing/knitting instructions. Swatches, $2.

Pineapple Appeal, P.O. Box 197, Owatonna, MN 55060, 507/455-3041. Sweatshirts, jams, pillows, windsocks, and tote bags kits for the beginning sewer. Free#.

Prime Moves, P.O. Box 8022, Portland, OR 97207. Authentic aerobic wear. $1#.

Raindrops & Roses, 8 SE 199 Ave., Portland, OR 97233. Maternity and nursing wear patterns. $1#.

Richard the Thread, 8320 Melrose Ave., West Hollywood, CA 90069. Historic period patterns and notions. $2#.

Seams Sew Easy, P.O. Box 2189, Manasses, VA 22110. Swimwear patterns (two-piece). L-SASE#.

Serging Ahead, P.O. Box 45, Grandview, MO 64030. Knit patterns and supplies. $1#.

Stretch & Sew Inc., P.O. Box 185, Eugene, OR 97440. Multisized patterns for women, men, and children. Free#.

Sunrise Designs, Box 277, Orem, UT 84059. Infant, toddler, and children's patterns. Several easy-to-sew designs in each multisized pattern. Free#.

Susan's Sewing Center, 68-720 Highway 11, Cathedral City, CA 92234. *Patterns by the Yard.* L-SASE#.

U-Sew-Knits, P.O. Box 43078, Phoenix, AZ 85080. Precut women's sportswear and children's clothing kits. SASE#.

Yes Mam Lingerie & Fashions, 106 S. Third Street, Leesburg, FL 32748. Kits for lingerie, men's lounge wear, and women's fashions. $1 and SASE#.

Embellishments

Badhir Trading, Inc., 8429 Sisson Hwy., Eden, NY 14057, 716/992-3193. Appliqués, bead/pearl fringe, sequins, and jewels for bridal and evening wear. $2*#.

Baubanbea Enterprises, Box 1205, Smithtown, NY 11787. Rhinestones, sequins, beads, jewels, lace, appliqués, feathers, silk flowers, fabrics, and more. $4#.

Collections, P.O. Box 806, Ithaca, NY 14851. Laces, 3/8" to 60" wide, including Rose Garden, Point d'esprit, lingerie, stretch and fiberfill lace. Free#.

Creative Trims, 18 Woodland Drive, Lincroft, NJ 07738. Lace, embroideries, and ribbons. Free#.

Donna Lee's Sewing Center, 25234 Pacific Hwy. S., Kent, WA 98032, 206/941-9466. Imported laces and Swiss embroideries; silk ribbons and French trims; Swiss batiste and China silks. $3#.

Elsie's Exquisiqués, 513 Broadway, Niles, MI 49120, 616/684-7034. French-reproduction laces, trims, silk ribbons, hand-crafted ribbon roses, and insertion laces.

Greatest Sew on Earth, P.O. Box 214, Fort Tilden, NY 11695. Sequin and jeweled trims and appliqués, eyelet embroideries, bridal laces, and pearls. $1#.

Lace Place, 9250 N. 43rd Ave., Ste. 6, Glendale, AZ 85302. Assorted laces. $2#.

Lace Plus, Inc., P.O. Box 3243, Fort Lee, NJ 07024. Fine quality Schiffli laces in a variety of widths and designs. $2# w/swatches.

Lacis, 2982 Adeline, Berkeley, CA 94703. A multitude of new and antique laces. Also, lacemaking supplies and interesting needlework tools and notions. $1.50#

Pioneer Specialty Products, Box 412, Holden, MA 01520. Laces, ribbons, eyelet, tape. $1*#.

Notions Specialists

Aardvark Adventures, P.O. Box 2449, Livermore, CA 94551, 415/443-2687. Books, beads, buttons, bangles, plus unusual assortment of related products. Decorative thread, including metallics. $1#.

The Bee Lee Company, P.O. Box 36108-B, Dallas, TX 75235. Complete selection of threads, zippers, notions, and trims, including Western styles. Free#.

Bobette Industries, 2401 S. Hill St., Los Angeles, CA 90007-2785, toll-free in CA, 800/237-6462 (orders only). Notions, tools, threads, books, machine parts, and accessories. $1#.

C. J. Enterprises, 2219 E. Thousand Oaks Blvd., Ste. 336, Thousand Oaks, CA 91362, 818/702-6029. Unique sewing machine feet for special applications, made to fit all makes and models. Ask for dealer referrals. L-SASE#.

Catherine's, Rt. 6, Box 1227, Lexington, NC 27292, 704/798-1595. Threads and more at wholesale prices. Minimum order, $35. School quantity discounts. $2 and L-SASE for thread color card.

Clotilde, Inc., 1909 SW First Ave., Ft. Lauderdale, FL 33315, 305/761-8655. Catalog of over 1,200 items, including special threads and notions, sewing tools, and supplies, books, and videos. $1#.

Custom Zips, P.O. Box 1200, So. Norwalk, CT 06856. Zippers cut to order. $2#.

D & E Distributing, 199 N. El Camino Real, Ste. F-242, Encinitas, CA 92024. Decorative threads and yarns, including silk, rayon, and Madeira metallics. L-SASE#.

The Embroidery Stop, 1042 Victory Dr., Yardley, PA 19067. Threads, yarns, needles. $1#.

Fit For You, 781 Golden Prados Dr., Diamond Bar, CA 91795, 714/861-5021. Sewing notions, accessories, videos, and square-dance patterns. L-SASE#.

Hemming's, 2645 White Bear Ave., Maplewood, MN 55109, 612/770-4130. Sewing machine accessories and furniture, professional pressing supplies, and a wide range of notions. Free#.

Home-Sew, Dept. S, Bethlehem, PA 18018. Basic notions, trims, coned threads, and tools. Free#.

Jacquart's, 505 E. McLeod, Ironwood, MI 49938, 906/932-1339. Zippers. $1#.

Madeira, 30 Bayside Court, P.O. Box 6068, Laconia, NH 03246. Decorative threads—from metallics and sequin strands, to trendy neons and rayons. $30 minimum. L-SASE#.

Maryland Trims, P.O. Box 3508, Silver Spring, MD 20901. Laces, sewing notions, and supplies. $1.75#.

Mill End Store, Box 02098, Portland, OR 97202, 503/236-1234. Broad selection of notions, trims, threads, and accessories. SASE#.

Nancy's Notions, Ltd., P.O. Box 683, Beaver Dam, WI 53916, 414/887-0391. Over 300 sewing notions and accessories, threads, and tools, interfacings and fabrics, books and videos. Free#.

National Thread & Supply, 695 Red Oak Rd., Stockbridge, GA 30281, 800/847-1001, ext. 1688; in GA, 404/389-9115. Name-brand sewing supplies and notions. Free#.

Newark Dressmaker Supply, P.O. Box 2448, Lehigh Valley, PA 18001, 215/837-7500. Sewing notions, trims, buttons, decorative threads, and supplies. Free#.

Oregon Tailor Supply Co., Inc., P.O. Box 42284, Portland, OR 97242, 800/678-2457 (orders only). Every kind of notion imaginable. L-SASE#.

The Paris Connection, 4314 Irene Dr., Erie, PA 16510. A wide variety of notions, feet, books, and patterns, including old sewing-machine manuals. $1.50#.

The Perfect Notion, 566 Hoyt St., Darien, CT 06820, 203/968-1257. Hard-to-find notions and threads (including their *ThreadFuse*™ melt adhesive thread). $1#.

Serge & Sew Notions, 11761 99th Ave. N., Maple Grove, MN 55369, 612/493-2449. Threads, books, patterns, furniture, fabrics, and more, priced 20-40% below retail. Free#. Swatch club, $6 for six months.

Serging Ahead, P.O. Box 45, Grandview, MO 64030. Threads, books, and patterns. $1#.

Sew-Art International, P.O. Box 550, Bountiful, UT 84010. Decorative threads, notions, and accessories. Free#.

SewCraft, P.O. Box 1869, Warsaw, IN 46580, 219/269-4046. Books, decorative threads, and notions.

Sew/Fit Co., P.O. Box 565, La Grange, IL 60525, 312/579-3222. Sewing notions and accessories; modular tables for serger/sewing machine setup; cutting tools and mats, books. Free#.

Sewing Emporium, 1087 Third Ave., Chula Vista, CA 92010, 619/420-3490. Hard-to-find sewing notions, sewing machine cabinets, and accessories. $2#.

The Sewing Place, 18870 Cox Ave., San Jose, CA 95070. Sewing machine needles and feet, plus books by Gale Grigg Hazen. Specify your brand and model if ordering machine accessories. L-SASE#.

The Sewing Workshop, 2010 Balboa St., San Francisco, CA 94121, 415/221-SEWS. Unique designer notions and supplies. L-SASE#.

Solo Slide Fasteners, Inc., P.O. Box 528, Stoughton, MA 02072, 800/343-9670. All types and lengths of zippers, other selected notions. Free#.

Speed Stitch, 3113-D Broadpoint Dr., Harbor Heights, FL 33983. Machine art kits and supplies, including all-purpose, decorative, and specialty threads, books, and accessories. $3*#.

Thread Discount & Sales, 7105 S. Eastern, Bell Gardens, CA 90201, 213/562-3438. Coned polyester thread. SASE#.

Threads & Things, P.O. Box 83190, San Diego, CA 92138, 619/440-8760. 100% rayon thread. Free#.

Threads West, 422 E. State St., Redlands, CA 92373, 714/793-4405 or 0214. Coned thread, machine parts, and accessories. SASE for free thread color list.

Treadleart, 25834 Narbonne Ave., Ste. I, Lomita, CA 90717, 800/327-4222. Books, supplies, notions, decorative threads, and creative inspiration. $1.50#. Bimonthly color catalog/magazine, $12 annually.

T-Rific Products Co., P.O. Box 911, Winchester, OR 97495. Coned thread. Thread color chart, $1.25.

Two Brothers, 1602 Locust St., St. Louis, MO 63103. Zipper assortment. SASE#.

YLI Corporation, 45 W. 300 N., Provo, UT 84601, 800/854-1932 or 801/377-3900. Decorative, specialty, and all-purpose threads, yarns, and ribbons. $1.50#.

Sensational Silks

Fabric Fancies, P.O. Box 50807, Reno, NV 89513. White silks, satins, and jacquards for wedding gowns and lingerie. Imported laces, English illusion, and French net. $10# w/swatches.

Oriental Silk Co., 8377 Beverly Blvd., Los Angeles, CA 90048, 213/651-2323. Tussahs, chiffons, voiles, brocades, velvets, and more. Samples, $1*/for each fabric type specified.

Sureway Trading, 826 Pine Ave., Ste. 5, Niagara Falls, NY 14301, 716/282-4887. Silk fabrics and threads; silk/wool blends. Samples: naturals/whites, $8; colors, $12.

Thai Silks, 252 State St., Los Altos, CA 94022, 800/722- SILK; in CA, 800/221-SILK. Every type of silk imaginable. Fabric club, $10/year (three swatched mailings). Full swatch set (over 600), $20 ($18*).

Top Drawer Silks Ltd., 1938 Wildwood, Glendale Heights, IL 60139. Range of silk fabrications. Annual membership, $13# w/swatches.

Utex Trading, 710 Ninth St., Ste. 5, Niagara Falls, NY 14301, 416/596-7565. Silk fabrics, yarns, and threads. Complete sample set, $35*.

For Formals, Proms, and Weddings

Bridal-by-the-Yard, P.O. Box 2492, Springfield, OH 45501. Imported and domestic laces and fabrics. $7# w/ swatches.

Bridal Elegance, 1176 Northport Dr., Columbus, OH 43235. Bridal Elegance patterns, sizes 4-22, and Wedding Gown Design Book. $.50#.

Bridals International, 45 Albany St., Cazenovia, NY 13035. Imported laces and fabrics; button loops and covered buttons for wedding gowns. $7.50*#.

Fabric Fancies, 501 Evans Ave., Reno, NV, 89512, 702/323-0117. Complete line of wedding supplies. Lace catalogue, $10*. Bridal silks, $10*. Embroidered satin samples, $10* and embroidered organza samples, $10* (both sets, $16*). Bridal Elegance® Patterns brochure, $1. Wedding gown design book, $9. Historical bridal patterns brochure, $1. Also, books and videos.

La Sposa Veils, 252 W. 40th St., New York, NY 10018, 212/354-4729 or 944-9142. Bridal headpieces. $3*#.

Mylace, P.O. Box 13466, Tallahassee, FL 32317, 800/433-8859; in FL, 800/433-8857. Extensive selection of trim and French bridal laces from 1/4" to 50" wide. $3.50#.

Patty's Pincushion, Inc., at Grande Affaires, 710 Smithfield St., Pittsburgh, PA 15219, 412/765-3010. Fabrics for the bridal party plus personalized service for planning wedding gowns. Swatches available.

Sew Elegant, 15461 Dorian St., Sylmar, CA 91342. Custom wedding gown kits, containing fabrics, laces, notions, and multisized patterns. $5*# w/ swatches.

S-T-R-E-T-C-H & Knit Fabrics

ABC Knits, 13315 433rd Court, S.E., North Bend, WA 98045 Acrylic, cotton, and wool-blend knits; coordinated ribbing. L-SASE#.

Artknits by Clifford, 2174 Gary Rd., Traverse City, MI 49684, 616/943-8218. Custom-knit ribbing. SASE#.

Bead Different, 1627 S. Tejon, Colorado Springs, CO 80906, 303/473-2188. Stretch fabrics for dancers, skaters, and gymnasts. Send SASE with inquiry.

Beth McLeod, 1113 87th St., Daly City, CA 94015, 415/992-8731. Cotton/ Lycra® and nylon/Lycra® stretch knits. $1 and SASE#.

Cottons Etc., 228 Genesee St., Oneida, NY 13421, 315/363-6834. Knits, sweatshirting, Lycra®, and more. L-SASE# w/swatches.

Everitt Knitting Co., 234 W. Florida St., Milwaukee, WI 53204. All types of sweater yardage, plus matching ribbing and trims. Write for retailer referrals.

Golden Needles, 2320 Sauber Ave., Rockford, IL 61103. Custom knit sweater yardage, sweater bodies with knitted name, and ribbing. Free swatches.

Just Rite Fabrics, RR3, Box 83B, Norton, KS 67654. Interlocks with matching ribbing, wool knits, stretch terry, and more. L-SASE and $2# (swatches included).

Kieffer's Lingerie Fabrics & Supplies, 1625 Hennepin Ave., Minneapolis, MN 55403. Swimwear nylon/cotton *Lycra*® blend stretch knits, sweatshirting, lingerie tricot. Also, many coned threads at bargain prices. Free#.

LG Fashions and Fabrics, P.O. Box 58394, Renton, WA 98058. *Lycra*® blend knits of cotton and nylon. $2*# w/swatches.

Marianne's Textile Products (formerly Diversified Products), Box 319, RD 2, Rockwood, PA 15557. Sweater bodies, ribbing, knit collars. $2 and L-SASE#.

Rosen & Chadick, 246 W. 40th St., New York, NY 10018. Cotton/*Lycra*® and nylon/*Lycra*® stretch knits. SASE#.

Sew Smart, P.O. Box 776, Longview, WA 98632. Ribbed knit collars, trims, and snaps. L-SASE#.

Stretch & Sew Fabrics, 1165 Valley River Dr., Eugene, OR 97401. Stretch & Sew patterns, plus a complete assortment of knit fabrics and notions. L-SASE#.

Stretch & Sew Fabrics, 19725 40th Ave. W., Lynnwood, WA 98036. A complete selection of knits, Stretch & Sew patterns, and related notions. L-SASE#.

The Thrifty Needle, 3232 Collins St., Philadelphia, PA 19134. Sweater bodies and ribbing. $2 and SASE# w/swatches.

Cycling, Hiking, Dancing, and Skiing Materials

Altra, Inc., 100 E. Washington St., New Richmond, IN 47967, 317/339-4653. Precut and pattern sportswear kits for outdoor activities, including skiing, backpacking, and cycling; skiwear fabrics and fleece; outerwear hardware and supplies. $1#.

DK Sports, Daisy Kingdom, 134 N.W. 8th, Portland, OR 97209, 503/222-9033. Kits and patterns for active sportswear and outerwear (skiing, bicycling, aerobics, swimwear, and rainwear). Outerwear fabrics, including *Taslan*®, mountain cloth, *Cordura*®, *Gore-tex*®, and vertical stretch ski pant fabric. $2#.

Donner Designs, Box 7217, Reno, NV 89510. Outerwear and activewear kits featuring water-repellent fabrics. Outerwear fabrics, including *Tasnylon*, one- and two-way stretch, and *Gore-tex*®. Teacher discounts. $1#.

Frostline Kits, 2512 W. Independent Ave., Grand Junction, CO 81505, 800-KITS USA. Fabrics and precut kits for sportswear, outdoor clothing, luggage, camping gear, and more. Free#.

Green Pepper, Inc., 941 Olive, Eugene, OR 97407, 503/345-6665. Active and outerwear patterns and fabrics, including nylon/*Lycra*® and polypropylene/*Lycra*® knits, water-repellent fabrics, and insulating battings. $2#.

The Rain Shed, 707 N.W. 11th, Corvallis, OR 97330. Large selection of outerwear fabrics, kits, sewing notions, and tools. $1#.

Sundown Kits, 23815 43rd Ave. So., Kent, WA 98032-2856. Kits for assorted outerwear. $1#.

Timberline Sewing Kits, Inc., Box 126-SUB, Pittsfield, NH 03263, 603/435-8888. Fabrics and kits for outerwear and gear. $1#.

Wardrobe Fabrics

Amanda Scott Publishing, P.O. Box 40425, Cincinnati, OH 45240, 513/851-8936. Fake-fur fabrics, patterns, and kits. Swatch set, $8#*.

Baer Fabrics, 515 E. Market St., Louisville, KY 40202, 800/288-2237; 502/583-5521. Comprehensive selection of fabrics. Seasonal sample sets (prices vary). Custom swatching available. Notions, $2#.

Britex-by-Mail, 146 Geary, San Francisco, CA 94108, 415/392-2910. Designer fabrics, including unusual sweater knits. Personalized swatching and special offerings. L-SASE#.

Camille Enterprises, P.O. Box 615-N, Rockaway, NJ 07866. Variety of fabrics, from the usual to designer. Four swatch mailings a year, $3 each; $10* a set.

Carolina Mills Factory Outlet, Box V, Hwy. 76, West Branson, MO 65616, 417/34-2291. Designer fabrics from major sportswear manufacturers, 30-50% below regular retail. Sample swatches, $2.

Classic Cloth, 2508-D McMullen Booth Rd., Dept. UN, Clearwater, FL 34621, 813/799-0417. Austrian boiled wool, dyed-to-match wool trim, and coordinating paisley challis. Swatches, $5* a set.

Clearbrook Woolen Shop, P.O. Box 8, Clearbrook, VA 22624, 703/662-3442. Variety of fabrics, with emphasis on wool. 8-10 sample sets per year. Free swatched mailings—send name and address to be placed on the mailing list.

The Cloth Cupboard, P.O. Box 2263, Boise, ID 83701, 208/345-5567. Japanese woodblock prints. Swatches, $2.50 and SASE.

The Couture Touch, P.O. Box 681278, Dept. UN, Schaumburg, IL 60168, 312/310-8080. Famous-name fashion fabrics, including Anglo, Landau, and Logantex. Complimentary seasonal swatch collection available.

Creative Fabrics, 3303 Long Beach Rd., Oceanside, NY 11572. Fine wool and polyester suitings, silk and silky polyesters, and challis. Swatches, $5*; $7 Canadian.

Creative Line Fabric Club, 101 Tremont St., Boston, MA 02108, 617/426-1473. Exclusive Italian imports, all natural fibers: silks, wools, cashmere, linens. Annual membership $25 (Canada, $35)—three swatch collections.

Cy Rudnick's Fabrics, 2450 Grand, Kansas City, MO 64108, 816/842-7808. Extensive collection of designer and specialty fabrics. Swatching service available. $3*, plus your personal color and fabric request.

Designer's Touch, 7689 Lakeville Hwy., Petaluma, CA 94952, 707/778-8550. Imported and domestic designer fabrics offered through representatives nationwide. Fashion Club membership also available—$50/year for 9-10 mailings of swatched fashion portfolios.

Elegance Fabrics, 91A Scollard St., Toronto, Ontario M5R IG4, Canada, 416/966-3446. Finest European fabrics—wools, silks, linens, cottons. Seasonal swatch catalogs: 300-swatch edition, $60*; 460 swatches plus notions, $100*; 460 larger swatches plus notions, $150*.

Exquisite Fabrics, Inc. (formerly Watergate Fabrics), Dept. SUB, 1775 K St. NW, 1st Floor, Washington, DC 20006, 202/775-1818. Exclusive fabrics from France, Switzerland, and Italy: exquisite bridal fabrics and laces, silks, cashmeres, cottons, and worsted woolens. Complimentary swatching service.

The Fabric Club, P.O. Box 28126, Atlanta, GA 30358. Exclusive designer fabrics at a 50-75% savings. Annual membership, $8, for four coordinated fabric brochures.

Fabric Gallery, 146 W. Grand River, Williamston, MI 48895, 517/655-4573. Imported and domestic silks, wools, cottons, and better synthetics. $5/year for four swatched mailings.

Fabrications Fabric Club, Box 2162, South Vineland, NJ 08360. Fabrics from designers, ready-to-wear manufacturers, and mills. Four mailings, $10/year ($5*).

Fabricland, Inc., Box 20235, Portland, OR 97220, 800/255-5412. Full bolts of fabric or boxes of notions available. Minimum order, $50. Write for price list.

Fabrics by Mail, 1252 Woodway Rd., Victoria, BC V9A 6Y6 Canada, 604/384-9573. Coordinated cottons, silks, wools, and synthetics. $5#(*2.50 refundable voucher).

Fabrics in Vogue, 200 Park Ave., Ste. 303 E., New York, NY 10166. Imported wools, silks, linens, cottons, and blends featured in Vogue Patterns. Six swatch mailings, $10/year.

Fabrics Unlimited, 5015 Columbia Pike, Arlington, VA 22204, 703/671-0324. Better fashion fabrics from designer cutting rooms.

Fashion Fabrics Club, 10490 Baur Blvd., St. Louis, MO 63132. Variety of quality designer and name-brand fabrics at moderate prices. Swatches monthly, $7/year.

Field's Fabrics, 1695 44th S.E., Grand Rapids, MI 49508, 616/455-4570. *Ultrasuede®, Facile®, Caress®*, and *Ultraleather®* swatches, $10; silk, *Pendleton®* wool, metallics, and more (write for swatch information).

Four Seasons Fabric Club, 811 E. 21st St., North Vancouver, BC V7J 1N8, Canada. Coordinated fabric selections identified by personal color season. $25/year for four swatch mailings.

G Street Fabrics, 11854 Rockville Pike, Rockville, MD 20852, 301/231-8998. Extensive selection of better fabrics. Over 20 basic fabric charts available, including cotton, wool, silk, *Ultrasuede®, Facile®* ($10 each). Sample subscription ($35/six months, $50/year) for 60 swatches per month. Custom sampling, $1/garment. Notions, $4#. Professional discounts.

Ginette's Haute Couture Fabrics, 36 Charles St., Milton, Ontario L9T 2G6, Canada. Cottons, linens, silks, denims, and easy-care blends at a savings of 20% to 50% off regular retail prices. Two catalogs, $15 Canadian/year.

Grasshopper Hill Fabrics, 224 Wellington St., Kingston, Ontario K7K 2Y8, Canada, 613/548-3889. Fine fabrics at competitive prices. Semiannual catalog, $5 Canadian ($2.50*).

House of Laird, 521 Southland Dr., P.O. Box 23778, Lexington, KY 40523, 606/276-5258. Designer fabrics offered through fabric showings by representatives nationwide. Write or call for information.

Imaginations, PO Box 2749, Westport, CT 06880, 800/343-6953. Discounts on coordinated groupings of knits and wovens, many from top label cutting rooms. Yearly subscription, $10 (Canada, $15).

J. J. Products Ltd., 117 W. Ninth St., Ste. 111, Los Angeles, CA 90015, 213/624-1840. Imported wool at discount prices. Swatch cards, $3* each.

Jehlor Fantasy Fabrics, 730 Andover Park W., Seattle, WA 98188, 206/575-8250. Variety of stretch fabrics, $2.50#. *Baubles, Bangles and Beads* catalog, $2.50. Ballroom dance costume patterns—SASE#.

Katsuri Dyeworks, 1959 Shattuck Ave., Berkeley, CA 94701, 415/841-4509. Fabrics from Japan. $5*#.

Left Bank Fabric Co. by Mail, 8354 W. Third St., Los Angeles, CA 90048, 213/655-7289. European silks, wools, cottons. Membership, $25*/year, for three collections.

The Material World, 5700 Monroe St., Sylvania, OH 43560, 419/885-5416. Imported and domestic silks, wools, and cottons. Quarterly swatch collections, $6/year.

Maxine Fabrics, 62 W. 39th St. Ste. 902, New York, NY 10018, 212/391-2282. Moygashel linens and blends, Liberty prints, *Ultrasuede®* and *Facile®*, coordinated silks, cottons, and novelties. $3# w/swatches.

Natural Fiber Fabric Club, 521 Fifth Ave., New York, NY 10175. 100% wools, cottons, silks, and linens at 20% savings over regular retail. Membership, $10/year for four swatched mailings and basic 24-fabric portfolio.

Oppenheim's, Dept. 394, N. Manchester, IN 46962, 219/982-6848. Classic fashion fabrics at a savings. Swatches, $2*. Free swatch mailing after first order.

Portfolio Fabrics, 4984 Manor St., Vancouver, BC V5R 3Y2, Canada. Bimonthly portfolios of imported fine fabric swatches. SASE#.

Samuel Lehrer & Co., 7 Depinedo Ave., Stamford, CT 06902. Fine clothing fabrics, primarily menswear. Swatch kit of over 50 samples, $9.95.

Seventh Avenue Designer Fabric Club, 701 Seventh Ave., Ste. 900, New York, NY 10036. Fabric selections from top-name Seventh Avenue designers at discount prices. Membership, $10/year for four swatched mailings.

Sew Easy Textiles & Trims, P.O. Box 54, Hudson Bay, SK S0E 0Y0, Canada, 306/865-3343. Quality fabrics, low prices. Volume discounts. Notions and patterns. $5# w/swatches.

South Sea Curios, Box 3927, Pago Pago, American Samoa 96799. Pacific Island prints and Polynesian motifs in 100% cotton and blends. Swatches, $4 ($2*).

Southern Fabrics by Mail, 1210 Galleria Mall, Houston, TX 77056, 713/626-5511. Large selection of exclusive imports and designer fabrics at reasonable prices. Membership, $15/year for four swatched mailings.

Southwest Design, 1356 County Road 128, Dept. UN, Hesperus, CO 81326, 303/588-3337. "Practical fabrics for less," including uniform fabrics, satin, lingerie tricot, and matching laces. Send $1* and L-SASE#.

Stitches and Stuff, 1212 72nd Ave. N., Minneapolis, MN 55430. Large selection of cottons, silks, polyesters, linens, wools, and blends. $1 and SASE#.

The Stitchin' Post, 161 Elm, P.O. Box 280, Sisters, OR 97759. Cottons and silks; trims. Catalog, $1.

Tanya's Fabrics, 1039 N. Mills Ave., Orlando, FL 32803, 407/896-1581; 800/331-8986. Color-coordinated Moygashel linen, silks, *Ultrasuede®,* and fine cottons. Swatch collection and fabric club membership, $3*.

Thimbleweed, 2975 College Ave., Berkeley, CA 94705. Cottons, silks, and linens. SASE#.

27th Street Fabrics, 2710 Willamette St., Eugene, OR 97405, 503/345-6224. Fine fabrics and notions plus personalized service for your sewing needs. L-SASE#.

Warren of Stafford, 99 Furnace Ave., Stafford Springs, CT 06076, 800/325-9019; in CT, 203/684-2766. Fine yarns and fabrics of cashmere, camel hair, and wool woven in Stafford's own mill. Swatches, $4* per request.

Winston's Fabrics, 8515 Delmar Blvd., St. Louis, MO 63124, 314/432-5005. Fine designer, classic, and bridal fabrics. SASE#.

The Yardage Shop, 423 Main St., Ridgefield, CT 06877, 203/438-6100. *Ultrasuede®, Sofrina, Lamous II®, Suedemark,* silk, linen, and more. $1#; swatches, $8.50.

Real Leathers

Berman Leather, 25 Melcher St., Boston, MA 02210-1599. Catalog and complete sample set, $5*.

C.T. Textiles, 340 E. 57th St., New York, NY 10022, 212/486-1299. Full color range of smooth-grain skins, suede pigskin, metallic leathers and pearlescents. Minimum order. $1 and SASE with color choice for sample.

D'Anton, Rte. 2, Box 159, West Branch, IA 52358, 319/643-2568. Sueded, smooth, and novelty leathers. L-SASE#.

Iowa Pigskin Sales Co., Box 115, Clive, IA 50053. Suede and smooth, full-grain pigskin, in a range of colors. Sample set, $4*.

The Leather Factory, P.O. Box 50429, Ft. Worth, TX 76105, 800/433-3201. Leather skins, lacing, tools, and books. $3*#.

Leather Unlimited Corp., 7155 County Hwy "B," UN 800, Belgium, WI 53004, 414/994-9464. Leather, tools, kits, belts, and buckles. Minimum order, $30. $2*#.

The Leather Warehouse, 3134 S. Division, Grand Rapids, MI 49508. Complete line of leather and leather-craft products. Free#.

Leo G. Stein, 4314 N. California Ave., Chicago, IL 60618, 800/831-9509. Garment pig suede, cowhide, embossed leather, and exotics. Minimum order, $25; quantity discounts. $3# w/ swatches.

M. Siegel Co., Inc., 120 Pond St., Ashland, MA 01721, 508/881-5200. Large assortment of colored garment leathers. Minimum order, $30; quantity discounts.

Prairie Collection, RR 1, Box 63, Meservey, IA 50457, 515/358-6344. Incredible fishskin leather, among others. Also, remnants available. $3*#w/samples.

Quintessence, P.O. Box 723544, Atlanta, GA 30339, 404/435-7441. Exotic skins (such as fish and frog), leathers, suedes, and metallics and trims (stone, shell, and bead), plus hand-painted cottons—swatched catalog, $5.

Tandy Leather Co., P.O. Box 2934, Ft. Worth, TX 76113. Smooth leathers, suedes, and exotics. Swatches, $2*; $1#.

Leather-likes: *Ultrasuede®*, *Ultraleather®*, etc.

✎ **Note:** Most retailers who carry better fabrics also inventory *Ultrasuede®* fabrics (e.g., *Facile®* and *Caress®*), plus other synthetic suedes and leathers. Those included on this list, however, are mail-order specialists and most offer these fabrics at everyday discounts.

Baer Fabrics, 515 E. Market St., Louisville, KY 40202, 800/288-2237; 502/583-5521. Sample set of *Ultrasuede®*, *Facile®*, *Caress®*, and *Lamous*, $7.50. $2#.

Clearbrook Woolens, P.O. Box 8, Clearbrook, VA 22624. Inquire about *Ultrasuede®*-brand scraps at special prices. L-SASE#.

Fabrics Unlimited, 5015 Columbia Pike, Arlington, VA 22204, 703/671-0324. Complete *Ultrasuede®* line. L-SASE#.

Field's Fabrics, 1695 44th S.E., Grand Rapids, MI 49508, 616/455-4570. *Ultrasuede®*, *Facile®*, *Caress®*, and *Ultraleather®* swatches, $10* (refundable with order).

G Street Fabrics, 11854 Rockville, MD 20852, 301/231-8960; 800/333-9191 (orders only). Sample chart of *Ultrasuede®* and *Ultraleather®*, $10* each.

Mary Jo's, 401 Cox Rd., Gastonia, NC 28054, 800/MARYJOS (800/627-9567). *Ultrasuede®*, *Facile®*, and some *Caress®* colors, all at discount prices. Call for more information.

Michiko's Creations, P.O. Box 4313, Napa, CA 94558. All shades of *Ultrasuede®*, *Ultraleather®*, *Facile®*, and *Caress®*. Ask about discounted remnant pricing. Swatched catalog, $5. L-SASE#.

UltraMouse, Ltd., 3433 Bennington Ct., Birmingham, MI 48010. *Ultrasuede®* scraps, sold by the pound. L-SASE plus $1.50#.

Ultrascraps, P.O. Box 98, Farmington, UT 84025, 801/451-6023. *Ultrasuede®* scraps and accessory patterns. L-SASE#.

The Yardage Shop, 423 Main, Ridgefield, CT 06877, 203/438-6100. Full line of *Ultrasuede®* fabrics and *Ultraleather®*. Also, *Lamous II®*, *Suedemark*, and *Sofrina*. For 350 swatches of these and assorted other swatches, send $9.50. $1#.

Special Buttons

Button Creations, 3801 Stump Rd., Doylestown, PA 18901, 800/346-0233. Buttons from all over the world, including wood, pearl, children's, hand-painted, leather, military, pewter, and cloisonné. $2#.

The Button Shop, P.O. Box 1065, Oak Park, IL 60304, 312/795-1234. Assorted button selections, plus notions for sewing and tailoring needs. Free#.

Buttons & Things Factory Outlet Store, 24 Main St., Rt. 1, Freeport, ME 04032, 207/865-4480. Matching service with buttons from all over the world. Free#.

Dogwood Lane, RR5, Box 162A, Sullivan, IN 47882. Handmade stoneware and porcelain buttons. L-SASE#.

Fashion Touches, Box 804, Bridgeport, CT 06601. Belts and buttons custom covered with your fabric. Free #.

The Hands Works, Box 386, Pecos, NM 87552, 505/757-6730. Handmade ceramic buttons. $2*#.

Mill Run Pottery, Box 95, Acworth, NH 03601. Handmade ceramic buttons in 3 sizes and several colors. SASE#.

Paco Despacio, Buttonsmith, P.O. Box 261, Cave Junction, OR 97523. Handmade buttons and earrings of silver, copper, brass, bone, clay, semiprecious stones, and other natural materials. $4#.

Randy Miller Pewter Buttons, North Road, East Alstead, NH 03602. Pewter buttons. $1 and SASE#.

Stella Buttons, University Station, P.O. Box 5632, Seattle, WA 98105. Mother-of-pearl buttons.

Wildwood Works, Lasqueti Island, BC, V0R 2J0, Canada. Wood buttons in a range of tones and sizes. Custom staining available. L-SASE#.

Body Doubles: Dress Forms

✎ **Note**: Complete-line notions catalogs also carry dress forms. See Hard-to-Find Patterns and Designs, pages 161 – 162

Dress Rite Forms, 3817 N. Pulaski, Chicago, IL 60641, 312/588-5761. Non-adjustable forms, either standard or custom-sized. L-SASE#.

Pattern *BODIFORM®*, 161 Seventh Ave., San Francisco, CA 94118, 415/752-2215. Custom, adjustable dress forms. Free#.

Uniquely You® Dress Form, 112-C Edwardia Dr., Greensboro, NC 27409, 800/334-0524. Custom-fit dress forms. L-SASE#.

Wolf Form Co., 39 W. 19th St., New York, NY 10011, 212/255-4508. All types of forms for all sizes—women, men, and children. L-SASE#.

References

- Sewing Books
- *Update Newsletter* Sewing Booklets
- Sewing Videos

- Sewing Publications
- Associations

Sewing Books

Gail's sewing library includes hundreds of sewing books. She relies on her library daily for references, referrals, and inspiration. (Yes, she even totes selected volumes for in-the-car, on-the-plane, or at-the-beach reading.)

If you are intrigued by new or improved techniques, start building a sewing library. You'll depend on the books for frequent reference and inspiration. (Or take a breather and indulge in some hassle-free armchair sewing.)

The following books are some, but certainly not all, of our favorites in the fashion and furnishing categories. (Due to lack of space, we had to leave out quilting and craft titles.) Ask for them at your local fabric, book, or sewing machine store; if you are unable to locate the books, order directly from the publishing or mail-order companies listed here. **(For serging-related books, refer to the list on page 174 of *Innovative Serging*.)**

✎ **Note:** Several of the books on this list are available through Open Chain Publishing. Their address is P.O. Box 2634-IS, Menlo Park, CA 94026. Additional copies of *Innovative Sewing* can also be ordered from Open Chain; send $16.95 ($18 for CA residents) postpaid.

Appliqué the Kwik-Sew Way, by Kerstin Martensson, ©1988 Kwik-Sew Pattern Co., 3000 Washington Ave. N., Minneapolis, MN 55411-1699. Three of the best appliqué methods are delineated, and master patterns for over 160 motifs are included. Find it where Kwik-Sew patterns are sold, or send $14.55 postpaid.

Bright Ideas for Your Home, by Per Dalsgaard and Elisabeth Erichsen, ©1978, Harper and Row, 10 E. 53rd St., New York, NY 10022. Absolutely the most clever, practical, and attractive home decorating projects we've seen. Unfortunately, the book is now out-of-print, but the ideas are still incredibly fresh. Check for it at your local library or used-book stores.

The Busy Woman's Fitting Book, by Nancy Zieman with Robbie Fanning, ©1989, Open Chain Publishing. Utilizing the simple-to-understand pivot-and-slide method, Nancy explains how to fit dresses, blouses, and jackets. $12 postpaid ($12.65 for CA residents).

The Busy Woman's Sewing Book, by Nancy Zieman with Robbie Fanning, ©1988, Open Chain Publishing. A wonderfully uncomplicated approach to the essentials of time-saving sewing—setting in sleeves, perfect plackets, and semi-lined blazers. $12 postpaid ($12.65 for CA residents).

Claire Shaeffer's Fabric Sewing Guide, by Claire Shaeffer, ©1989, Chilton Book Company, Radnor, PA 19089. Claire outdid herself compiling this comprehensive text. One-of-a-kind in the sewing book market, it focuses on every conceivable fabric used for fashion sewing. Your library shouldn't be without it. $27.95 postpaid ($29.57 for CA residents) from Open Chain Publishing.

The Complete Computer Sewing Book, by Myra Coles, ©1987, William Heinemann Ltd. Distributed in the United States by David & Charles, Inc., North Pomfret, VT 05053. This British author was one of the first to discuss the how's, why's, and wonders of computerized sewing. $19.95 postpaid.

The Complete Book of Machine Embroidery and *The Complete Book of Machine Quilting,* both by Robbie and Tony Fanning, ©1986 and 1980, Chilton Book Company, Radnor, PA 19089. Yes, Robbie is our editor and friend, but even if she weren't, we'd recommend these books. Indisputably, they rank among THE references for sewing machine embroidery and quilting, whether you're a beginner or a fiber-arts professional. Available from Open Chain Publishing for postpaid prices of $18.95 and $19.95, respectively ($20.20 and $21.25, respectively, for CA residents).

Country Style Appliqués, by Mary Mulari, ©1987, Mary Mulari, Box 87, Aurora, MN 55705. Mary's distinctive handwriting and illustrations take the reader step-by-step through dozens of country-inspired appliqués. Motif patterns included. Also inquire about her other titles. $9.45 postpaid.

The Fabric Lover's Scrapbook, by Margaret Dittman, ©1988, Chilton Book Company, Radnor, PA 19089. Don't let the title fool you—there's not one poodle-dog toilet-paper cover in this book. Margaret describes her scrap-sewing projects as "frivolous and fun, experimental and exciting." And they are. Available from Open Chain Publishing for $16.95 ($18 for CA residents) postpaid.

Innovative Serging: The Newest, Best, and Fastest Techniques for Overlock Sewing, by Gail Brown and Tammy Young, ©1989, Chilton Book Company, Radnor, PA 19089. The companion book to *Innovative Sewing.* Brand-new techniques for serging garments and home decorating. Available from Open Chain Publishing for $16.95 ($18 for CA residents) postpaid.

Know Your Sewing Machine, by Jackie Dodson, ©1988, Chilton Book Company, Radnor, PA 19089. Jackie, a real sewing pro, amazed us with the creative and functional potential of any sewing machine. $14.95 postpaid from Open Chain Publishing. Also, don't miss the brand-specific books in this series, also available from Open Chain Publishing: *Know Your Bernina, Know Your Brother, Know Your Elna, Know Your New Home, Know Your Pfaff, Know Your Simplicity, Know Your Singer, Know Your Viking,* and *Know Your White.*

Necklines Made Easy, by Ann Person, ©1989, Stretch & Sew, Inc, P.O. Box 185, Eugene, OR 97440. Take a basic knit top pattern: vary the neckline to create an entire wardrobe. Multisized patterns are included with the book. The book sells for $12.98 at stores that carry Stretch & Sew patterns and books. For information on the nearest retail outlet, call 1-800-547-7717.

Owner's Guide to Sewing Machines, Sergers, and Knitting Machines, by Gale Grigg Hazen, ©1989, Chilton Book Company, Radnor, PA 19089. Gail imparts insightful tips about the inner workings and care of sergers and sewing machines. Valuable and interesting information, presented humorously by one of the industry's leading machine experts. Available from Open Chain Publishing, for $16.95 ($18 for CA residents) postpaid.

Pants for Any Body, by Pati Palmer and Susan Pletsch, Palmer/Pletsch, Inc., P.O. Box 12046, Portland, OR 97212-0046 ($8.20 postpaid). If you want to sew more flattering pants, this book promises to be one of your most-used references. Although Pati and Susan are thorough in their presentation of practical solutions to common pant-fitting and pant-sewing problems, they never let the copy or illustrations slip into tedious overkill.

Rags, Making a Little Something Out of Almost Nothing, by Linda and Stella Allison, ©1979, Clarkson Potter, Inc., One Park Ave., New York, NY 10016. For fabricholics and junk-store junkies only, but irresistible nonetheless. The Allison sisters' whimsical wanderings include scarf clothes, button jewelry, and incredibly fun T-shirt yarn (made from stripped knit or T-shirt scraps). It's out-of-print, but *Rags* often still shows up regularly in remaindered book catalogs and used book stores. Originally $14.95 (hardback). Also see *The Fabric Lover's Scrapbook.*

Sensational Silk, by Gail Brown, ©1982, Palmer/Pletsch Inc., P. O. Box 12046, Portland, OR 97212. Obviously it's difficult for Gail to be objective about her own book. But if you want to sew silks or silkies, hassle-free, consult this book. The time-saving techniques apply to most blouse and dress construction. $8.45 postpaid.

Sew, Serge, Press/Speed Tailoring in the Ultimate Sewing Center, by Jan Saunders, ©1989, Chilton Book Company, Radnor, PA 19089. Ideal tools, organization, and techniques are explained. Fascinating profiles of sewing celebrities, photographed in their own sewing rooms. $16.95 postpaid ($18 for CA residents) from Open Chain Publishing.

Sew Smart with Wovens, Knits and Ultrasuede® Fabric, by Judy Lawrence and Clotilde, ©1977, Sewing Knits., Inc, P.O. Box 1493, Boulder, CO 80306. Professional sewing secrets for achieving professional results. Covers all phases of construction, plus a section on *Ultrasuede®* fabrics. Available for $17.60 postpaid from Clotilde, Inc. (see page 163 of the "Sew-by-Mail Directory").

Simplicity's Simply the Best Sewing Book, ©1988, Simplicity Pattern Company, 200 Madison Ave., New York, NY 10016. One of the best efforts to integrate serging and conventional sewing how-to's. The spiral-bound paperback is $16.20 postpaid from Simplicity, 901 Wayne St., Niles, MI 49121.

Singer Sewing Reference Library's 101 Sewing Secrets, coauthored by Karen Drellich and Sue Green, ©1989, Cy DeCosse, P.O. Box 3040, 5900 Green Oak Drive, Minnetonka, MN 55343. Intriguing techniques and a plethora of luscious photography. $14.95 postpaid.

Singer Sewing Reference Library's Sewing Update 2, edited by Nancy Restuccia, ©1989, Cy DeCosse, P.O. Box 3040, 5900 Green Oak Drive, Minnetonka, MN 55343. Another beautiful presentation of interesting sewing how-to's and commentary, ranging from ruching to twin-needle seaming of stretch knits (Gail's contribution to the book). $14.95 postpaid. Also look for annual releases in the *Update* series.

Speed Sewing, by Jan Saunders, ©1985, Speed Sewing Ltd., 3895 West Henderson Road, Columbus, OH 43220. A classic book that's delightfully explicit about how to maximize your machine and productivity. $15.95 postpaid ($16.83 postpaid for OH residents).

The Shade Book, by Judy Lindahl, ©1980, Judy Lindahl, 3211 N.E. Siskiyou, Portland, OR 97212. Judy was the pioneer in fabric-decorating how-to's, and her concise handbook still reigns as one of the most complete and easy-to-follow. $7.95 postpaid. Also, ask about her other books, *Energy Saving Decorating* and *Decorating with Fabric.*

Update Newsletter Sewing Booklets

The following are *Update Newsletter* sewing publications. They are sold by fabric stores, machine dealers , and mail-order sewing supply companies. Or you can order individual titles for $3.95 each from the *Update Newsletters,* 2269 Chestnut, #269, San Francisco, CA 94123.

Beyond Straight Stitching, the Basics of Creative Machine Stitchery, by Barbara Weiland O'Connell, ©1988. Barbara simplifies decorative machine stitchery—necessary tools, variations on satin stitching, tailor-tacking fringe, machine open work, and more.

Fashion That Fits, by Nancy Zieman, ©1989. Nancy, well-known host of the T.V. show, "Sewing with Nancy," explains her fool-proof fitting program, step-by-step — from measuring and correct pattern size selection to easy pivot-and-slide alterations.

Fashion That Flatters, by Marilyn Thelen, ©1989. This fashion expert shows how to make the most important decision in sewing: choosing the best, most flattering style for you.

Feet Smarts, by Jackie Dodson, ©1989. If you've always wondered what to do with all the feet in your machine attachment box, read this book. Learn the best ways to use basic, cording, hemming, buttonhole feet, and zipper feet, among others.

For Kids: Sew Fast, Sew Fun! by Barb Griffin, ©1988. This talented designer/author makes sewing for kids a wonderful creative adventure. Appliqués (patterns included), embellishments, and newborn necessities are just a few of the many subjects covered.

Make Room for Sewing, by Leslie Wood, ©1988. How to transform any available space (no matter how small) into an efficient sewing center. Tips on lighting, furniture, fabric and notion organization.

The Newest Knit Know-How, by Gail Brown, ©1988. The best, fastest, and most professional methods for edge-finishing, hemming, and seaming. Also, understand what stretch ratios really mean.

Shaping Fashion, a Guide to Today's Interfacings, by Barbara Weiland O'Connell, ©1988. A concise compilation of the interfacing types and how-to's, updated (after Stacy Fabric Corporation went out of business) to include all the currently available brand names. Techniques for both fusibles and sew-ins are covered.

Sewing Videos

These days, books aren't the only references in sewing libraries. How-to videotapes are fast becoming the "other" category of educational mainstays. Because television has the unique capability of focusing on techniques, step-by-step, in full color, you're sure to pick up some new tips.

With few exceptions, most sewing machine companies have produced one or more instructional videos; some come with the machine, while others are sold separately. Ask your dealer about video rentals or sales; if you have difficulty locating a brand-specific video, write to the sewing machine company (addresses are listed on page 159).

Other training tapes deserving your consideration are being produced, sold, and rented by freelance sewing specialists. You'll find these videos at fabric stores, machine dealerships, and through mail-order catalogs.

Staying current on video titles is an ongoing task; sewing titles are discontinued and added on a frequent basis, so instead of a title list, we are including a comprehensive list of those who are producing or distributing tapes. Write these firms for a list of current titles, prices, and dealer referrals or mail-order prices. For those not offering catalogs, send a large, self-addressed and stamped envelope.

American Home Sewing Association, 1375 Broadway, New York, NY 10018.

Burda Patterns, P.O. Box 2517, Smyrna, GA 30031.

Clotilde, Inc., 1909 S.W. First Ave., Ft. Lauderdale, FL 33315. Catalog, $1 (for first-class delivery).

DME, P.O. Box 1624, Manchester, NH 03105.

Donna Salyers, c/o Amanda Scott Publishing, P.O. Box 40425, Cincinnati, OH 45240.

Islander School of Fashion Arts, Inc., P.O. Box 5216, Grants Pass, OR 97527.

June Tailor, P.O. Box 208, Richfield, WI 53076.

Learn By Video, 3404 South 50 West, Bountiful, UT 84010.

Nancy's Notions, Ltd., P.O. Box 683, Beaver Dam, WI 53916. Free color catalog. (Their Video Club has one of the most comprehensive around, with over 120 titles; lifetime membership is $15.)

Palmer/Pletsch Associates, P.O. Box 12046, Portland, OR 97212-0046.

Power Sewing, P.O. Box 2702, San Francisco, CA 94126.

Roberta Carr/Landes Communications, P.O. Box 32120, San Jose, CA 95152-2120.

Sew Sensational, P.O. Box 1936, Orem, UT 84057.

Sew/Fit, P.O. Box 565, La Grange, IL 60525.

Sewing Update Videos, P.O. Box 31715, St. Louis, MO 63131.

Theta's®, 2209 N.W. 46th St., Oklahoma City, OK 73112, Attn: Theta Happ.

Ultra Fit, 237 Van Corlandt Park Ave., Yonkers, NY 10705.

Sewing Publications

Butterick Home Catalog, 161 Sixth Avenue, New York, NY 10013. $8 for four issues annually.

McCall's Pattern Magazine, 230 Park Avenue, New York, NY 10169. For a four-issue annual subscription, $10.

Serger Update, 2269 Chestnut, #269, San Francisco, CA 94123. The only periodical devoted entirely to serging news and techniques. Published monthly ($36 annual subscription).

Sew It Seams, P.O. Box 2698 Kirkland, WA 98083. $22 per year for this quarterly magazine.

Sew News, P.O. Box 1790, Peoria, IL 61656. $15.97 for an annual subscription (12 monthly issues). Look for the "Machines in Motion: Sergers" column, written by Gail Brown and Sue Green.

Sewer's SourceLetter, CraftSource, 7509 7th Place S.W., Seattle, WA 98106. Published quarterly. $15/year (single copy, $4).

Sewing Update (address is the same as *Serger Update*). Newsletter format without advertising (sister publication to *Serger Update* newsletter). Sent every other month—$18 per year. Also, see the special sampler offer on page ____.

Vogue Patterns Magazine, 161 Sixth Ave., New York, NY 10013. Subscriptions are $12.95 annually for six bimonthly issues.

Associations

Connecting with other seamsters is another way to expand your sewing horizons. Besides, we've never met a diehard home-sewer we didn't like.

✎ **Note:** When you write these associations, identify yourself (as a consumer, retailer, or wholesaler), and request membership information.

American Home Economics Association, 2010 Massachusetts N.W., Washington, D.C. 20036.

American Home Sewing Association, 1375 Broadway, New York, 10018.

American Sewing Guild, National Guild Headquarters, P.O. Box 50976, Indianapolis, IN 46250-0976.

Bishop Method Sewing Council, P.O. Box 764, College Park, MD 20740.

Canadian Home Sewing & Sewing Needlecraft Association, 224 Merton St., Suite 204, Toronto, Ontario, M4S 1A1 Canada.

Custom Clothing Guild of America, 620 Market Street, Kirkland, WA 98033.

Independent Sewing Machine Dealers Associaton (I.S.M.D.A.), P.O. Box 338, Hilliard, OH 43026.

Michigan Bishop Sewing Council, 1549 E. Atherton Rd., Box 144, Flint, MI 48507.

National 4-H Council, 7100 Connecticut Ave., Chevy Chase, MD 20815. (Also, call your county extension office for local 4-H information.)

About the Authors

Gail Brown is one of the most widely read writers in home sewing and is recognized for her serger expertise, extensive research, and fast, innovative methods. She is Contributing Editor for the *Serger Update* newsletter, is the coauthor of three best-selling books on serger sewing, including *Creative Serging Illustrated* and *Innovative Serging*, and was also an instructor for the Palmer/Pletsch Serger Workshops. Her work appears in *McCall's Pattern Magazine, Needle and Craft, Sewing Update, Sew News, The Singer Sewing Library*, and *Vogue Patterns Magazine*. Although this home economics graduate started her career nearly 20 years ago in New York City, she now transmits via modem from the small coastal town of Hoquiam, Washington. Her patient husband, John Quigg, and two children, Bett and Jack, put up with her deadlines and growing collection of sergers, sewing machines, needlework collectibles, and computer paraphernalia.

Tammy Young has combined creativity and practicality in her writing and publishing career. Having worked for several years in the ready-to-wear fashion industry, she is known for her ability to translate retail trends into home-sewing techniques. Tammy is a graduate of Oregon State University and is a former extension agent, high school home economics teacher, and manager of the Palmer/Pletsch Serger Workshops. Her recent titles include *Innovative Serging, Distinctive Serger Gifts and Crafts, An Idea Book for All Occasions*, and *Serged Gifts in Minutes!* Her office and home are now located in downtown San Francisco, where she oversees all facets of *Update* newsletter and book production—editing, illustration direction, layout, and printing. When her hectic schedule allows, Tammy travels stateside and abroad, frequently picking up fashion and fabric trends for the *Sewing* and *Serger Update* newsletters and books.

Index